JAVA® SE 7
PROGRAMMING
ESSENTIALS

JAVA® SE 7 PROGRAMMING

ESSENTIALS

Michael Ernest

WILEY

John Wiley & Sons, Inc.

Senior Acquisitions Editor: Jeff Kellum
Development Editor: Kathi Duggan
Technical Editors: Dr. Ernest J. Friedman-Hill and Paul Nahay
Production Editor: Christine O'Connor
Copy Editor: Judy Flynn
Editorial Manager: Pete Gaughan
Production Manager: Tim Tate
Vice President and Executive Group Publisher: Richard Swadley
Vice President and Publisher: Neil Edde
Book Designer: Happenstance Type-O-Rama
Compositors: Cody Gates, Craig Johnson, and Kate Kaminski, Happenstance Type-O-Rama
Proofreader: Candace English
Indexer: Nancy Guenther
Project Coordinator, Cover: Katherine Crocker
Cover Designer: Ryan Sneed
Cover Image: © nullplus / iStockPhoto

ISBN: 978-1-118-35910-5
ISBN: 978-1-118-46385-7 (ebk.)
ISBN: 978-1-118-41695-2 (ebk.)
ISBN: 978-1-118-43409-3 (ebk.)

Dear Reader,

Thank you for choosing *Java SE 7 Programming Essentials*. This book is part of a family of premium-quality Sybex books, all of which are written by outstanding authors who combine practical experience with a gift for teaching.

Sybex was founded in 1976. More than 30 years later, we're still committed to producing consistently exceptional books. With each of our titles, we're working hard to set a new standard for the industry. From the paper we print on, to the authors we work with, our goal is to bring you the best books available.

I hope you see all that reflected in these pages. I'd be very interested to hear your comments and get your feedback on how we're doing. Feel free to let me know what you think about this or any other Sybex book by sending me an email at nedde@wiley.com. If you think you've found a technical error in this book, please visit http://sybex.custhelp.com. Customer feedback is critical to our efforts at Sybex.

Best regards,

Neil Edde
Vice President and Publisher
Sybex, an Imprint of Wiley

To Jocelyn, my love

ACKNOWLEDGMENTS

Just hours before this writing, I received an email from Kathryn Duggan, this book's development editor, saying the last chapter had now entered the pitiless, gaping maw of production. Let the grinding and forging begin. For this part of the process, I have to listen at a distance and make sense of the whirs and groans this material might force from the machine. I have to wonder what rough edges I missed that will now be cast in bronze, buffed into a high relief, and given prominence. What best parts will end up in some corner shadow or made to rest against the wall? I don't know. The wait is almost as hard as the writing.

What we've put into this book, though, is our combined best effort to oil that machine, a result of collaboration, faith, rerevising, and just a little lip biting. As this book goes into the mill, I am proud to have worked with every one of its contributors.

Kathi guided this project with an unfailingly positive spirit and saw it through more than one rough patch, all the while having to pick up and move several hundred miles, then find a house. Without her diligence, kind words, and tolerance for my sprint-and-coma style of submitting chapters, I am not sure I'd have gotten this far, at least not in 2012. Thank you, Kathi; no one can expect the level of effort and encouragement you put into this book.

Ernest Friedman-Hill served as my technical editor, checking both the code and the rationale of the narrative for accuracy and consistency. You, good reader, will never again see such a bargain struck for a book of this sort. Ernest is an accomplished computer scientist, a professional of talents and abilities beyond my ken, an author in his own right, and a JavaRanch colleague whose work and contributions I have admired for over a decade. This book could have become a pale farce without his attention, his advice, and his drive on improving, well, everything. Yes, everything, right down to creating an alternate cover (which was ignored, sadly). I owe him big-time. I pledge here to pay his generosity forward. When you come across a section you think is especially sharp, I'd be pleased if you remembered Ernest for it (too).

Paul Nahay reviewed the manuscript and, so far as I could tell, observed each punctuation mark with suspicion. He uncovered error after error we somehow missed. These are errors an author might forgive as understandable lapses, but errors that a disinterested eye might view as a sign of wavering competence. It can be a thankless role, and Paul did it fearlessly. Thank you, Paul.

Jeff Kellum, the acquisitions editor, might have had to vouch for me more than once. Several of my first drafts came in like a New Year's Eve walk home: late, unintelligible, and in dire need of more solids. Thank you, Jeff, for this opportunity and for your faith. I hope the work here adds to your credit.

Pete Gaughan, the editorial manager, watched this process throughout and kept me grounded in the demands of publishing, He reminded me, tactfully and more than once, one must feed Production properly. He threw a lot of rules at me, sure, of the sort I accept with quiet grudging and irritation. He did it without apology, however, and I can't say how much I appreciate that. Thanks, Pete, for holding the line and keeping me honest.

Many people play a part in getting a book to print, and I'm sorry I haven't met the people who worked to make this book handsome and well-lit. The people at Sybex I did talk to made me feel it was all in good hands. I'd do this again with them. On a practical note, their attention to detail, from comma splices to color schemes, impressed me. I'd have had better luck throwing pork chops past a wolf. Thank you to production editor Christine O'Connor, copyeditor Judy Flynn, and compositors Cody Gates, Craig Johnson, and Kate Kaminski at Happenstance Type-O-Rama.

What was possible here, however, begins with my students and colleagues. I taught my first Java course in 1995. Today, I wonder how I ever got the nerve. For everyone who said you learned a concept or a technique from me that still pays off, or just told me I added something to the good, thank you. You're the reason I still teach this subject and why I thought some written words might help a few more people on their way.

About the Author

Michael Ernest entered the world of Java programming the way many people do. He spent three years as a bank teller, operated a forklift, earned a degree in English at an aggie college, spent four years as a firefighter, earned an advanced degree in English literature, sold baseball cards and comic books, began doctoral studies at Claremont Graduate School, and taught night classes. He then took an entry-level job in data processing at Bank of America, followed by a job at a global chemical-manufacturing concern and then jobs at Access Graphics, Lockheed Martin, General Electric, Synergistic Computer Solutions, and FusionStorm. He still has all the never-quite-vested retirement plans and darling little 401(k) accounts to prove it.

In that time, Ernest was once left alone for three weeks with a shelf of abandoned O'Reilly books and a SPARC IPX computer. One entire 435 MB drive and 48 whole MB of RAM! He discovered a passion for Sun Microsystems technology to add to his passion for adult learning and has enjoyed teaching computing courses ever since.

Ernest started his own subject matter–expert group, Inkling Research, in 1999. He currently consults, teaches, writes, and speaks on several topics, including Solaris-based technologies such as ZFS, Containers, and DTrace; Java SE/EE programming; software architecture; fault analysis; and performance management. He writes and maintains his own courses in several technologies and products, including DTrace, Solaris 11, GlassFish, Tomcat, ActiveMQ, and ServiceMix. He has written some standard courses for Sun and Oracle and served as an adviser and reviewer for a few more.

Often asked to speak on minor topics of limited appeal at the last minute, Ernest has spoken at JavaOne, TheServerSide Java Symposium, and Oracle OpenWorld. He very nearly spoke to five people at a conference session in 2011, but then they announced snacks over the loudspeaker.

Ernest lives in the San Francisco Bay Area with his wife, Jocelyn; a teenage daughter who loves marching band; and a son who will attend a college you've never heard of in the fall of 2012. Ernest studies Kung Jung Mu Sul and tai chi and claims the record for the least possible aptitude for the guitar among people who won't give up. His first and only 500 GB hard drive is holding steady at one-third full.

Contents at a Glance

Contents

CHAPTER 6   Encapsulating Data and Exposing Methods in Java   119

CHAPTER 7   Using Java Methods to Communicate   147

CHAPTER 8   Using Java Constructors   173

CHAPTER 9   Inheriting Code and Data in Java   203

CHAPTER 10   Understanding Java Interfaces and Abstract Classes   231

CHAPTER 11   Throwing and Catching Exceptions in Java   259

APPENDIX A   Answers to Review Questions   289

APPENDIX B   OCA Certification Program   301

INTRODUCTION

As Java nears its 20th birthday, I think it's time people stopped using the term *cool* to describe this technology and *rock star* to describe the people who have made shining contributions to it. In dog time, Java is 140 years old. In Internet time, that's a millennium or so. Java today is more like the Roman Empire than a cultural phenomenon. It is pervasive and far-flung, a world power, a Goliath its neighbors fear and loathe. It supports a culture at least as worried about its decline as it is hopeful about its advance. And it is a well-guarded prize that those nerd barbarians on the steppes dream of sacking every day, as they should.

Java has a canon of literature devoted to it, books worth reading twice and keeping close at hand. There are websites loaded with friendly (or cagey) advice, open-air markets of tech articles, and Java experts. Java prophets hold forth at every forum; everyday users, mostly held together with caffeine and product logos, roam convention halls everywhere for popular talks and prime wireless signal. There is even a pantheon of major and minor Java deities, some of whom appear at so many conferences you might wonder when they write code or if they do anything else.

Java has been serious business for some time, and still is. Tens of thousands of people talk every day about its use, its applications, its rightful owners, and its future developments. It is all a conversation, as they like to say in the academic world. But what has not kept pace with this activity, in my view, is attention to how we should teach Java with this bustling culture in view.

The recent introductory books I have browsed take a pedagogical approach, as if you must recapitulate the learning process you got in middle school to learn anything new. These books introduce the elements of the language, a functional grammar, and a thin, neutral style for observing it. They skip lightly for hundreds of pages, emphasizing a necessary breadth of topics. The authors believe in developing your competence across this terrain: new element, brief example, relevant exercise, next topic.

This stuff is all about *identifying* the conversation I have just described. In this book, I want to help you *join it*. I believe you want that too. You want to learn to participate in it, contribute to and learn from the exchange, and get more from it over time. Even though spelling bees are fun for competition, and maybe course grades gave you a sense of accomplishment, that's not the primary way you learn anymore.

Certification is, in my view, a low rung. If you want to find work in this field, it's my failure to let you believe a high score on the exam will do more than bolster your confidence. The most common complaint I hear from colleagues is that the people they interview can't say anything *about* Java programming. They can recite facts and answer stock questions if they aren't too nervous. And certification may have been required to get the interview, but now what? If you cannot, in that moment, participate in a small conversation with a trained professional who engages in it every day, the interview is a waste of everyone's time, including yours.

For that reason, I've included my opinions on Java usage and style in this book, as well as rules and rote facts. In the later chapters, I give you quite a bit more information on form and uses for Java than you need to get certified. I include some ideas that, if you learn to apply them, can raise your interviewer's eyebrows: *You know that already?* In this book, you'll learn more than someone who is trying only to meet expectations.

I have no idea what amount of time or knowledge is required for you to pass the exam. I don't much care. This book will help you enter the conversation, using full sentences, discussing ideas on good practice and knowing there are multiple ways to write any program. If you're new to this field, you can start by mimicking what I have to say (and hopefully not get spotted too soon). If you're a skeptic who reads widely, you can balance this material against your other sources and start some conversations yourself. If you're smarter or more informed than I am, you can prove me wrong and burn me in effigy on Amazon. Bring whatever you have, but above all *show me what you have learned*, not your exam score. Passing is passing.

In this book, you will learn the way adults learn: by relating what you know to what you don't know, by interacting with people who know a bit more and a bit less than you do, by treating your mistakes as just another way to learn, and by doing something new with Java every day. I will talk to you about moving around this subject more like a planet and less like an electron. If you want to join this conversation—and pass the exam in due time—this book is for you.

Who Should Read This Book

This book is for people who want to learn Java programming well enough to recommend themselves for entry-level work in this field. Earning the Oracle Certified Associate, Java SE 7 Programmer certification is a constructive step in that direction. I've covered all the stated requirements for that exam in this book.

To profit fully from this book, in my view, you must invest time and effort in reading and writing Java code, not just reading about it. Before you can do that, you need to learn elements of the language, and before you can do that, you need a guide who can tell you something about the practice of programming. You should also ask whether you fancy sitting for hours at a time writing code, making it work, testing its reliability, and—here's the killer—explaining how it works to someone else.

If you're taking a college course, I believe this book is the best available guide to start learning and writing simple programs. If this book isn't on your syllabus, propose it to your instructor. If it is, awesome! Yay for me! As for you, you'll get two teachers for the price of one. I offer advice on good practice, provide a context for the skills you're acquiring, and a few exercises to get the ball rolling. This is your chance to take on an occasional curveball, as you will at any job, but without people watching or expecting quick results.

If you're the self-teaching type, this book will help you write better code along the way to preparing for the exam. This book is *not* just enough Java to get you over that hurdle. I aim to teach you Java itself. I want you to develop enough skill to help you get a job. Your ability to define keywords, identify faulty lines of code, and answer 68 questions correctly in 150 minutes or less—that's all fine. It's one bump in the road and, in my opinion, a minor one. You need to see Java in motion, set it in motion, and identify its motion in a few dozen lines of code. If that sounds like something you want to know how to do, this book is for you.

What You Will Learn

At a minimum, you'll cover all the topics you need to prepare for the OCA, Java SE 7 Programmer exam. With proper study, you will apply the fundamentals of the Java programming language to increasingly complex Java program examples, learn how to write small tests and sample programs, and distinguish between code that merely works and code that is easier to read, maintain, and reuse. You'll start by writing simple Java classes that contain only a `main()` method; go on to design methods and classes following some simple, easy-to-remember guidelines; and finally, create your first abstract types for adapting existing Java code to a wider range of use. You'll wrap it all up by seeing how exception handling can help you protect and preserve the state of a running program as it encounters errors.

What You Need

- ▶ A computer with Java Development Kit (JDK) SE version 7 fully and properly installed—Some examples in this book will work with JDK 6, but many of the examples apply features that are specific to JDK 7.

- ▶ A text editor—I used vi to write every code example in this book. You might prefer a program that will highlight Java keywords and so on. Please do avoid an integrated development environment (IDE) like Eclipse or NetBeans for now, if you can. A beginner, in my opinion, should start with few tools and type things out. An IDE is more a crutch than a conveyance when you're first learning to walk. Your legs can't form right, in my opinion, if you don't first train them to work on their own.

- ▶ A user community—There are opinions in this book that other knowledgeable people may disagree with. That's healthy and I encourage it. If you don't know where to go, try the JavaRanch website. I may even see you there.

- ▶ Time to write code—Don't cheat yourself. People like me can separate, from yards away, those who have written a lot of code from those who cut, paste, compile, and call it learning. We'll figure you out fast. Do the work.

What Is Covered in This Book

Java SE 7 Programming Essentials includes all the topics that make up the Oracle Certified Associate, Java SE 7 Programmer exam. It is organized to take the beginning student from language basics to understanding how Java programmers use inheritance, abstract types, exception handling, and fundamental design techniques in practice every day.

Chapter 1: Introducing the Basics of Java   You'll write your first Java program, learn how to import code into a program, and take a first look at using variables.

Chapter 2: Applying Data Types in Java Programming   You'll get your first look at working with primitive types, classes, and objects in Java. You'll take a full look at two classes that manage text, the `String` and `StringBuilder` classes.

Chapter 3: Using Java Operators and Conditional Logic   You'll review Java's built-in operators and use them to form expressions. You'll learn how to test objects for equality and use tests in general to form decision statements.

Chapter 4: Using Java Arrays   You'll examine the anatomy of a Java array and test it in a sample program. You'll also take a close look at the ArrayList class and learn its method interface.

Chapter 5: Using Loops in Java Code   You'll learn how to apply looping statements to call code repeatedly and how to break out of loops on specific conditions.

Chapter 6: Encapsulating Data and Exposing Methods in Java   Starting here, you'll address issues of design and style when writing Java code. You'll learn how encapsulation works, how to manage class member visibility, and what is meant by abstracting data.

Chapter 7: Using Java Methods to Communicate   You'll design Java methods to clearly express their purpose and review the rules for passing primitive and object types from one method to another.

Chapter 8: Using Java Constructors   You'll write constructors to suit a variety of specials needs when making objects out of your classes.

Chapter 9: Inheriting Code and Data In Java   You'll learn how one class inherits from another and how it differs from encapsulation. You'll also write subclasses that have to pass parameters to their parent classes before they'll work.

Chapter 10: Understanding Java Interfaces and Abstract Classes   You'll learn how to form a *type system* in this chapter and review a complete program example—using an interface, an abstract class, and an enumeration type—to model a hypothetical business.

Chapter 11: Throwing and Catching Exceptions in Java   You'll throw and catch exception objects, learn the difference between checked and unchecked exceptions, and identify commonly seen exception classes.

Appendix A: Answers to Review Questions   This appendix includes solutions and explanations for the questions at the end of each chapter.

Appendix B: OCA Certification Program   This appendix outlines the requirements of the Oracle Certified Associate, Java SE 7 Programmer exam, including the format, minimum passing score, and exam duration. It also maps each exam topic to the chapter in which it is discussed.

You can also download Appendix C: Answers to Additional Exercises online at www.sybex.com/go/javase7essentials. This appendix includes solutions and explanations for the exercises at the end of each chapter.

The Essentials Series

The Essentials series from Sybex provides outstanding instruction for readers who are just beginning to develop their professional skills. Every Essentials book includes these features:

- ▶ Skill-based instruction with chapters organized around projects rather than abstract concepts or subjects.

- ▶ Suggestions for additional exercises at the end of each chapter, where you can practice and extend your skills.

- ▶ Digital files (via download) so you can work through the project tutorials yourself. Please check the book's web page at www.sybex.com/go/javase7essentials for these companion downloads.

Certification Objective
The certification margin icon will alert you to passages that are especially relevant to Oracle Certified Associate, Java SE 7 Programmer certification. See Appendix B, "OCA Certification Program," for more information.

How to Contact the Author

If you have feedback for this book, please write to me at michael@javaranch.com. My other email addresses aren't big secrets, but I do filter my inboxes without let or hindrance. If you subscribe to JavaRanch, you can post longer comments and critiques in a forum there and let me know you did. Please don't use their private message facility to contact me.

You have a short comment? I'm @mfernest on Twitter; you can use #Java7Essentials if you like. I have a profile on LinkedIn that you can consult if you'd like more information on my professional background. If you want information on the custom courses, seminars, and training I provide, *and* you have some dates in mind, please write to marnie@inklingresearch.com. We are a small word-of-mouth business driven by human contact and long-term business relationships. There's no website.

I maintain a tech-ish blog at http://radio.javaranch.com/michael. I don't post there so often, but if I have something more to add about this book, and it's not the kind of thing Sybex considers a useful supplement, I'll post it there.

Sybex strives to keep you supplied with the latest tools and information you need for your work. Please check www.sybex.com/go/javase7essentials, where I'll post additional content and updates that supplement this book if the need arises.

CHAPTER 1

Introducing the Basics of Java

From this page to the end of the book, there is one goal in mind: to show you how to consume Java code as well as anyone else. By understanding how Java programs can be composed, what language tools there are to assist you, and how written code can be read in a methodical, straightforward fashion, you'll be ready to manage existing code and even write some small programs yourself.

The shorter-term goal is to help prepare you for the Java SE 7 OCA exam. topics are organized with the long-term goal in mind, however, and the discussion is not limited to the exam objectives. If you're a literal, need-to-know-only type, a map of the exam objectives to each chapter appears in the back of the book. You can decide what to ignore.

To start, some basic questions will be answered: How is Java code organized? How do you write a Java program? How do you use existing Java code in a program you write? And how do you manage the state of a program as it runs?

In this chapter, we'll cover the following topics:

▶ **Understanding Java class structure**

▶ **Writing a `main()` method**

▶ **Importing other Java classes**

▶ **Understanding variable scope in Java code**

Understanding Java Class Structure

Certification Objective

Java has a few top-level structures for containing code. There are structures called *interfaces* and *abstract classes*, for example, which we'll discuss in Chapter 10, "Understanding Java Interfaces and Abstract Classes." The one to understand right away is a simple Java class. The one thing you'll do most often with Java classes is make *objects*. An object is a runtime instance of a class somewhere in the memory space of a Java program. All the different objects of all the different classes you use to create one program, taken as a whole, represent the *state* of that program.

Java classes have two primary elements: *methods*, often called functions or procedures in other languages; and *fields*, more generally known as variables. Together these are called the *members* of the class. Methods operate on the state of objects to which they belong. If the change is important to remember, a variable stores that change. That's all classes really do. It is the programmer who creates and arranges these elements in such a way that the resulting code is useful and, ideally, easy for other programmers to understand.

Program state is a concept I'll repeat and elaborate upon throughout this chapter.

A Java class can be quite simple. It can include variables to represent something you're calling data, such as personal contact information, defined in a class you name to express that concept:

```
public class ContactInfo {
    String firstName;
    String lastName;
    String address;
    String city;
    String cell;
}
```

The ContactInfo class is about as simple as a Java class can get. It contains data, expressed as a number of fields, you could use in a program to track people who matter to you. You can represent each person's information as one ContactInfo object, which you can then use to add, access, or modify this information over time.

Each field is declared as a String type, which is another class. In Java, you always create new classes from existing types. A few of these types, called *primitives*, don't have their own fields and methods, but you'll tend to focus on classes and objects because you can define them to do exactly what you think they ought to do. In the case of a String, you get to use a type that lets you put text in an object, manipulate it, and retrieve it.

ContactInfo methods, once you add them, would perform these same general actions. What they provide that is new is a context: a named type with operations that are specific to contact information, something that isn't expressed well or fully by a bunch of named strings alone.

Of course a Java class gets a little busier once you devise methods for it—again, a subject we'll explore throughout this book. For the sake of illustration, let's say you wanted the ContactInfo class to provide methods that read or write the value of its firstName variable. The methods to support that might look like this:

```java
public class ContactInfo {
...
    public void setFirst(String newName) {
        firstName = newName;
    }

    public String getFirst() {
        return firstName;
    }
}
```

The ellipsis in this example is a placeholder, not legal code. Pretend your variables were listed here instead. You have now added two methods in the ContactInfo class, called setFirst() and getFirst(). One lets a caller retrieve the value of the firstName field; the other lets the caller provide a new value to replace the current one.

Following this same syntax, you could write methods to represent each of the remaining fields. You might even end up with code that will compile. You'd need just a little luck because there are several requirements I haven't yet spelled out. For now, you're just getting an idea what Java code looks like.

A method is an operation that can be *called* by other methods. The called method may require information from the *calling* method in the form of *parameters*. A method also declares what kind of value it *returns* in the form of a *type*. Parameters and return values are stored and represented in code as variables. The full declaration of a method, then, is said to have a *signature*, like this one:

```java
int getJellyBeans(int howMany)
```

The parameter howMany has to be an integer. More specifically, it must correspond to Java's int type. The parameter name should at least hint at its intent. The method getJellyBeans() returns an integer too. Maybe it's the number of jelly beans the caller receives; maybe it's the number remaining. You won't know unless the method's author tells you; you just know it will be an int type.

Some languages infer a variable's type by the assigned value. If you declare x = 5, for example, it's assumed you mean the integer 5, not the character 5.

UNDERSTANDING WHY TYPE IS IMPORTANT

Java is a *type-safe* language. The tools that validate Java code before it runs do what they can to ensure, for example, that only integer *operators* are applied to integer values. Before they convert Java code to an executable form, every operation and its *operands* are tested for correct type. This rule obliges the programmer to track variables carefully, which is not a small amount of work. But the benefits, including code that is easier to read and maintain, are also substantial.

Java, and other *object-oriented* languages like it, promotes a way of writing software that keeps data and the methods that operate on them close to each other (ideally, in the same file). The idea is to develop software that is easier to maintain and reuse over time. In practice, this goal often proves surprisingly difficult to achieve.

One way to reinforce simplicity is by visualizing classes with simple diagrams, like the one shown in Figure 1.1.

Object-oriented languages encourage the programmer to think in terms of software pieces that can be combined to make larger programs.

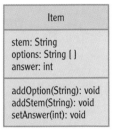

FIGURE 1.1
A proposed Java class item

UML itself is beyond this book's scope. I use simple UML class diagrams to illustrate a concept when the equivalent code requires a foundation you don't yet have.

This diagram loosely applies visual conventions described by the *Unified Modeling Language (UML)*, a widely used design language. The class name `Item` appears in the top section. Immediately below we list the class fields `stem`, `options`, and `answer`. We also indicate each field's type, which are `String`, an *array* of `String` (signified by the brackets), and an integer (`int`), respectively.

At the bottom, we list three methods: `addOption()`, `addStem()`, and `setAnswer()`. Each method name, along with the parameter types specified, implies a direct relationship with one of the members, but we'd probably like more information to be sure.

As with variables, a good method communicates purpose through its name. In our diagram, we could further clarify things by including the type required for each parameter and the return to the caller, but we don't aim to be thorough. Instead we try to strike a balance between useful information and an easy-to-digest depiction. If we're really good, the details we leave out are something a savvy reader can infer. If the reader is really good, they can fill in the blanks in a matter that best suits the overall project. Naturally those skills take time and experience to develop.

A WORD ON JAVA TERMINOLOGY

The terms *method* and *field* reflect a design philosophy that is (or was) important to Java's original designers. In everyday programming, you can use these terms without regard for those issues, but be careful with bringing in terms from other languages. If you referred to a Java method as a *function*, for example, you might receive some strange looks from other programmers. Saying *variable* when you meant *field*, on other hand, is unlikely to cause distraction. The terms *function* and *procedure* don't sound right to the Java ear, but the term *variable* is merely less precise than the term field.

Distinguishing between Classes and Objects

So what's the purpose of a class again? Most of the time, we use it to make *objects*. An object is a runtime entity whose type is defined by its class. All Java objects have a type. All types have methods. All types have fields that, taken as a whole, reflect the object's *state*. Every time a field in an object changes value, the overall state of that object also changes.

As an example of what is meant by object state, let's imagine a class called Point3D. We'll give it three integer fields: x, y, and z. It will include methods setX(), setY(), and setZ(), which allow a caller to modify any one element of a Point3D object at a time. A diagram of this class might look like Figure 1.2.

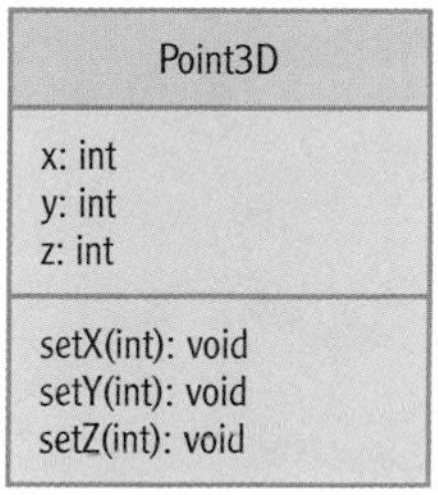

Point3D
x: int y: int z: int
setX(int): void setY(int): void setZ(int): void

FIGURE 1.2 A
sketch of the Point3D class

We can assume, while designing, that these methods will do the work suggested by their names. Whether they operate correctly and predictably is, of course, a code concern. But the objects made from this class will have the Point3D type. Each object will expose the methods setX(), setY(), and setZ(). The state of each object is based (mostly) on the three integer values listed. In that sense, a Point3D object whose x, y, and z values are, say, 1, 2, and 3, has a different state than one whose values are 3, 5, and 9.

DISTINGUISHING BETWEEN OBJECT STATE AND OBJECT EQUALITY

What if two Point3D objects have the same values? How do you tell them apart? As it turns out, the answer depends on the class's programmer. Two Point3D objects could be considered equal if they have matching states. They could also be considered unequal because they have different locations in memory. *Equality* is a fundamental concept in Java: An object is always equal to itself, but it is equal to another object with the same type and state only if the programmer encodes that relationship. We'll discuss this matter in depth in Chapter 3, "Using Java's Operators and Conditional Logic."

One way to think of overall Java program state is to list all the different objects that make it up. Most of the time, the sheer number of objects in play makes this approach impractical. There are thousands of objects, even in a modestly sized Java program, so we usually take this approach only when there's big trouble. If a program runs too slowly, for example, or consumes more resources than expected, and there is no quicker way to isolate the cause, then it's time to sift through the objects individually.

Understanding Other Elements of Java Class Structure

There are other elements we can use to complement a Java class. I'm keeping things as simple as I can for now, but I should mention those other elements and where in the book we'll discuss them fully.

Constructors are a key element in many Java classes. A constructor is method-like in its form, but its only role is to define the way objects of the class are created. Every constructor has the same name as its class, has no return type, and may accept parameters. When the programmer doesn't need to alter default object construction, the Java *compiler* will include one in the class file it generates. Constructors are discussed fully in Chapter 8, "Using Java Constructors." Until then, if we need a specialized constructor to complete an example, we'll show it but keep commentary on it to a minimum.

Java classes may also contain other Java classes. These are called *inner classes*, and they are handy when you want to include a new type that depends completely on the class that contains it. Inner classes fall outside the scope of this book, but you should know about them. Many Java programmers use them and, in some circles, how they use them raises a bit of controversy.

You should also know what are called *class* members in a class. We discuss them at length in Chapter 7, "Using Java Methods to Communicate." For now, I mention them to qualify a statement I made earlier: Classes are primarily used to make objects. That statement still holds, but there are times when you'll want to name methods or variables that actually belong to the class itself.

Static members exploit a difference in the way classes are loaded into memory. A class loads into memory as part of the class itself, that is, without the possibility of changing over time the way objects do. That means you can call a static method without making an object from its class first, as you'll see in the next section. You can access a static variable by its class name or by an object of that class's type. Its value will be visible to all objects of the class and will be the same for all objects: more on that in Chapter 7. For now, bear in mind there's something more to classes than just making objects.

The compiler converts Java source code into *bytecode*. Java thus straddles a traditional distinction between interpreted (human-readable) and compiled (machine-readable) code.

Writing a *main()* Method

Earlier I described a method as an operation that can be called by another method. You might have wondered where the calling starts? Which method is the first to get called, and who calls it?

Certification Objective

The answer for a Java program is its main() method. A main() method is the gateway between the startup of a Java process, which is managed by the Java Virtual Machine (JVM), and the beginning of the programmer's code. The JVM calls on the underlying system to allocate memory and CPU time, access files, and so on. This happens behind the scenes normally, so if you run java -version on a JVM-configured system, you don't see anything happening beyond the intended output. Like any other executable program, however, the JVM gets permission from the operating system to run and asks for the resources it needs to set itself up. When that is done, the JVM processes the -version flag, prints the result, releases the resources it allocated, and tells the operating system it's ready to terminate.

The main() method lets us hook our code into this process, keeping it alive long enough to do the work we've coded. The simplest possible class looks like this:

```
1. public class EntryPoint {
2.     public static void main(String[] args) {
3.         // this line is a comment only
4.     }
5. }
```

This code doesn't do anything useful (or harmful). It has no instructions other than to declare the entry point. It does illustrate, in a sense, that what you can put in a main() method is arbitrary. Any legal Java code will do. In fact, the only reason we even need a class structure to start a Java program is because the language requires it. To compile and execute this code, type it into a file called EntryPoint.java and execute the following:

```
$ javac EntryPoint.java
$ ls
EntryPoint.class      EntryPoint.java
$ java EntryPoint
$
```

To compile Java code, the file must have the extension .java. The name of the file must match the name of the class. The result is a file of *bytecode* by the same name, but with a .class filename extension. Notice that we must omit the .class extension to run the program because a period has a reserved meaning for the JVM.

The rules for what a Java code file contains, and in what order, are more detailed than what has been explained so far. You can in fact store several Java classes in one file under certain conditions. To keep things simple for now, we'll follow a subset of the rules: one, that each file can contain only one class, and two, the file name must match the class name, including case, and have a .java extension.

If we replace line 3 in EntryPoint.java with System.out.println("Hello world!"); then compile and run the code again, we'll get the line of output that matches what's between the quotes. It is not required that a class with the same name as the file be declared public. Please try it.

▶

The class file is a specific format for bytecode. The JVM validates the bytecode before running it to ensure *type safety*.

UNDERSTANDING THE "HELLO WORLD" EXAMPLE

After 15 years of using this example in teaching, I must say it has lost what little charm it ever had. Many people consider the "Hello world!" program to be the first program one should learn in any language. In my view, it raises for Java beginners too many questions that they have no foundation to answer on their own: What is System? What does the dotted notation do? Is the out element a field? If so, how do fields have methods? Where do you find the println() method, and where can you learn the parameter it takes, legal types, and so on? Hold those questions in mind; they will be answered all in due turn.

Let's first review the words in the main() method's *signature*, one at a time. The *keyword* public is what's called an *access modifier*. It declares this method's level of exposure to potential callers in the program. Naturally, public means anyone in the program. The least-open access modifier is private, which restricts visibility to methods in the same class.

The keyword static binds a method to its class so it can be called by just the class name, as in, for example, EntryPoint.main(). In fact, the JVM does this, more or less, when loading the class name given to it. If a main() method isn't present in the class we name with the java executable, the process will throw an error and terminate.

The keyword void represents the return type. A method that returns no data returns control to the caller silently. In general, it's good practice to use void for methods that change an object's state. In that sense, the main() method changes overall program state from started to finished.

Finally we arrive at the main() method's parameter list, represented as an array of java.lang.String objects. In practice, you can write either String[] args or String args[]; the compiler accepts both. The variable name args hints that this list contains values that were read in (arguments) when the JVM started. We will discuss the String type in Chapter 2, "Applying Data Types in Java Programming" and the array type in Chapter 4, "Using Java Arrays."

Let's say we wanted to remake our Point3D class so the values for x, y, and z could be read in at start time with a command like this:

```
$ java Point3D 15 28 7
```

We cover access modifiers in Chapter 6, "Encapsulating Data and Exposing Methods in Java."

There are four access modes altogether: *protected* is one. The *default access mode* has no keyword.

Java keywords are reserved by the language for a special purpose. These words can't be used to name a class, method, or variable.

Arrays are the simplest form of a *collection* Java provides.

These values are each interpreted by the JVM as a series of character sequences separated by white space. Each sequence is used to create a `String` object, which is then assigned to an array *index* in the order received. Using the example, we'd expect to find a 15 in args[0], a 28 in args[1], and a 7 in arg[2]. To convert each one to a numeric type, we need to know a little bit more.

To see how this works, add a `main()` method to the `Point3D` class and put the following statements in it:

```
System.out.println(args[0]);
System.out.println(args[1]);
System.out.println(args[2]);
```

Compile and run the program. You'll see that the values added to the program output in the order they were input. And if you don't use these specific numbers, or numbers at all, it still works! That's because these values aren't being processed by the class; they're just passing through. Values introduced at program start usually influence program operation in some way. When you see a `main()` method's args array used just to initialize one object, it's usually toy code: That kind of work can also be handled by a constructor.

MOVING ON FROM "HELLO WORLD!"

Of course a Java "Hello World" program works fine, and it's easy to modify into something a little more interesting. But there's plenty going on that's just not apparent to a beginner. For example, there's a default constructor lurking about somewhere. One thing you don't know yet is that every class *inherits* code from the Java ecosystem. Another thing you haven't seen is how or which other classes are used to help you run a Java program. I'll shed some light on those last two points right now.

Importing Other Java Classes

Certification
Objective

Executing code written in any language relies on some amount of routine setup work. Toolmakers for a language will bake some of that routine into their works to save us all a bit of tedium. You can see some that work, in Java, with the following command. Use a window with an output buffer and scrolling capability:

```
java -verbose -version
```

This incantation produces 275 lines of extra output on my system, using an early release of Java SE 7. Each line reports a class that was loaded into the JVM because some already-loaded class asked for it. The name and order of classes can vary, depending on the Java version you're using (and possibly your operating system). In all cases, however, the first classes you should see loaded are `java.lang.Object` and `java.io.Serializable`.

The JVM *imports* these classes to help build the runtime process itself. The `java.lang.Object` class comes first because it is the parent class to all other Java classes. It provides the fundamental methods and state every object needs to operate in the JVM ecosystem. You should therefore commit the names of the `java.lang.Object` methods to memory, even if they don't mean a lot to you right now.

Figure 1.3 diagrams the key methods we'll discuss in this book.

Java objects receive `java.lang.Object` information by inheriting it.

```
java.lang.Object

clone( ): Object
equals(Object): boolean
finalize( ): void
getClass( ): Class
toString( ): String
```

FIGURE 1.3
Partial list of
java.lang.Object methods

From the diagram, it's apparent that any Java object should be able to make a copy of itself (`clone()`), determine if another object is equal to it, return its class/type, and convert itself into a `String` form. The `finalize()` method prepares an object for removal from memory by releasing the system resources it was using. I'll describe these methods in more detail as they become relevant to discussion.

There are thousands of different classes in the Java runtime alone, all of which inherit from `java.lang.Object`. With so many classes, there has to be some way to ensure that any name you give to a class won't conflict with someone else's. Java supports this by using *packages*. `java.lang` is a package; so is `java.io` (short for input/output).

The methods of one class are sometimes described collectively as the class's *behavior*. They are also called the *interface* of the class.

The first part of a package name indicates who produced the code. Subsequent package name elements, separated by dots, often name a category or subdomain of the classes. Third-party code packages usually start with the company's Internet domain name in reverse, such as, for example, `org.apache`.

The `java.lang` package includes types that are used by the JVM and are essential to the foundation of every Java program. Almost every package included in the Java Development Kit (JDK) starts with `java` or `javax` (extended).

But again, there are thousands of Java classes, and certainly many, many more that have been written the world over. The `-verbose` flag shows us a mere 270+. How does the JVM find just the ones it needs?

Each class has a *fully qualified package name*, or FQPN for short. To use it, your system environment must be configured to find these classes in the filesystem. The environment variable the JVM uses is called the *classpath*. The classpath lists one or more directories (folders) that contain Java packages.

In Java code, we use *import* statements to leverage the classpath environment. An import statement lets you declare the full package names for the classes you want to use. You can refer to any imported class by its class name alone (that is, `Object` instead of `java.lang.Object`) and save yourself some typing.

There's no practical limit to listing imported classes, other than your limit for reading through them and staying awake. Be aware that classes you import but don't use cause no harm. The compiler won't complain. Some code-development tools will warn you about unused import statements. It's not illegal to leave them in, just misleading.

Import statements also serve as an inventory of the classes used in a code file. You can import each class, one per statement, to create a cast of characters for the program, like this:

```
import java.lang.Object;
import java.io.Serializable;
```

Looking again at the output from `java -verbose`, I noticed that 99 of the classes my system loaded came from the `java.lang` package. Who wants to read through that many `import` declarations for one package? Instead, you can import all the classes from one package with a wildcard:

```
import java.lang.*;
import java.io.*;
```

However, because you need `java.lang` classes in all cases, the toolmakers just bake that one in. That's why you don't see `import` statements in simple test programs.

Another reason you don't see `import` statements in example code is that classes you commonly use are responsible for their own imports. Take the `java.lang.System` class as an example. Its member out (short for *output*

▶

A fully qualified package name is like an absolute path to a file, only it is globally unique.

▶

How the classpath is written depends on whether the operating system supports case-sensitive variables.

▶

Unlike #include or require directives used in other languages, a Java `import` imposes virtually no overhead on the compilation process.

stream) is in fact a variable of type java.io.PrintStream. To access it, the System class imports the java.io package. Even classes belonging to the same group from the same author need import statements to get to the other packages in that group.

Classes from other packages you try to use without a supporting import statement will make the compiler complain. To fix that problem, you might end up using a mix of FQPN and wildcard imports. There's no right or wrong to that, but mixing those conventions can be distracting to people who need to review or debug your code. Sticking to one approach is, at the least, a common courtesy and a sign of a consistent coder.

The package wildcard does *not* apply to packages organized under the imported package. If you want to use both java.awt.Dialog and java.awt.applet.Applet in a file, for example, you must provide an import statement for each.

out **is also a** *static* **member of** System, **which is why we can use it without making a** System **object.**

Understanding Package Declarations

Small code examples aside, all Java classes should declare their own package too. This practice helps the reader understand where the current code is organized relative to a larger body of code. The import statements also help a code reviewer understand which classes support the current class. Classes in the same package don't need to do this; they have a built-in *scope* that precludes the need for importing.

The package declaration is always the first *statement* in a Java file, followed by import statements, followed by class definitions. The internal arrangement of classes and their members, however, is a matter of preference. Most Java programmers will list fields first, constructors second (if any), and then methods, but the compiler will accept any arrangement.

A package declaration is a simple statement:

```
package com.ernestco;
```

Configuring your system so the compiler and JVM can find them shouldn't be hard, but there are rules you must follow. Remember the full path to the rt.jar file in the verbose example output? The JVM seems to find that critical file on its own (but it's another baked-in convenience). The classes we create have to be locatable by the classpath. If the class files reside in an archived format, known as a JAR file (like rt.jar), the classpath must include the filename as part of the path.

Tools called integrated development environments (IDEs) will manage these configuration details like this for you. The most popular free IDEs are NetBeans and Eclipse. Others, like IntelliJ's IDEA, are available for a price but are usually free for a trial period. Eventually you will want to know how to configure your own environment. You want to think of these tools as conveniences, not crutches. If a tool gets misconfigured and you don't know how to write code without it, the day in front of you might become very long.

Understanding Variable Scope in Java Code

Certification Objective

So far we've covered simple class structure, executing code in the JVM, and importing classes from other packages. You can now write a HelloWorld example program and appreciate how much Java you need just to run more Java. But we haven't yet written a non-static method or dug further into using variables. Let's do that now with the Point3D class outlined earlier.

The code we need to store and modify one coordinate in a Point3D object looks like this:

```
public class Point3D
{
    int x;

    public void setX(int xcoord) {
        x = xcoord;
    }
}
```

The method setX() will receive an int named xcoord and assign its value to the field x. This is how methods *communicate* in Java, by passing values from the calling method to the caller. The called method declares the type of information it accepts for a *message*. The name of the method should, as always, imply what the message is for; the parameter name should clarify that intent.

This message is also known as a *temporary variable*. It has a name and value that expire as soon as the called method returns control to the caller. Any

Objects have individual states and behavior. In the sense of that vocabulary, we also say methods communicate with messages.

variable that is *declared* in the parameter list, or inside a method body, lasts in memory only for the duration of the method call.

We consider the term *variable* less precise than the term *field* because it refers to program data storage for any *duration*. A field is available as long as the object containing it remains in memory (and is therefore called a *member* of that object). How long other variables remain in memory depends on the context, or *scope*, in which we declared them.

We refer to this aspect of variables as their *lifetime*. Every time you use a French curly brace in Java (the { symbol), whether it's to open a class, method, or other construct you haven't yet learned, you create a *scope* for the variables it contains.

Each scope not only has a lifetime, it also has a *namespace*. Let's say you have a variable i you'd like to use for a variety of temporary purposes. With one global namespace only, you could use it only once. Because each method has its own scope, you can use i without getting any baggage related to a previous use. But there is also a drawback, which the following code fragment illustrates:

```
int x = 1

public void setX(int x) {
    x = x;
}
```

How do you know which x is which? You don't. And, as it turns out, neither does the compiler. In this case it cannot figure out that member x is on the left and parameter x is on the right, as you might expect.

Fortunately, Java provides means to distinguish the two. The keyword this refers to *the current object* and can be used to access any member of the object. Using it, the meaning becomes unambiguous:

```
public void setX(int x) {
    this.x = x;
}
```

In doing so, you realize one more benefit. Now you don't have to conjure two names for the same datum in straightforward situations like this one. And there are other ways the this keyword helps resolve sticky situations, which we'll cover in Chapter 9, "Inheriting Code and Data in Java."

Understanding Program State

You will use lots of variables for lots of purposes in a busy Java program. Some of them will act as *counters* or placeholders or serve another role useful for temporary storage. The ones that store values you want to track over the life of an object are its fields, and contribute to what I've been calling the object's state. As fields change, so does the state of the object; these fields *are* the object's state. In fact, if a field changes often in a class but it never seems to matter to the program, ask yourself why you're using it.

The more fields a class contains, the more complex its state changes become. It's never too early to think about limiting a class to just the fields it needs to reflect state changes. You'll get way ahead in becoming an effective and economical Java programmer by keeping this goal in mind.

THE ESSENTIALS AND BEYOND

In this chapter, we covered some basic elements of writing Java programs, including the structure of a Java class and how to write a `main()` method. We also discussed how one Java class can incorporate classes from other packages. To dig a bit deeper, we also looked at the role fields play in maintaining an object's state and the role methods play in altering object state or providing some other kind of service.

ADDITIONAL EXERCISES

1. Use the Java runtime with a class that has a `main()` method, but leave the `.class` filename extension on. What result do you get and what does it mean?

2. Sketch your own diagram of a physical object as if you were going to make a Java class from it: perhaps an apple, coin, or magazine. What state data do you think the class should hold? What behaviors (methods) should it support?

3. Obscure a `main()` method in one of your Java classes by using comment markers (`//`) at the beginning of those lines. Re-compile the code and run it as you normally would. What result do you get and what does it mean?

4. Run a `java` command with the `-verbose` option again and review the different package names you see. Note which classes are not in the `java.lang` package. In particular, note any package names that don't start with `java`.

We didn't review Java's online documentation, but you'll use it a lot. Start by browsing the `java.lang.System` class here:

> `http://docs.oracle.com/javase/7/docs/api/java/lang/System.html`

Use the navigation links provided to learn about the `System.out` member.

5. Complete the `Point3D` class so each member variable has a `set` method.

(Continues)

REVIEW QUESTIONS

1. Select the two options that name basic components of a Java class:

   A. Methods   **B.** Blocks

   C. Instances   **D.** Fields

2. True or false: The compiler will insert a `main()` method in a Java class if the programmer doesn't specify one.

3. How does Java define equality between two objects?

   A. Two object variables have the same values.

   B. Two object variables refer to the same location in memory.

   C. Always B; possibly A.

   D. Always A; possibly B.

4. A field's lifetime (scope) is the same as which of the following?

   A. Object   **B.** Class

   C. Method   **D.** JVM

5. Which classes are visible to your code if you import `java.util.*`?

   A. All classes in the `java.util` package

   B. All classes in the `java.util` package plus every package below it

   C. All files in the `java.util` folder

   D. None of the above

6. The state of any Java object is directly related to which of the following?

   A. Member variables   **B.** Non-static methods

   C. Home address   **D.** Parameters

7. Which pair of terms describes separate aspects of variable scope?

   A. Statement and expression

   B. Namespace and duration

   C. Duration and lifetime

   D. Opening and closing braces

(Continues)

THE ESSENTIALS AND BEYOND *(Continued)*

8. Which statement is true regarding command-line arguments used when starting a Java program?

   A. They must be `String` objects.

   B. They must have white space in them.

   C. They should be reasonable.

   D. They are processed into the `args` array as parameters.

9. True or false: Every Java class has at least one constructor.

10. What does the classpath do?

    A. It points to every Java directory in the filesystem.

    B. It decides which files have bytecode in them.

    C. It lists directories that have Java packages.

    D. It makes Java archives into filenames.

CHAPTER 2

Applying Data Types in Java Programming

In the examples in Chapter 1, you saw casual use of data types to help you understand Java class structure. Now we dig in a bit deeper to understand the two basic types of data we have in Java, objects and primitives. As you learn about them, you'll get a better understanding of the rules that support them and the cases the drive their use.

We'll also take our first look at two key Java classes, `String` and `StringBuilder`, which you'll need quite frequently in everyday programming.

In this chapter, we'll cover the following topics:

▶ **Creating, using, and destroying objects**

▶ **Distinguishing between object references and primitives**

▶ **Declaring and initializing variables**

▶ **Default initialization of variables**

▶ **Reading and writing object fields**

▶ **Using the `StringBuilder` class and its methods**

▶ **Creating and manipulating strings**

Creating, Using, and Destroying Objects

 Certification Objective

Creating an object of a Java class occurs through a process called *construction*. While the programmer can exert some control over how construction takes place, the process itself is so important that it will be inserted into every class at compilation time if the programmer does nothing with it.

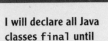

I will declare all Java classes final until further notice.

You don't have to include a constructor in a class, but you can, even if you just want to write what the compiler would produce. The default constructor, also known as the no-arg constructor, looks like the one shown in Listing 2.1.

LISTING 2.1 NewThing class with default constructor

```
$ cat NewThing.java
public final class NewThing {
    public NewThing() { }
}
```

As you can see, a default constructor takes no parameters and includes no code. All the necessary steps to construct a NewThing object in memory are built into the JVM, so a programmer is never directly responsible for object construction. Rather, the constructor form gives the programmer a way to alter or elaborate upon the construction process. You'll learn how to do both with the default constructor in Chapter 8, "Using Java Constructors."

Before we explore further with objects and data types, we need the help of two new terms, *referent* and *reference*. A referent is an actual object in Java memory. A reference is a variable. It has a declared type and a name, and it can point to the location of one referent with the same type. In a casual discussion, it's common for a speaker to point to a variable in some code and call it "such-and-such an object" instead of calling it the thing that represents an object.

Primitives are discussed in the next section, "Distinguishing between Object References and Primitives."

Normally it's not important to be more precise because the speaker expects that their listeners know the difference and don't mind the shortcut in conversation. If you're new to such presentations, however, and you never hear it any other way, you might think the two are more or less the same thing—but they *really* aren't. Distinguishing between an object reference and the thing it points to—the referent—will not only help you better understand the *life cycle* of Java objects, it will also help you understand how they are very different creatures from what Java calls a *primitive*.

You can observe this relationship, in a sense, by printing a java.lang.Object referent, as shown in Listing 2.2.

LISTING 2.2 PrintObject class with output

We'll stick to simple Unix commands for listing, compiling, and running code. To follow along on Windows, you'll need to translate the commands as needed.

```
$ cat PrintObject.java
public final class PrintObject {
    public static void main(String args[]) {
        Object obj = new Object();
        System.out.println(obj);
    }
}
```

```
$ javac PrintObject.java
$ java PrintObject
java.lang.Object@12b6651
```

When printed, the `obj` reveals the contents of the referent: the object's type and a value that, for the sake of simplicity, we'll say is a location where the object resides. Notice the reference `obj` doesn't appear to point to the *content* of the referent, just its location. Even this location doesn't mean too much. It's simply an address the JVM assigned the object. The value you see won't be the same. In fact, you may not even see the same address if you run this program more than once. It will depend in part on what system you use to run the code.

This relationship between reference and referent is an indirect but powerful one that has several benefits. First, since a reference points only to a memory address and not actual content, it only has to have room to store the address. Referent addresses have one size, so it doesn't matter what type of object you want to refer to. All object references have a common size. The referent is of course as big as it needs to be, up to the limit the JVM allows. The reference only has to get you to it.

Second, references are a way of expressing interest in the referent. When we remove all references to a referent—either by assigning them to other referents or the keyword `null`—the referent becomes expendable. The memory it consumes can be released and made available for future objects. The *lifetime* of any referent, therefore, depends on how many references (variables) point to it. In particular, it remains active for as long as its longest-living reference refers to it.

To better appreciate this relationship, let's write a Java class called `FreeCopy` with a method that will return a reference to itself to the caller. Listing 2.3 shows the `FreeCopy` class with example output.

LISTING 2.3 The `FreeCopy` class with output

The process of finding expendable objects in memory and removing them is called *garbage collection*.

```
$ cat FreeCopy.java
public final class FreeCopy {
    FreeCopy local;

    FreeCopy getOne() {
        return this;
    }
    // "this" lets the called method
    // refer to its own object

    public static void main(String args[]) {
        FreeCopy fc1 = new FreeCopy();
        FreeCopy fc2 = new FreeCopy();
        FreeCopy fc3 = fc2.getOne();
```

```
        fc3.local = fc1.getOne();
        System.out.println(fc1);
        System.out.println(fc2);
        System.out.println(fc3);
        System.out.println(fc3.local);
    }
}

$ javac FreeCopy.java
$ java FreeCopy
FreeCopy@12b6651
FreeCopy@4a5ab2
FreeCopy@4a5ab2
FreeCopy@12b6651
$
```

Study the output first. The addresses printed show that the first and fourth references point to one referent. The second and third references point to another. Thus there are four different references but only two FreeCopy objects among them.

Next read each statement in this program carefully and make sure you get what's happening. (If it doesn't turn your brain to jelly the first time through, you're going to outgrow this book quickly.) First, note that the FreeCopy class has a member variable of type FreeCopy. The variables fc1 and fc2 each get assigned their own FreeCopy objects. fc3 is assigned the same referent as fc2. The member variable fc3.local is assigned to the same referent as fc1. The program prints out each referent's type and location.

THINKING OF JAVA CLASSES AS CONTAINERS

Let's take a moment to consider how an object can contain an object of its own type. If it doesn't look odd to you on first sight, congratulations! It sure did to me, and it took me longer than a moment to think through it.

On one hand, you can think about it as one box that holds another box. One box has to be big enough to hold the other, of course. And while boxes are conceptually one thing, each instance is a different thing with its own properties. We don't let the concept of a box distract us from the material reality of boxes.

THINKING OF JAVA CLASSES AS CONTAINERS *(Continued)*

In Java, we can think of a reference as the conceptual thing and a referent as the material thing. When we declare a FreeCopy variable inside a FreeCopy class, we're saying that the referent can contain a reference of the same type. The reference is a referent location holder. It doesn't become "real" until we assign it a referent, and it can't get a referent until after the object that holds it is created. There's no real potential for confusion once you think it through.

There are two ways to reduce the reference count we have on our FreeCopy referents. One, we could assign a variable to a different FreeCopy instance. Two, we could change their value to the keyword null, which reassigns the variable so it refers to no referent. What we *can't* do is release or destroy the variable. Variables go away only when the scope in which we declared them expires. Two good object conservation practices derive from this lesson: One, you should declare object references (variables) in the narrowest scope where they still do something useful for you, and two, you should assign variables to null as soon as you no longer need the referent.

Distinguishing between Object References and Primitives

You've now learned an important subtlety of creating objects in Java. How they consume and release memory is removed from our direct view as a matter of language design. And, as you will no doubt hear, programmers who assume this memory management takes no effort to support often have painful stories to tell about bloated server programs that regularly have to be restarted. The two guidelines previously given can go a long way to avoiding that outcome: Keep your object references in as narrow a scope as you can and assign them to null as soon as you can. When you assign an object reference to null, you allow JVM to determine whether the original referent may be cleared from memory, making the space available for a future object.

Certification Objective ▶

Boolean values have one of two possible states: true or false.

Still, there are many cases where using an object provides no benefit for the overhead required. For example, if you just need to store a simple value—an integer, floating-point number, or Boolean value—it's easier and cheaper to use a variable that actually contains that value, not a reference to an object's type and location. For such cases, Java provides a set of types called *primitives.*

Each primitive *is* a type. It just isn't defined by a class. Instead, Java represents them with *keywords* that are enforced by the compiler and virtual machine. Keywords have special meaning in the language and cannot be used as variables or names. Primitives contain a literal, type-legal value only, no methods or members. Table 2.1 lists each primitive keyword and its meaning.

TABLE 2.1   Java primitives

Keyword	Type
boolean	true or false value
byte	8-bit integral value
short	16-bit integral value
int	32-bit integral value
long	64-bit integral value
char	16-bit Unicode value
float	32-bit floating-point value
double	64-bit floating-point value

▶

Number storage is defined at the bit level. Java integers follow a storage scheme known as signed-two's complement.

There are several things to notice here. A boolean variable can store only the value true or false. These words are also *reserved* in the Java language. Many other languages allow zero or nonzero values to represent false or true. Java insists on type-specific values.

The types byte, short, int, and long all store integer values. The *range* of each type is defined by how many bits it gets for storage. An 8-bit range allows for 2^8, or 256, possible values. To allow for negative values, the highest bit holds the sign, leaving room for 2^7 nonnegative and 2^7 negative values. Zero is included in the nonnegative range. A byte variable, therefore, can store any value from -128 to 127. A short variable can store any value from -32768 to 32767, and so on.

The char type is a funny case. Its 16-bit value range is the same as an unsigned integer, allowing for 2^{16}, or 65,536, values. Instead of mapping to a numeric range, however, the char type maps to Unicode values, a collection of character sets that spans the major written languages of the world but they are still stored as numbers. You can perform numeric calculations with char values; you just won't get a numeric result from them..

Floating-point values are trickier things to understand. How, for example, do you store 1/3, or a transcendental number like π, in a fixed amount of space? And how do you represent the decimal point in bit form? The short answer is that however you do it, you end up sacrificing some *precision* of your value in the process.

There are other issues as well, such as how to deal with values very close to zero. The definition for a floating-point primitive therefore has to lay out rules and conditions the numbers-focused programmer can rely on for storing and retrieving these values. The types float and double follow the same rules but offer different levels of precision based on their bit ranges.

Just because we call these types primitive doesn't mean they are simple. In fact, many Java programming puzzles merely test the reader's intimate knowledge of primitive types and their behavior in uncommon cases. For example, what happens when you add 1 to a byte variable that currently stores 127? What happens when you try to divide a number by zero and store it in a floating-point variable? Both questions have answers that have nothing to do with intellect and everything to do with knowing the rules for representing numbers in machine storage. If the kind of code you write relies on intimate knowledge of these types, you'll need to know them inside and out. Even if you don't, not knowing the rules means, up to a point, leaving the outcomes of your code to chance.

Primitive types behave like *registers*. That is, they store literal values and have no concept of pointing to a memory location. Even if you declare several primitives of one type and assign them all the same value, they will each get independent storage locations.

With that in mind, each primitive variable is said to hold a *copy* of some literal value. An object variable holds a copy of a referent address. In the same way that three int variables, all holding the value 7, are distinct elements of storage, so are three object references all pointing to the same referent.

This distinction causes no small amount of misunderstanding for beginning programmers. A variable that is just another name for the value 7 is different from a variable that knows where to find a 7 object in memory. Still, each variable only holds a *copy* of its content. No variable in Java ever has an exclusive copy of any value. We'll study the implications of this meaning in detail in Chapter 7, "Using Java Methods to Communicate."

Declaring and Initializing Variables

I've defined several aspects of variables already. For the sake of review, and to collect those points under an easy-to-find heading, I'll repeat those points and elaborate on them.

When you declare a variable in Java, you fix the type and name of one storage element in your code. These two properties endure for as long as the scope in which the declaration was made.

When you declare instance variable in a class (one that is not defined as static), that variable is part of every object made from that class. It expires only when the object referent has no more references to maintain it.

If you declare a variable inside a method, it expires once the method returns control to its caller. These variables are sometimes called *automatic* or *local* variables because their lifetime is limited to the enclosing method. This immediate context allows a method body to name variables without concern for names in the enclosing class or in other methods.

We initialize variables by assignment with an *expression*. In the statements

```
int y = 25;
Object obj = new Object();
```

the value 25 is a numeric literal; the result of the expression new Object() is a referent. We call both of them expressions because we want to establish, even for the simplest case, that they must *resolve* to a value the compiler can match to the variable's declared type.

The individual *operands* of an expression, however, do not have to observe this rule. That is, you could subtract one large int value from another and assign their difference to a short, assuming the difference falls within short range. Consider the class in Listing 2.4.

LISTING 2.4 The Short class with a variable assignment

```
public final class Short {
    public static void main(String args[]) {
        short stack = 64000-60000;
        System.out.println(stack);
    }
}
```

The variable stack is a short, a 16-bit signed integer type that cannot store values greater than 32767. Thus the numbers used in the expression are too large for a short, but the difference between them is not. By the same token, if

There are other scopes in Java we won't discuss in this guide, but these rules will apply for them as well.

Certification Objective

An expression is sometimes referred to as the right-hand side (RHS) of an assignment statement.

we assign a sum of two short values, say 32000 and 8000, that exceed what a short can contain, the compiler will reject it. It is therefore only the result of an expression you have to worry about. That said, you will encounter more than one expression in your programming career that will oblige you to work out on paper why the compiler won't accept it.

There are several ways to mislead a programmer with expressions that seem inappropriate to a variable in code of this sort, but if you remember that the compiler cares only about the resulting type of the expression, you'll catch most attempts to fool you, if not all of them. Declaring and initializing a variable in one statement makes code easy to read, but it's not always practical. When and where you initialize a variable is influenced by factors that are sometimes at odds with each other. In methods, for example, you will often use the parameters received from a caller to modify the value of a class variable. Consider the example in Listing 2.5.

It's common in test questions to assign an expression to a char or byte variable and test the programmer's understanding of range and type.

LISTING 2.5 EasyMath class with addTwo() method

```
public final class EasyMath {
    int sum;
    public int addTwo(int x, int y) {
        sum = x + y;
        return sum;
    }
}
```

The variable sum is a class member. The value we want to assign it is the sum of two method parameters. If we declared sum inside the method, it would still receive the assignment, but then we'd lose the sum variable when the method returns.

I don't mean to make separating a variable's declaration from its initialization sound like a problem. It is in fact a necessity. It is how one object *communicates* with another, by identifying a method through its name and parameter list and asking it to operate on the values provided. The only way the called object can remember that action is by providing a store for the result.

For simple code examples, this figurative language may sound fancy or academic. When discussing complex program design, however, it's often easier to exchange ideas first using these abstract terms. I explain these terms now so you'll be prepared for readings and conversations you'll have in the future. There is a problem in all of this, sort of, but it has to do with managing class code well, not the act of separating variable declaration from initialization. Consider a case where we declare a member variable in a class with many methods. Perhaps the first listed method that initializes the variable doesn't appear in the code for

To extend the communication metaphor, we sometimes refer to the parameters passed to a method as a *message*.

another 50 lines. Perhaps there are several methods that initialize or modify the variable.

Class code doesn't determine the order in which these methods are called. The callers do that. If there is a necessary process to setting or getting a member's value, the programmer has some options. One is to document the necessary steps, thereby delegating responsibility to the calling programmer. Another is to enforce the behavior through code, which takes more knowledge and skill than we have at the moment. Either way, this interaction between member variables and callers through the class's methods has to be thought out carefully in a large class.

One bit of good news, as mentioned previously, is that each method has its own scope and namespace that is separate from other methods. Any number of methods can use the same name for a local variable without worry, including reusing names declared at the class level. The variable names declared by method parameters belong to the same scope.

Keep to simple, obvious cases when reusing variable names between member and method scopes. As Listing 2.6 illustrates, it's not hard to get into trouble.

LISTING 2.6 ScopesTrial **class with multiple place variables**

```java
public final class ScopesTrial {
    Object place = new Object();
    public void setObject(Object newObj) {
        Object place = newObj;
    }
}
```

It appears the setObject() method should update the member variable place. As written, however, a temporary variable place is assigned the value of the parameter, and the method exits. The member variable place doesn't change. What was the intended result? It may be easy to figure out in a short code example, but as a class's code gets longer and more complex, it gets harder to tell the difference between poor name choices and an actual code bug.

If you allow more than one method to modify the same member variable, you must think through the consequences of call order. This issue will grow in proportion to the number of methods involved, so it's important to catch it early in a growing class. Listing 2.7 is a simple case.

LISTING 2.7 Converter **class with implied call order**

```java
public final class Converter {
    float temp;
```

```java
void setTemperature(float newTemp) {
    temp = newTemp;
}

void subtract() {
    temp = temp-32;
}

void divide() {
    temp = temp / 1.8f;
}

public static void main(String args[]) {
    Converter co = new Converter();
    float myTemp = 68.0f;
    co.setTemperature(myTemp);
    System.out.println(co.temp + " degrees F");
    co.divide();
    co.subtract();
    System.out.println(co.temp + " degrees C");
}
}
$ javac Converter.java
$ java Converter
68.0 degrees F
5.7777786 degrees C
```

In the `main()` method we create a `Converter` object, call set temperature to set a Fahrenheit value. We call the methods that each perform part of the conversion and print the result. If you live in the United States, it may take longer for the horror to set in, but the result is wrong: 68 degrees Fahrenheit is much closer to 20 degrees Celsius. To produce the right result, the program must subtract 32 first and divide by 1.8 second.

It's an easy problem to fix, but it's far better to prevent it altogether. You could document the class warning potential callers about the need to follow order. You could combine the methods into a single call so the class member temp is updated in one place. You could write another method that calls `subtract()` and `divide()` in the right order on behalf of the caller.

Each solution has benefits and trade-offs. Documenting sounds weak, but it means you don't have to change the code at all, and you might need it the way it is for other reasons. Combining the methods seems ideal to me, but maybe the methods in question are used by other callers with different needs. A method that calls these methods for us also works, but then we have to make sure the caller uses the right one.

For code that just doesn't work as expected, we don't have to be so delicate. But for code that works mostly well, the most straightforward fix is sometimes out of the question.

Default Initialization of Variables

I hope you noticed something in reading the previous section. The state of an object "in between" method calls can become a question mark in otherwise legal code. As programmers writing Java classes, we have to plan how we will let methods touch the *state* of the object, that is, the fields that store its values.

The compiler and the JVM have a similar job at a lower level. In order to support type-safety in our code, their checks must ensure that each member has a legal value as soon as it is declared. But as you just saw, declaring and initializing every member ourselves may not have any meaning to our code: What is a default temperature? Fortunately, the compiler and JVM don't have to figure that out either. They just have to make sure each member has a type-appropriate value before they become accessible.

Let's say you wrote a class like the one in Listing 2.8.

LISTING 2.8 A busy Java class

```
public final class Mess {
    Object obj1;
    public void setObject1(Object obj1) {
        this.obj1 = obj1;
    }
    Object obj2;
    public void setObject2(Object obj2) {
        this.obj2 = obj2;
    }
// additional code here
}
```

It's ugly to read but legal code. Once the Mess class is created, its members obj1 and obj2 become accessible to a caller. To protect the system's type rules, the compiler has to ensure that these members refer to valid referents before they are ever accessed. It doesn't matter to the compiler whether a value is usable in a program, only that it's legal. This issue is important enough that the compiler will always initialize members in class scope if the programmer

Notice you can declare members anywhere in the class's scope. This way you can declare variables close to where they are initialized.

doesn't. Consequently, it is always the programmer's responsibility to establish a starting value for each field if the compiler's default assignment makes no sense to the program.

The default value for each type is shown in Table 2.2.

TABLE 2.2 Default initialization values by type

Variable type	Default initialization value
boolean	false
byte, short, int, long	0 (in the type's bit-length)
float, double	0.0 (in the type's bit-length)
char	'\u0000' (NUL)
All object references	null

Inside method code, it's a different matter. The compiler does not concern itself with variables that are declared inside a method. The programmer is responsible for initializing local variables before they are used in an expression. If you use a variable in an expression without initializing it, however, the compiler will complain, as shown in Listing 2.9.

LISTING 2.9 Using a variable before initializing it

```
public final class DeclareInitialize {
    public void setValue() {
        int x;
        int y;
        y = x;
    }
}

$ javac DeclareInitialize.java
DeclareInitialize.java:5: variable x might not have been
initialized
        y = x;
            ^
1 error
```

The variables x and y are declared inside the setValue() method. Notice the compiler does not complain about y; it hasn't been used in an expression. It is x, once the compiler tests its value, that becomes suspect. The language of the complaint suggests the compiler doesn't even know for sure. What it does know is that x is not initialized for *every* possible case, and that's the standard.

Seems like a raw deal, doesn't it? The compiler won't do the work and complains if you don't. Why? The compiler only has to enforce type-safety in your program. It doesn't have to assist, according to the rules in the Java Language Specification. It provides default initialization for class members; it doesn't for local variables. And those are the rules.

This error can also occur if the variable x was redeclared by mistake and should have referred to a class member. Remember, every method body gets its own namespace. In a large class, it's easy to forget why or if you meant to shadow a member variable with a local one by the same name. Limit reuse of variable names for simple cases, like giving an incoming parameter the same name as the field you mean to modify, and you'll make this mistake less often.

Reading and Writing Object Fields

**Certification
Objective**

By now you might imagine there's not much left to say about object fields. They're variables in a referent that must be addressed by an object reference, or by using the this keyword. In Chapter 6, "Encapsulating Data and Exposing Methods in Java," we'll discuss why, in typical Java code, you *don't* want to allow open access to your fields in this manner. For now, however, you're learning one thing at a time, starting with Java code that is legal. Your long-term goal is writing legal code that is easy to read, reflects common practices, and looks more like the working code as you understand more what it should look like.

Relying on direct field access for now, we can use a version of our Point3D class without methods and just set the values for x, y, z as shown in Listing 2.10.

LISTING 2.10 Using a Point3D class without methods

```java
public final class Point3D {
    int x, y, z;
    int uselessSum;

    public static void main(String args[]) {
        Point3D point = new Point3D();
        point.x = 5;
        point.y = 12;
```

```
            point.z = 13;
            point.uselessSum = point.x + point.y + point.z;
    }
}
```

Once we've made a `Point3D` object, we can use the reference to access each field. In this example we just set each member's value, but we can also use them in expressions. If we wanted to calculate `point`'s linear distance from (0,0,0), for example, we could write an expression using the appropriate formula and store the results to a variable, either a temporary one or a class member.

> **It is legal to declare multiple variables of one type in a single statement, as was done in Listing 2.8. Mostly it saves a little space.**

A WORD ON DIRECT FIELD ACCESS IN OBJECTS

As simple as this mechanism is, it is not useful in general programming. Direct field access implies that whoever handles the object reference will always set values in a useful way or retrieve values at the right time (before or after a state change).

Say you wanted to use some `Point3D` objects to populate a map of 10000×10000×10000 points. How do you make sure no `Point3D` object has coordinate values that exceed the map's limit? And if the map supports only nonnegative coordinates, how do you guard against an object with any of its coordinates set to a negative value?

You need code to *guard* the storage and *validate* any changes made to it. That's where methods come in. Whatever services a method provides to its callers, it must also help protect the *integrity* of the object data from accidental or intentional misuse. For reasons that are less obvious, you might also want to protect a field from being read directly at any time by any reference holder. Again, we'll investigate the means for managing fields in Chapter 6.

We've discussed type-safety a few times so far and emphasized the compiler's role in enforcing it. This discussion might lead you to wonder how exactly you can print an object reference. How is it that any type can be printed? It's a fine question. Answering it will help you better understand how all objects, in some way, can be converted to a stream of printable characters. Let's start by adding the following lines to the end of the `main()` method in Listing 2.8.

```
System.out.println(point.x);
System.out.println(point.y);
System.out.println(point.z);
```

The answer is that the program prints 5, 12, and 13, each on a separate line. When we read an object field, we treat it as an expression, meaning we ask the JVM to evaluate it. Whether it evaluates to a literal or a referent location, it also resolves to a type. The receiving method must accept that type as a valid parameter. The type is int in all three cases here, but this println() method will in fact accept any type our expression resolves to.

It's not magic; the output still has to be converted to a number of printable characters (in proper sequence) for the operating system to receive and process them to an output channel (such as a terminal window). Therefore, the JVM must perform some kind of conversion behind the scenes, first by reading the object field, then by converting its type to something the operating system can handle. With that in mind, we should discuss string types; they are fundamental to every meaningful program you will ever write.

Using the *StringBuilder* Class and Its Methods

You now have both motive and information enough to learn your first *class interface*. A class interface is just a list of fields and methods you can access through an object of that class.

On a higher level, a class interface also communicates its capabilities by the types it uses (as parameters and return values) and the names it uses for its methods and fields. When these elements are well-chosen and documented, the class usually takes less time to learn and apply. It also tends to be easier to maintain and debug.

One thing you'll notice about string types in general is how many of their methods let you manage a string as an *array of characters*. A string is basically that: an ordered list of characters. It could make sense as a human-readable word or a stream of words. It could also *encode* complex information intended for a specific application, perhaps one that can parse it into smaller units of meaning and convert it to primitive values or other types.

You're ready to start reading JDK class interfaces, so let's examine the one for java.lang.StringBuilder. All JDK classes are published online by their major release version, so make sure you find the Java SE 7 version, which is here:

You can find other JDK classes by replacing the package name elements of this link with the one you want and appending .html to the class name.

    http://docs.oracle.com/javase/7/docs/api/java/lang/StringBuilder.html

Just scrolling, it looks like the StringBuilder class has a lot of methods, but many of them are variants of the same method. Two of StringBuilder's methods, append() and insert(), account for 25 of the method entries, so it's not as much to absorb as it looks like.

A Word on the *java.lang.String* Class

Strings are an essential type. Historically, Java programmers have learned the `java.lang.String.` class first for that reason. And they have learned an odd thing along the way: If you declare and initialize a `java.lang.String` type in one statement, you don't have to make an object. It is in fact legal to write `String name = "Michael";` the compiler knows what to do.

This exception seems to provide a minor convenience—you don't have to type the new keyword—but it really has to do with performance. Understanding why Java allows assignment without construction, however, means you have to think about this exception to your class-object model before you've spent enough time with the rules. We discuss `java.lang.StringBuilder` first for that reason. We'll address the `String` class and the reasons behind its exceptional syntax in the next section.

I'll use the diagram in Figure 2.1 to cut things down and focus on the key methods. In diagrams of this sort, you should usually be less concerned with full details of parameters and more concerned with the names of methods, or *operations*, the class makes available.

java.lang.StringBuilder	
append(...)	: StringBuilder
insert(...)	: StringBuilder
delete(int, int)	: StringBuilder
setCharAt(int, char)	: void
charAt(int)	: char
substring(...)	: String
capacity( )	: int
length( )	: int
trimToSize( )	: void
reverse( )	: StringBuilder

FIGURE 2.1 Selected methods from the StringBuilder class

The class name appears at the top followed by fields (if they are significant to what the diagram wants to illustrate), which are in turn followed by methods. Diagrams of this sort aren't used just to convert Java code into a graphic form, although that is a useful benefit. They're meant to focus on aspects of the class that promote one discussion topic or another. Think of these diagrams as suggestive rather than exhaustive.

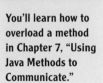

You'll learn how to overload a method in Chapter 7, "Using Java Methods to Communicate."

Notice that I've replaced some parameter lists with an ellipsis (...) to indicate that the method accepts several different parameters. This technique is called *overloading.* If we couldn't vary parameter lists for the same method easily, we'd probably have to rename the methods to signify their accepted types, like appendBoolean() or appendDouble(). It's better to have two methods to think about generally instead of 25 to think about specifically. Overloading, when it's well done, can take a big bite out of the chore of learning a new class.

In Figure 2.1, the methods are also grouped with related behavior to hint at the general services the class's methods provide. The intentions of each method group are described here:

Modifying object content

append(): Converts to string form any primitive or object and adds it to the end of the current object

insert(): Puts the parameter data supplied at a specified location in the current object

delete(): Removes characters using starting and ending index numbers

setCharAt(): Changes the character at the specified index

Retrieving part of a string

charAt(): Retrieves the character at the specified index

substring(): Retrieves characters using starting and ending index numbers

Managing the actual and available size of object data

length(): Returns the number of characters in the object

capacity(): Returns how many characters the object could hold without allocating more space

trimToSize(): Reduces the capacity of the object to its current length, if possible

Providing surprisingly useful services

reverse(): Inverts the current order of the characters

Also, there are four ways to construct a `StringBuilder` object:

- ▶ No parameter: the initial capacity is 16 characters; initial length is 0.

- ▶ With an `int`: capacity is set to the value given (must be non-negative).

- ▶ With a `String` object.

- ▶ With a `CharSequence` object.

A WORD ON READING CLASS INTERFACES

Breaking a class interface into smaller, logical groups takes time. You'll get faster and more precise with experience. Here are some basic tips to start:

- ▶ For one method name, ignore any parameter differences.
- ▶ Look for logical name pairs (open/close, add/remove).
- ▶ Create your own categories. You can refine them as you go.

To learn how to apply these methods and constructors, you'll want to do two things. One, write simple test programs for them to confirm your understanding. Two (and more important), get into the habit of writing test code. Sooner or later, working knowledge of any class comes from using it; there is no substitute. Listing 2.11, as an example, tests the `StringBuilder` no-arg constructor.

LISTING 2.11 A test of the default `StringBuilder` constructor

```
public final class StringBuilderNoParam {
   public static void main(String args[]) {
      StringBuilder sb = new StringBuilder ();
      System.out.println("capacity: " + sb.capacity());
      System.out.println("length: " + sb.length());
   }
}
$ javac StringBuilderNoParam.java

$ java StringBuilderNoParam

capacity: 16
length: 0
$
```

As expected, the object's `capacity` was set to 16 and `length` was set to zero. It's nice (or a relief!) when your findings match the documentation, but you should also write tests you expect to fail. A good starting point for such tests is to apply values that are type-legal but don't make sense in the context of the class, as Listing 2.12 shows.

LISTING 2.12 A test of the `StringBuilder(int capacity)` constructor

```
public final class StringBuilderTestNegativeInt {
    public static void main(String args[]) {
        StringBuilder sb = new StringBuilder (-5);
        System.out.println("capacity: " + sb.capacity());
        System.out.println("length: " + sb.length());
    }
}
```

The code in Listing 2.12 will compile because -5 falls within a Java integer's range. It should not work because a new with negative capacity has no meaning. What we need to know is *how* the `StringBuilder` class handles this input. Let's run it and find out:

```
$ javac StringBuilderTestNegativeInt.java
$ java StringBuilderTestNegativeInt
Exception in thread "main" java.lang.NegativeArraySizeException
        at java.lang.AbstractStringBuilder.<init>
(AbstractStringBuilder.java:64)
        at java.lang.StringBuilder.<init>
(StringBuilder.java:97)
        at StringBuilderTestNegativeInt.
main(StringBuilderTestNegativeInt.java:3)
```

The output we receive is what's called a *stack trace*. At the top of the stack, we are told what went wrong. In Java, the term *exception* applies to an error in the program. Errors in Java also take the form of a class, in this case a `NegativeArraySizeException` class.

The JVM traced this exception back to line 3 of our code, where we called the constructor and passed in -5. It turns out the `StringBuilder` constructor passes this value along to a class called `AbstractStringBuilder`, which *throws* the exception. In short, our code got past the compiler but then crashed the JVM. We're fortunate in a sense, though: the name of the exception alone tells us what's wrong with the program. Or, in our case, confirms that the class won't tolerate a negative value for the object's capacity.

That's all it takes to write a simple test for any `StringBuilder` method, including the ones that were outlined in this chapter and the ones that weren't.

Exceptions are the topic of Chapter 11, "Throwing and Catching Exceptions in Java."

We say exceptions are thrown because they alter the desired flow of the program when they occur.

I didn't describe the methods that I don't think will mean much to you right away, but you may feel differently upon browsing the documentation. Express what you think is useful by testing it! Make sure the methods you want to use behave as expected and fail as expected. Sure, it can be slow and tedious work, but the idea that you can blindly rely on code from another source has far bigger consequences for code you will truly depend on.

Creating and Manipulating Strings

There are actually quite a few classes that operate on strings. There's no simple way to list all of them from the JDK, but you can find the class names that start with the word `String`. For starters, browse this web page:

```
http://docs.oracle.com/javase/7/docs/api/allclasses-noframe.html
```

You can search for all the class names that have the word `String` in them to give you an idea. So why so many string types? Why isn't `java.lang.String` enough? One reason is that certain kinds of string data or forms, such as XML content or a URL, are easier to manage using an object with methods that are dedicated to handling them. But we seem to have more than one general-purpose string class available too. I said before that the `String` class has a special place in the compiler's heart. If I simply assign a literal string, signified by double-quotes around a sequence of characters, to a String reference, the compiler will accept it:

```
String name = "Michael";
```

But why? Shouldn't we have to construct an object? As it turns out, there are a couple of factors that make the `String` class special.

It turns out the `String` class tries to reduce the cost of its own objects. In some production applications, String objects can consume 25 to 40% of the memory spaced required. Object creation cost adds up fast on that scale, and repeatedly using the same strings is usually a big part of that. To mitigate object creation cost, the `String` class maintains what is called an *intern pool*, a cache that stores `String` values. These are referents that survive even when no object reference points to them.

Certification Objective

You know from Chapter 1 that the `String` class loads very early in the start process of any program, so the intern pool is available at the beginning. "Interned" strings, or just "interns," when they are added, stick with the class. If a `String` assignment introduces a new value, it's added to the intern pool.

When a subsequent assignment that does not use the new keyword matches an existing intern, the reference is made to point to it, The intern pool itself is not free of course, but it provides a net reduction in resource demand. By trading off

Caching is a common technique for storing frequently reused data in a more convenient memory location.

object construction for a lookup of existing strings, the class prefers to pay with additional memory for the savings in performance.

The intern pool stores these referents as efficiently as it can. One thing it cannot do, as a result, is allow for the referents to change, either in size or in content. Unlike a `StringBuilder` referent, which directly supports changing its capacity, a `String` referent is *immutable*. Its content and size are not open to change.

You can think of a `String` object as a storage box you have packed perfectly full and whose sides can't bulge. There's no way to add objects, nor can you replace objects without disturbing the entire arrangement. The trade-off for optimal packing is zero flexibility. Notice, however, that the `String` class interface doesn't say anything about immutable objects. In fact, methods like `concat()`, `replace()`, and `toLowerCase()` all encourage modifying a referent's contents, whether you used direct assignment or construction to make it.

In fact, these methods end up constructing new objects behind the scenes and pointing you to the new referent. There's a great deal of convenience in this approach, but it's expensive. You may not appreciate the cost until you've used a very large number of these operations. Consider the example in Listing 2.13.

LISTING 2.13 Sample code manipulating a string

```java
public final class ImmutableTest {
    public void stringFun() {
        String test = new String("Jackpot!");
        test = "bingo";
        test = test.toUpperCase();
        test = test.concat(test);
        System.out.println(test);
    }
    public static void main(String args[]) {
        ImmutableTest it = new ImmutableTest();
        it.stringFun();
    }
}
$ javac ImmutableTest.java
$
```

Here we treat the method stringFun() as a *procedure*. It changes the object's state over a number of statements but returns no value. If you have several tests you want to run as a single program, you can write each one as its own procedure, then use main() to call each one in turn. Take care that each method returns the data to a state the other tests can use, or write a testSuite() method that governs the call order, resetting data, and so on.

In Listing 2.13, we assign a constructed referent for test, then reassign it to an interned string. We call some methods to modify the content and print the result. You can of course insert additional println() calls to observe each change.

First ask yourself what the output should be. Answer before you run this code. It is practice that will absolutely pay off on your exams, so don't cheat yourself. Add in the println() statements if you can't see why the output is what it is. It's a common and honorable tactic when you're really unsure why your code works the way the does. However you go about it, however, you can figure out the results.

What's completely hidden is the number of String objects that were made in the course of this program? It's certainly more than the one explicit construction we have. If String referents are immutable, then every change to the data requires a new referent to assign the object reference.

Proving this action, unfortunately, takes more knowledge and skill than you have the foundation to accept. But if you wondered why you should learn StringBuilder in the first place, and you trust what you've read so far, you have a likely answer. StringBuilder is a better choice for performance than String if you intend to manipulate your referent's content with wild abandon. It was in fact introduced to the JDK for that specific purpose.

Let's not assume, however, that StringBuilder never constructs temporary objects behind the scenes on its own. It certainly does, and when we get to Chapter 4, "Using Java Arrays," we'll dig into the dark secret all string types share. To know exactly how each string class goes about this business, you'd need documentation that details their inner workings or the source code itself. Until you're ready for that, you have to rely on what the methods tell you and hope it's all to the good.

If you haven't already, do look at the class interface and documentation for the String class.

On a closing note, here's the output for Listing 2.13:

```
$ javac ImmutableTest.java
$ java ImmutableTest
```

THE ESSENTIALS AND BEYOND

This chapter covered the fundamentals of Java's two general data types: objects and primitives. You learned how to declare and initialize them at the class and method level and why the compiler's role is different for each. You also learned how to distinguish between variables that are object references and those that store primitive values. We then reviewed the interface of the StringBuilder class and why you should prefer it, in the general case, to the String class.

ADDITIONAL EXERCISES

1. Using Listing 2.3, draw boxes to contain each reference and circles to contain each referent as declared in the main() method. Draw arrows from each reference to its referent.

2. Write a class called BadShort. In its main() method, declare a short variable and assign it the value 60000. Compile the code. What does the output mean?

3. Write a class that declares a member of each primitive type and one Object reference. Do not initialize them. In the main() method, create an object of the class and print out the value of each member using System.out.println().

4. Using the code in Listing 2.8, write a colloquial expression that will calculate the distance between (0,0,0) and (point.x, point.y, point.z).

5. Write some code to construct a StringBuffer object using a familiar phrase or sequence of characters. Print out the reverse of the phrase.

REVIEW QUESTIONS

1. What would the following statement in a main() method do?

   ```
   new Object();
   ```

   A. Nothing; there's no reference for it.

   B. Create a referent.

   C. Halt the program.

   D. Throw an exception.

   (Continues)

THE ESSENTIALS AND BEYOND *(Continued)*

2. What does immutability mean?

   A. The object reference can't be modified.

   B. The object referent can't be released.

   C. The object reference can't be released.

   D. The object referent can't be modified.

3. What's the largest positive value the `long` type can contain?

   A. $2^{64} + 1$ B. $2^{63} + 1$

   C. $2^{64}-1$ D. $2^{63}-1$

4. Which primitive types can hold the value 256?

   A. `byte` only

   B. `short`, `int`, and `long`

   C. `byte` and `short` only

   D. `byte`, `short`, and `int`

5. What is the `capacity` value of a `StringBuilder` object that is constructed as follows:

   ```
   StringBuilder sb = new StringBuilder("singleandLOVINGit!");
   ```

   A. 16 characters   B. 18 characters

   C. 19 characters   D. 34 characters

6. Identify the true statements. (Choose all that apply.)

   A. For a String, capacity would be a redundant property.

   B. A StringBuilder's capacity is always greater than its length.

   C. An empty String has a length of one.

   D. A StringBuilder's length is never greater than its capacity.

7. Which of the following is a Java keyword for a primitive type?

   A. Boolean   B. integer

   C. Char   D. byte

(Continues)

THE ESSENTIALS AND BEYOND *(Continued)*

8. Which of the following values can be used to create a `StringBuilder` object?

    A. 15 empty spaces   **B.** Nothing

    C. Any Java keyword   **D.** All of the above

9. In which case will the `String` class intern a new value?

    A. When it has been constructed the second time

    B. When it has been assigned for the first time

    C. When it has been declared in the main() method

    D. Anytime it has been directly assigned

10. Which variable type stores a copy of its assigned value?

    A. Primitives   **B.** Object references

    C. Both

CHAPTER 3

Using Java Operators and Conditional Logic

The fundamental unit of work in a Java program is the statement. To write useful statements, you must learn how to operate on your data. To write accurate statements, you must also learn the rules of the operation themselves. There is no substitute for understanding Java's operators very well. Your primary reward is a big one: You'll spend less time getting your code to do the right thing. Once your statements evaluate correctly, you'll need to test them and make sure all the decisions based on those statements evaluate as they should.

In this chapter, we'll cover the following topics:

▶ **Using Java operators**

▶ **Using parentheses to control operators**

▶ **Understanding object equality**

▶ **Using `if` and `if/else` statements**

▶ **Using a `switch` statement**

Using Java Operators

It's important to use clear, unambiguous terms as much as possible when describing operators because your code will rely heavily on using them correctly. We will first sort them into categories that make it easier to remember them. We'll discuss the basics of each group, paying particular attention to operators that are unfamiliar to a programmer just getting started.

In this book, we won't concern ourselves with the many technical subtleties that influence the way some operators work. Defining the rules of machine computation is a highly technical, detailed, and exacting discipline, in part because every valid case for using an operator must have a known, unambiguous result.

As a beginning programmer, you don't have to apply the same rigor to using these operators right away. A foundation in basic math and logic is sufficient to understand how most of them work. It is important to observe, however, that behind virtually every operator is some subtlety of implementation, and somewhere down the road you will confront them.

Every programming language must document how its operators work so that programmers know what to expect from testing and regular use. For Java, the authoritative document for these definitions is called the Java Language Specification, or JLS. It defines the meaning for each and every element allowed in the language, including the following elements:

▶ Reserved words

▶ Allowed types and values

▶ Legal names for classes, fields, and methods

▶ Variable declaration and initialization

▶ Exceptions

And it covers many other topics you're not yet acquainted with. For programs to run reliably on a machine, every code element has to be specified so there's no confusion over its role. Sometimes that leads to usage that seems ambiguous until you cover the rules carefully.

For example, the JLS distinguishes between what it calls *separators*—characters that signify the end of one program element and the beginning of another—and what it calls *operators*—characters that symbolize a complex action. You've seen the period (or dot) used to separate an object reference from a field or method. You'll also see it used to separate the whole and fractional parts of a floating-point value. You might not once think about, even years after using Java, but somewhere it has to be defined how the compiler is going to tell the difference.

Or consider the asterisk. In a declaration like `import java.util.*`, it *globs*, or expands to a list of, all the classes in the package. In an expression, it is of course a multiplication operator. Again, it's context that determines the meaning and the JLS that sets the rules for interpretation.

The characters that Java defines as separators are as follows:

```
(      )      {      }      [      ]      ;      ,      .
```

You can download or browse the Java Language Specification at `http://docs.oracle.com/javase/specs/`.

Parentheses, braces, and brackets are used as containers, as you'd expect. Braces contain a block of code. Brackets are used for declaring and accessing arrays. The semicolon is a statement *terminator*. Commas are used in a few different contexts to list things, such as multiple parameters in a method call. The dot also separates package names from class names. Used between an object reference and one of its members, it is actually considered an access operator. Once again, there's no way to know that without consulting the JLS.

We discuss arrays in Chapter 4, "Using Java Arrays."

Parentheses have several uses too. You've already used them with method calls to hold a list of parameters (zero or more), but they have other operational meanings as well. I'll describe those and other separator meanings as they occur in this chapter.

The JLS, section 3.12, lists 37 *tokens* as operators. The JLS does not, surprisingly, provide a table for these operators. To understand the reasons why, you need to know more about operators and how they are defined. Table 3.1 lists the tokens.

TABLE 3.1 Java operator tokens

Operators	Purpose	Associativity
[]	Array access	Left to right
.	Object access	
()	Method invocation	
++ --	Post-increment/decrement	Left to right
++ --	Pre-increment/decrement	Right to left
+ -	Unary plus/minus	Right to left
! ~	Logical/bitwise NOT	Right to left
()new	Casting	Right to left
	Object creation	
* / % + -	Arithmetic	Left to right
+	String concatenation	
<< >> >>>	Bit shifting	Left to right

TABLE 3.1 *(Continued)*

Operators	Purpose	Associativity
< <= > >= instanceof	Relational test Type test	Left to right
== !=	Equality test	Left to right
& ^ |	Bitwise operation	Left to right
&& || ?:	Conditional operation	Left to right Right to left
= += -+ *= /+ %= &= ^= |= <<= >>= >>>=	Assignment	Right to left

The tokens listed include some familiar figures, like the arithmetic symbols you'd see on a calculator. Some you might see on a programmable calculator. Others you will see only in a general-purpose programming language, and still one or two more are specific to Java. The second column describes the nature of each group; I'll explain each of these as we work our way down the list. The third column describes how these operators associate when they are used in the same expression.

This list also includes two Java operators that are also language keywords, new and instanceof. The new keyword is used to prompt object creation. The instanceof keyword checks the type of an object reference. You'll see an example of its use later in the chapter.

Understanding Operator Types and Properties

There are several different properties that help classify and describe the roles of our operators. Detailing each operator by its properties goes beyond the scope of this guide, but learning the primary concepts will make it easier for you to break down and absorb the set shown in Table 3.1.

One way we describe an operator is by how many operands it takes. It's important for the compiler to know, when it sees an operator in context, which of the surrounding elements are intended as *operands* to that operator. Each Java operator takes one, two, or three operands and is described as *unary, binary,* or *ternary,* respectively. Careful study of the table reveals that some symbols have more than one meaning. The designers did this to reduce the total number of characters needed to represent operator actions. Also, many of these tokens have a meaning that carries to other languages. Sometimes it's the number of operands that tells us which operator is intended.

There are two unary operators (++ and --) that have both a *prefix* and a *postfix* behavior. That is, they will modify an operand either before or after it has been evaluated in an expression. You might wonder how important it is to have both options. I can't recall the last time specifying a prefix or postfix increment spelled the difference between a groundbreaking new program and one that just didn't work. However, if you do need to express exactly when you are reading an integral value and when you are modifying it, these operators give you way to do it.

Some operators work in a *bitwise* fashion. That is, they exploit the way Java stores an operand in memory to manipulate it. Some veteran programmers, in particular ones who understand machine code well, prefer bitwise expressions because they are terse and efficient. For newcomers to programming, it is not always obvious on first sight when or why you'd use them, much less what another programmer intended by using them. When code efficiency is important, bitwise operations can be useful but also cryptic.

Some operators that are technically bitwise are instead called *shifting* operators. These operators move a value's bits to the left or right of their current position in storage. Consider the value two, which is represented in four bits as 0010. If you shift the bits to the left by one and fill in the low bit with a zero, it becomes 0100, or four. Shifting left amounts to multiplying by two.

The last category I'll call out here are *logical* operators. Also known as truth functions, a logical operator evaluates *Boolean* operands. Logical operators can be used to link two disjoint statements (such as "if it is raining and if I have a hat," or "if I play Tetris until sunrise or if I study for my final") to create a compound truth expression. You can use them to determine if several statements are collectively true or if at least one of them is true. Logical operators help us make decisions in a program based on their outcomes.

If the terms described previously are unfamiliar to you, here's a word of advice. Take time to research them. Understand how they are commonly used. Digesting this information may seem far removed from writing interesting programs. However, if you're serious about programming, you'll find you spend much more time reading code than writing it, and naturally that means reading code other people have written. Understanding *any* code at this level is essential preparation to becoming a more fluent programmer.

INTERPRETING OVERLOADED OPERATOR SYMBOLS

Java uses the same tokens to represent three bitwise and logical operators (&, ∧, and |). They are all binary operators, so we have to look at the type of the operands to know which operation is intended. If both operands are integers, the operation is bitwise. If both operands are boolean primitives (or object references), the operation is logical. If you provide operands of either type, the compiler will complain.

Precedence and Associativity

The remaining operators described here should be familiar to anyone who has used a calculator, so I add two more terms to our vocabulary that will help you understand how all operators in one expression relate to each other: *precedence* and *associativity*. We learn these terms in arithmetic and they apply more or less the same way to language operators but with a couple differences.

In arithmetic, precedence establishes the order of evaluation for multiple operators in one expression. Without precedence, the result of an expression like the following one below is potentially ambiguous:

$$3 + 4 \times 5$$

Should this statement evaluate to 35 (by adding first and multiplying second) or 23 (the reverse)? In math, we're taught that multiplication *precedes* addition in the order of evaluation, so the answer is 23.

Java applies the same principles of *infix notation*, in which operators are positioned between their operands. We need rules, therefore, to understand not only which operands belong to which operators, in a compound expression, but also which operators precede others. Not all programming languages do this. Languages like FORTH, for example, use a postfix notation style (also called Reverse Polish Notation) that places the operator after its operands. The previous expression would look like this in a FORTH statement:

$$5\ 4 \times .\ 3 +$$

That is, we input the values 4 and 5, then multiply them. The dot in FORTH retrieves the last value stored (the product of the last operation) to use as input. We input the value 3 and add them.

A computer can process expressions in postfix notation immediately and in the order given, so there's no precedence to work out. It's a more efficient scheme. It's also unfamiliar to anyone trained on infix notation. But much like trying to get the United States to prefer the metric scale of measure, getting programmers to prefer postfix notation is an uphill battle. We'll need precedence rules for the foreseeable future.

But precedence isn't sufficient to resolve potential ambiguity. Some operators, such as multiplication and division, have the same precedence. They are, after all, just inverse forms of the same operational process. How should Java evaluate an expression that contains two or more of these operators? Consider the following expression:

$$3 + 4 \times 14 \div 7 \div 7 - 8$$

Precedence alone doesn't yield a single reasonable interpretation. Say we decided that multiplying and dividing from left to right was the most efficient approach: We'd compute -4 (after truncating to get an integral value). If we processed these operations from right to left, we'd compute 51.

The interpretation that prevails is defined by associativity, or grouping rules. In most cases, operators of equal precedence associate from left to right, so the agreed-upon answer here is -4. Some operators do associate from right to left, however. We won't concern ourselves with the reasons why. They appear in Table 3.1, and we'll point them out as we go.

It is of course good practice (and a courtesy) to write the simplest readable expressions you can. At the same time, you should keep the rules of precedence and associativity close at hand when you need them. Relying on memory alone for the occasions you have to interpret someone else's long, complicated or highly technical expression is a bad bet.

In support of that advice, I'll list and discuss the Java operators in their order of precedence. The JLS lists operators by strict precedence because it has to, but many of the fine distinctions between levels of precedence have to make aren't significant to a beginning programmer. To make the business of learning them all easier, I've defined 11 categories:

**Certification
Objective**

1. Separators

2. Postfix/Prefix

3. Unary

4. Multiplicative

5. Additive

6. Shifting

7. Relational

8. Equality

9. Bitwise/Logical

10. Conditional

11. Assignment

I've also fashioned this list so you can use a mnemonic device to help memorize them. Here's one: *Some PUMAS Relate as Equals to BLack CAts*. Or devise your own. Once you get the categories down, there are details for operators in one category you'll want to commit to memory too. Get the categories down first and absorbing the smaller details will get easier.

Using Separators

Separators take precedence over all other operators. This category, however, does *not* include braces (for code bodies), the semicolon (for statement terminators), or the comma (for listing multiple elements). None of these symbols have meaning to any operand, and to parse the smaller units (statements and expressions) we must have to sort them out first.

Brackets (for array operations), parentheses (for method calls), and dots (member access) are different because they separate the pieces that make up one part of an expression. As the grouping agent for this "subatomic" level, they will *generally* evaluate first in an expression. There are some cases where they are ignored, such as when short-circuit operators are in play. I'll explain this effect when we get to them later in this section.

> **In Java, the comma may separate certain operands but it never operates on them.**

Using Postfix/Prefix Operators

There are two operators, ++ and --, that can *increment* or *decrement* an integral variable by one. If the operator prefixes the variable, the value changes before the expression is evaluated. If the operator follows the variable, its value changes after evaluation.

In practice, the high precedence of these operators means the difference between them can be minor or even unnoticeable. Consider the following expression:

```
i++ + ++i
```

If i is initialized to zero, this expression will evaluate to 2. To get a different result, the precedence of the addition operator would have to interpose itself between the other two.

It's convenient to discuss postfix and prefix operators together because they do the same kind of work, but they also have important differences. One, postfix operators take precedence over prefix operators. Two, postfix operators associate left to right, while prefix operators associate right to left. In an expression that includes several of both, the postfix operators would all evaluate right to left before the prefix operators, which would then evaluate in the reverse direction! That's two good reasons not to combine them.

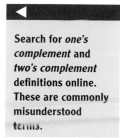

Because prefix operators have different precedence and associativity, some people group them with the unary operators.

You will often see these operators used as loop counters, which we discuss in Chapter 5, "Using Loop in Java Code."

Using Unary Operators

Unary operators take one operand; they associate right to left. That's about all these operators have in common with each other, as Table 3.2 shows.

TABLE 3.2 Unary operators

Operators	Operation
+ -	Sets the sign of a variable or value
~	Bitwise NOT (inverts all bits)
!	Logical NOT (inverts true or false)
(*type*)	Casts a reference to the given type
new	Object construction keyword

The sign operators (+ and -) will set the sign of any numeric value. The logical NOT operator returns the *complement* of a Boolean expression. The expression !true evaluates to false, and vice versa.

The bitwise NOT operator returns the *complement* of an integral type and is a little trickier to discern. It's not merely the opposite sign of the current value; rather, it inverts ("flips") the bits that represent the stored value, including the sign bit. The result is what's called the *one's complement* value of the operand.

Search for *one's complement* and *two's complement* definitions online. These are commonly misunderstood terms.

Integral types in Java do not have a symmetrical positive and negative range, as you may recall from Chapter 2, "Applying Data Types in Java Programming." They have symmetrical negative and nonnegative ranges, but that doesn't help much. The distinction may not even seem important—at least not until your calculations are all off by one—but without it you might write a fair number of nearly correct programs.

Java uses the all-zeroes bit representation—technically, a number without a negative sign—to represent zero itself. The *bitwise complement* of zero is therefore all bits set to 1s, including the sign bit. Java uses this pattern to represent the first number in the negative range, -1. Thus the bitwise representation for decimal 1 in 32-bit form is: 0b0000_0000_0000_0000_0000_0000_0000_0001

The bitwise complement of positive 1 is

0b1111_1111_1111_1111_1111_1111_1111_1110

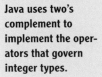

In Java SE 7, we can express literal integers in bit form and use underscores to break them up for easy reading: 0b0000_0000 _0000_0000_0000 _0000_0000_0001.

The prefix "0b" is required to indicate we mean a binary representation; without it, the compiler will interpret this as octal (base eight) representation. In the two's complement scheme, this value stands for negative two. The leftmost bit holds the sign. Therefore, as we increase the numeric scale in the negative range, we gradually replace ones with zeroes. Scaling in the nonnegative range does the opposite. The lowest number in the negative range is all zeroes except for the sign bit:

0b1000_0000_0000_0000_0000_0000_0000_0000

The absolute value of the maximum negative number does not equal the maximum positive number, but they are still bitwise complements. If you have to work with numbers in this form, all you can do is remember and embrace this fact. It's not something I've had to work with in my own experience, but I've seen it used in technical interviews and vendor trivia contests at some Java conferences. Programmer beware.

Java uses two's complement to implement the operators that govern integer types.

The two's complement scheme intervenes on the programmer's behalf. It can't create symmetry where it doesn't exist, but it can provide a simpler rule: "invert and add one." That's it. Take the bit representation of any integer, flip *all* the bits, and add one and you have the same scalar value with a sign change.

The last element in this group is the *casting operator*. Casting tries to evaluate an object reference to another type. It is expressed by parentheses that contain the Java class you want to cast. The reference is the operand. For example, if we used an Object reference to point to a String referent, we might then want to cast it back:

```
String str = new String("let's go casting!");
// Use an Object reference to refer to a String referent
Object obj = str;
// Cast the reference to a String to assign it again
String str2 = (String)obj;
```

We need the casting operator for reasons we won't discuss until Chapter 9, "Inheriting Code and Data in Java." Until then, don't assume the casting operator lets you convert one type to any other. It's useful, not magical.

Using Multiplicative and Additive Operators

These categories include the "basic calculator" functions: multiplication, division, remainder (also known as modulus), addition, and subtraction. They operate on all numeric primitives. Just as in math, the multiplicative operators take precedence over the additive ones.

```
The + operator has a second use. Given two operands that evaluate
to String values, the + operator will concatenate them into a third
String:
public static void main(String args[]) {
       String first = "snicker";
       String second = "doodle";
       System.out.println(first + second);    // prints snickerdoodle
}
```

What's less obvious is what occurs when you combine the addition and concatenation operators. To illustrate, you can add the following statements to the main() method immediately above:

```
int x = 212;
int y = 121;
System.out.println(first + x);    // snicker212
System.out.println(second + y);    // doodle121
System.out.println(second + x + y);    // doodle212121
System.out.println(x + second + y);    // 212doodle121
System.out.println(x + y + second);    // 333doodle
System.out.println(x + y + second + x + y);    // 333doodle212121
```

If the + operator appears more than once, it associates left to right, as expected. However, if either operand in the expression evaluates to a String type, concatenation trumps addition. Others values, such as x and y in our example, are silently converted to String literals and then concatenated. Notice in the last two statements that x and y were summed first. The additive operators associate left-to-right, therefore the sum of x and y comes first, then the concatenation of the sum and the value of the reference second.

Using Shift Operators

Shift operators use the bit representation of integral types to double or halve their value. Shift one bit to the left, multiply by two; to the right, divide by two. So if you left-shift the value four using the << operator, you'll get eight. Here it's shown using a short's worth of bits

```
short stack = 0b0000_0100 << 1; // (will equal 0b0000_1000 or 8)
```

Do it again to get 16, once more to get 32, and so on. Right-shifting 32 three times, using the >> operator, brings you back to four.

The sign bit is not modified by either of these operators. If you left-shift -8 by one bit, the sign remains in the high-order bit. The result is -16. If you shift once to the right it will be -4.

Shift operators are *binary* operators, meaning they require two operands. The first operand supplies the value you want shifted. The second operand specifies the *distance* (number of bit slots) to shift. That means the expression 2 << 3 evaluates to 2^4 (or 16). 16 >> 1 evaluates to the square root of 16, or $16^{1/2}$, or four. Bear in mind that bit-shifting is not the same as using exponents. 16^1 is the same as 16 << 0 *and* 16 >> 0, that is, no shifting at all. There is no equivalent expression for 16^0 using shift operators.

If you need to move the sign bit too, Java supplies the >>> (unsigned bit shift right) operator to do that. And if you do come across a valuable use for that operator, please send me an email. I've perhaps heard two uses cases for it in all the years I have used Java and I can't remember either one.

Using Relational Operators

Relational operators let us determine the type of inequality (less than or greater than) that exists between two values. Relational operators are by definition binary operators and especially useful for sorting through a collection of numbers or testing a value as it increases or decreases and approaches a limit.

The operators < (less than) and > (greater than) are the same as we use in math. Like most programming languages, Java also provides the <= (less than or equal to) and >= (greater than or equal to) tokens as conveniences. It's worthwhile to take a moment and recognize that these are also *compound* operators. That is, these two operators really make two decisions in a single step. They're possible because the underlying physical processor has machine-level instructions that let us to pretend just one operation is taking place.

Object references also have a relational operation in the form of the `instanceof` keyword. It evaluates to `true` if the first operand, an object reference, "relates" to the second operand, a Java object type, usually a class. Object references can relate to a type in a couple ways. The simplest case is one whose referent was constructed from the given type, as follows:

```
public static void main(String args[]) {
    Object obj = new Object();
    System.out.println(obj instanceof Object);
    obj = null;
    System.out.println(obj instanceof Object);
}
```

The expression `obj instanceof Object` will evaluates to `true` in the first test and false in the second. This outcome means *the `instanceof operator` tests the type of the referent, not the type of the variable.* You're not ready to fully appreciate that distinction, so I've italicized it. You might want to highlight or annotate it too ("the author is really hung up on this statement, I don't know why"). You will understand this operator better once you learn about inheritance. We'll have that discussion in Chapter 9.

A Java *interface* is also a legal operand with `instanceof`. We'll study them in Chapter 10, "Understanding Java Interfaces and Abstract Classes."

Using Equality Operators

Equality is another operator that sounds simpler than it is. Either two operands are equal to each other (`==`) or they're not (`!=`), right? Certainly that conclusion holds true for integral and Boolean values. For floating-point numbers, it's not as simple to define. Two fractional values you'd call equal in practical terms can nonetheless be unequal in absolute terms.

Consider the values 20.000005 and 20.0000049. Are they equal? In mathematical terms, of course they are not. In effective terms, however, the degree of *precision* you need in a program may change your perspective. Which is more helpful to your cause, an effective test or an absolute one? We don't need to sort that issue out in a beginner's book, but keep in mind there's more to equality for floating-point values than I've said.

Object equality is another matter entirely. What does it mean to test the equality of two object references? As it turns out, there are also two kinds of tests for them, one that is absolute, in a way, and one that is relative (kinda sorta). I devote a section to that subject later in this chapter to make sure I articulate the issue clearly.

Using Bitwise and Logical Operators

As mentioned earlier, Java uses the same three symbols to represent bitwise and logical operators. In order of precedence, the symbols are &, ∧, and |. The ampersand (&) is called the AND operator. The caret (∧) is called the XOR (eXclusive OR) operator. The pipe (|) is called the OR operator.

Each bitwise operator takes precedence over its logical counterpart. In either context the operators are binary, so we have to consider the operands in order to know which operation was intended. If the operands are integral values, we interpret the operator as bitwise. If both operands are Boolean values, we interpret the operator as logical. If we apply one operand of each sort, we will interpret the compiler's displeasure.

```
public final class Bitgical {
    public static void main(String args[]) {
        System.out.println(true ∧ false);
        System.out.println( 5 ∧ 24);
    }
}
$ javac Bitgical.java
$ java Bitgical
true
29
```

The ∧ operator determines if two bits or Boolean operands are different. Bitwise XOR evaluates to 0 if two bits *match*, 1 if they don't. The expression 11 ∧ 11, for example, evaluates to 0 (all bits are the same, which appears like subtraction). The expression 11 ∧ 4 evaluates to 15 (all bits are different, which appears like addition). Likewise, logical ∧ returns true if the operands are different or false if they are the same.

Interesting to note: The expression 11 ∧ 15 evaluates to 4, and the expression 15 ∧ 4 evaluates to 11. If you combine the result of an XOR with one of the original operands, it will always produce the remaining operand.

The bitwise AND operator compares the bit arrangement of two integral values, testing if both values are 1. If both numbers have the same bit set to 1, the result for that comparison is 1. In *all* other cases, the result is 0. Logical AND operates similarly for Booleans; if both operands evaluate to true, the operation evaluates to true. Otherwise, it evaluates to false as shown here:

```
public final class And {
    public static void main(String args[]) {
        System.out.println(true & false);
        System.out.println(5 & 24);
    }
}
```

```
$ javac And.java
$ java And
false
0
```

Notice the bitwise result is zero. That's because no bits in the comparison were both set to 1.

This isn't much of a revelation in math, but it's very useful when treating integers as *bit fields*, a collection of properties encoded by their position in a multibit storage type. You can think of an `int` as a way to store 31 different *flags*, or state values that are on/off, enabled/disabled, running/stopped, whatever. It's cheap, efficient storage, but you also then need bitwise operators to extract these values and code to interpret their meaning.

As with most solutions in programming, there's a trade-off. These days, in general-purpose programming, physical memory isn't the precious commodity it once was. As a result, the benefits of a bitset seem minimal. When you do have to fit a program into a small memory space, however, a bitset is an effective tactic.

The bitwise | operator tests whether either of two bits is 1. If so, the result is 1. The result is 0 only if both bits are 0. Similarly, the logical | operation result is true if either operand is true. The result is false only if both operands are false.

```
public final class Or {
    public static void main(String args[]) {
        System.out.println(true | false);
        System.out.println(5 | 24);
    }
}
$ javac Or.java
$ java Or
true
29
```

Using Conditional Operators

There are three conditional operators. Each one has its own level of precedence. The first two, conditional AND and conditional OR, are binary operators. They are represented by doubling the symbol of their logical counterparts. The conditional AND token is &&. The OR token is ||. These two are also called *short-circuit operators* because they will ignore the second operand if it doesn't affect the outcome of the whole expression.

With conditional AND, for example, evaluation stops if the first operand evaluates to `false`; the result of the second operand is moot. Using conditional OR, evaluation stops if the first operand evaluates to `true`. You can use this effect to write tests for the second operand that would normally make the compiler complain. If the compiler infers such operands never have to be evaluated, it won't verify them. Here's an example:

```
public static void main(String args[]) {
    int x;
    if ( true || x > 5 ) System.out.println("See?");
}
```

We haven't covered the `if` statement yet (it's coming soon), but the idea here is plain. Since the first operand is literally always `true`, the second one will never come into play. Consequently, the compiler ignores the fact that *x* hasn't even been initialized. Along with other subtle side effects I've noted, this one is prime material for exams that want to test your vigilance in analyzing code. You have been warned.

The third operator in this group is just called the *conditional operator*. It is also called "the" ternary operator because it's the only one that takes three operands. It has an arcane form that is easiest to understand by example:

```
String msg = (x == 15) ? ("Happy!") : ("Sad.");
```

The first operand is a Boolean expression. If it evaluates to `true`, the expression following the question mark is evaluated. If it evaluates to `false`, the expression following the colon evaluates next.

This terse form appeals to programmers who prize brevity. In the C programming language, it is a popular device in code obfuscation contests, where the goal is to write the least-readable working code. Fortunately, Java does not allow a programmer the same license with the ternary operator that C does.

When long expressions are involved, however, it's still easy to abuse. Here's an example statement using one level of nesting:

```
String msg = (guess > jellybeans) ?
"Sorry, over the top." :
(guess == jellybeans) ?
 "Winner!" :
 "Close, but no cigar.";
```

If the value guess exceeds the value of `jellybeans`, we assign the literal `String` "Sorry" to `msg`. If guess is equal to `jellybeans`, we assign the literal "Winner!". Otherwise, the remaining message is assigned. You can imagine what additional levels of nesting would look like. Few people will thank you if you give them a creation like this to read.

Using Assignment Operators

There are 12 assignment operations altogether, making the most populous category. The simple operator (=) takes precedence over the others, which are called *compound operators*:

| *= | /= | %= | += | -= | <<= | >>= | >>>= | &= | ^= | |= |

Each one of these tokens combines assignment with a multiplicative, additive, shifting, or bitwise operator. Instead of writing x = x * 5, for example, you can write x *= 5. It may seem like a small convenience, but if you do a lot of code work manipulating numbers, you'll come to appreciate it.

And if you think that minor convenience is all that's going on, you're in for a truly inscrutable surprise. Check this out:

```
public final class Compound {
    public static void main(String args[] ) {
        int i;
        float j;
        float w = 3.14f;
        i += w;
        j = i + w;
        i = i + w;
    }
}


$ javac Compound.java
Compound.java:8: error: possible loss of precision
        i = i + w;
                ^
  required: int
  found:    float
1 error
```

Let's walk this code carefully. We declare the variables i and m as integers and j and w as floating-point numbers. We use the compound assignment operator to set i equal to i plus w. We then assign to both j and i the sum of the two variables.

Two of these statements are fine. One fails. Why?

Let's first ask why the second statement doesn't fail. There is a property in Java at play here known as *implicit casting*. If you assign a primitive value of one type to another with equal or greater storage, the compiler allows it. You can assign an integer value to a `float` (or `double`) variable without a problem. Implicit casting follows this progression:

```
byte → short → char → int → long → float → double
```

It's allowed because there is no risk of losing the *precision* of the value. If instead you try to assign a `long` value to an `int`, even if the value at hand is within `int` range, the compiler reports an error. The term *possible loss of precision* means that allowing this assignment might truncate the value at hand, making it "less precise" than it was. Even though `int` and `long` have the same capacity, a `long` is considered more precise.

Variable j stores the sum of i and w as a `float`. The type of *i* gets lost in the implied casting, but the value maintains precision. To assign the same result to i, you'd have to tell the compiler you accept the possible loss of precision with an *explicit cast*, like this:

```
i = (int)(i + w);
```

The casting operation forces the result of addition into an `int` form, a mandate the compiler accepts.

So why does i `+=` w compile? It includes an explicit cast as part of its makeup. How would you know that? By reading the JLS, which tells you this behavior is included. *Why* is it included? Well, you could read the appropriate section of the JLS:

```
http://docs.oracle.com/javase/specs/jls/se7/html/jls-15.html#jls-15.26.2
```

It, however, doesn't say why, it just declares the rule. I'll steer clear of inferring the motive, at least in print.

Using Parentheses to Control Operators

Some PUMAS Relate Equally to BLack CAts: separators, post/prefix, unary, multiplicative, additive, shifting, relational, equality, bitwise, logical, comparison, assignment. Memorize that much and you'll be able recall the order of precedence more quickly when you need it. Also, remember that unary, conditional, and assignment operators associate right to left. All other operators (of equal precedence) associate left to right.

Certification Objective

Now let's use an expression from the previous section to consider how to alter the order of evaluation:

$$3 + 4 \times 14 \div 7 \div 7 - 8$$

Let's say you don't want normal associativity to order the evaluation of the multiplicative operators. Instead, you first want the two sevens reduced to one. To effect this, you need a means to override the default. Just as in math, you can use parentheses to do that. Let's rewrite the expression as follows:

$$3 + 4 \times 14 \div (7 \div 7) - 8$$

Now the last division in the expression will evaluate first. The whole expression then evaluates to 51.

Parentheses can override precedence as well as associativity. Let's say you wanted the additive operators to evaluate first, then the rest. You can achieve that with the following rewrite:

$$(3 + 4) \times 14 \div 7 \div 7 - 8$$

Now the expression reduces to $7 \times 14 \div 7 \div 7 - 8$, or -6.

If you're not careful, you can achieve complexity now by nesting parentheses and using all its various meanings—casting, method invocation, and evaluation overrides—all one expression. Consider the following made-up statement:

```
Widget pie = (Widget)(factory.fillCircle((22/7) * (circle.radius << 1));
```

Assume for the sake of discussion that the *factory* object reference fills a circle for you if you supply its area as a parameter. In this example you calculate it for a square with a radius of one using the approximation 22/7 in place of pi times the radius squared.

This statement uses parentheses three different ways: first, to cast the result to a *Widget* type; second, to invoke a method; and third, to order the calculation with explicit grouping. Statements like this aren't at all unrealistic. Reading them correctly and quickly takes some practice.

The language designers naturally want to use your knowledge from math and even your intuition to help you decipher such a statement. That's one reason to prefer infix notation over postfix notation, even if the latter is more efficient. Still, to be sure of your results, you must learn the rules of operation by heart. Remember, you can sometimes interpret them correctly only by knowing the number and type of operands necessary.

Test questions commonly present you with a few code statements and ask you to determine (a) which statement option is illegal, if any; (b) if the code will compile; (c) if the code will run; and sometimes even (d) how much of the code will run before it fails. By the end of this book, you'll have enough information to manage such questions for straightforward cases. The challenge is all about the accuracy, and to some degree speed, of your analysis.

◀

If I have any role in writing the exam, you can be certain you'll see several questions that follow this format.

Understanding Object Equality

Testing equality between two integral numbers is simple. When it comes to floating-point values, however, the precision of the operands may complicate the test. I mentioned earlier the idea of *effective equality*: two numbers that are close enough to be equal according to the needs of your program.

Let's say we're calculating interest on two money market accounts with slightly different balances. What's the difference between a calculation of $1.5800003 on one and $1.5800007 on the other? They're the same, practically speaking, but they're not mathematically equal. To make them practically equal, we might truncate the values. There's nothing wrong with that, but it does require we write code *and* a set of informing principles by which a calling programmer will understand how that code is designed to work.

Certification Objective

A similar issue arises when you want to test object references for equality. Given two references as operands, the equality operator (==) will tell you if they refer to the same referent. In a sense, this is like integer equality: Seven always equals seven. Anything that stores a seven must be considered equal to seven. Any reference that stores a location must be equal to any other reference storing the same location.

We expect this equality to resolve to true when one object reference has been assigned to an existing referent, as in this example:

```java
public static void main(String args[]) {
    Object ab = new Object();
    Object cd = ab;
    boolean sameRef = (ab == cd);
}
```

The test ab == cd will resolve to true, which is then assigned to the sameRef variable. Any two references, despite their differences in name or scope, are deemed equal if they access the same referent. This rule bears a resemblance to integer equality. And while it's an essential test, it doesn't let us define effective equality when we need it.

Let's say we constructed two String objects with the same literal value. We test them with the == operator and the result is false.

```java
public final class Equality {
    public static void main(String args[]) {
        String jack = new String("water!");
        String jill = new String("water!");
        System.out.println(jack == jill);
    }
```

```
}
$ javac Equality.java
$ java Equality
false
```

Our code tells us that much. But say we really wanted to know whether the referents pointed to by jack and jill had the same *content*. We need another way to define that effective equality. That's not a small need, by the way. It's easy to point out that content equality, so called, is far more important than referent equality for many needs. Fortunately, the Java language designers agree and provide the Object.equals() method to offer that flexibility.

Well, sort of. The source code for the Object.equals() method is similar to the following:

```
public boolean equals(Object obj) {
    return this == obj;
}
```

The Object class just wraps the equality operator in a method. If you compare any two Object references, you'll get the same result whether you use == or the equals() method. How do you get effective equality out of that?

The *Object* class supports what it calls the narrowest—meaning the least inclusive—test for equality. The narrowest possible sense of equality occurs when a referent is equal to itself (such as two references pointing to the same referent). For many Java classes, it would be better if you could compare the contents of two referents, using logic that determines if two different referents have the same value.

Notice what happens if we construct and compare two String objects with the same content and test with the equals() method instead of the equality operator:

```
public static void main(String args[]) {
    String str1 = new String("abc");
    String str2 = new String("abc");
    boolean strictEq = (str1 == str2);
    boolean effectiveEq = str1.equals(str2);
    System.out.println("strict: " + strictEq);
    System.out.println("effective: " + effectiveEq);
}
```

Should you compile and run this code, you'll get the following result:

```
strict: false
effective: true
```

There is something hidden this time, but it's not magic. The String class overrides the equals() method, defining equality as any two String references that have the same value (where two references pointing to the same referent is merely the narrowest case). In practice, this kind of effective equality, as shown in Figure 3.1, is what you need most of the time.

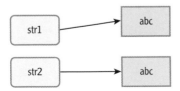

FIGURE 3.1   Effective equality between objects

Here you see two reference and referent pairs, and what we'd like to know more often than not is whether they have the same values, not whether they have the same referent. With strict equality, as we are calling it, you can only test the relationship shown in Figure 3.2.

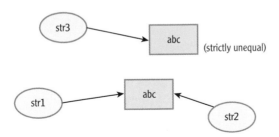

FIGURE 3.2   Strict quality between objects

Here the reference str3 has the same content but could not pass a strict equality test. In general, testing whether two references point to the same referent is a query on the state of the references. An effective test instead is a query on whether data, or state, is shared between two objects. The concern here usually derives from asking whether two objects have achieved the same state at the same time, and that is, generally speaking, the question you more often need an answer to in a program.

In all the example classes you've seen in this guide, we've inherited the equals() method as is from the Object class. In other words, we can test for strict equality only until we use (or write) classes that override the equals() method to support effective equality.

Implementing it, it turns out, is a rigorous exercise. There are several rules you must adhere to for reliable, accurate testing. That kind of programming is well beyond us for now. In Chapter 9 we will discuss the technique for overriding inherited methods and how to apply it, but you still will not have the foundation you need to implement effective equality on your own.

Using *if* and *if/else* Statements

The logical operators you've learned wouldn't be much use if you didn't use them to make *decisions* in your code. The ternary conditional operator was originally devised for that purpose: Based on the result of the first operand, only one of two paths of execution follows.

Reading a conditional operator in code gets harder the more you try to do with it, as you've seen. It's better for maintaining code if the language syntax helps you read it. Every programmer, through practice, learns to strike a balance between code that is clear and code that is brief. Just as terse code, full of bitwise and logical operators, can become cryptic, so can overly simplified code, saddled with many simple statements, become tedious to browse and digest.

When it comes to choosing among multiple paths of execution, the first syntax-friendly constructs to learn are if and if/else statements. Their simplest form looks like this:

```
if (boolean_expression)
    statement1;
```

In this context, the parentheses contain (or separate) the Boolean expression. If it evaluates to true, statement1 executes; otherwise, program control transfers to the statement delimiter. If you want to execute multiple statements, you use code block separators to contain them:

```
if (boolean expression) {
    statement1;
    statement2;
    statementN;
}
```

Whether the expression evaluates to true or false, any statements that follow the terminating code block separator will execute normally. If you want mutually exclusive paths of execution, append an else statement to the if statement:

```
if (boolean_expression)
    statement1;
else
    statement2;
```

To incorporate multiple statements for either statement, use code block separators:

```
if (boolean_expr) {
    statement1;
    statement2;
} else {
    statementA;
    statementB;
}
```

Now you can achieve a similar effect to the ternary conditional operator and use multiple statements without making a spaghetti mess. The indenting I've shown promotes readability only, by the way; it's not required. Combined with the syntax, it makes the code much easier to browse.

Then there are times when you need to execute statements where there are more than two outcomes to a decision. Those outcomes, while they are related in some sense that derives from the program logic you're writing, probably don't reduce nicely into a number of either-or paths.

Here's an example concept: "If it is Monday, I'll write some code. Otherwise, if it's Tuesday, I'll test my operator knowledge. Otherwise, if it's Wednesday, I'll review the current chapter." For some reason, as this list of statements implies, you want to consider Wednesday's plan *only* if Monday and Tuesday can be ruled out.

To support this *nested logic* approach, you can use the else statement to create another if statement, as shown here:

```
if (boolean_expression)
        statement1;
else if (boolean_expression)
        statement2;
```

The process of revising code without breaking its callers or dependencies is called *refactoring*.

You can nest if statements indefinitely, but this technique also becomes harder to read the further you take it. Deeply nested if statements are often a sign that the logic hasn't been thought through. It's a common outcome when programmers add conditional cases to an existing structure instead of changing the structure to a simpler or more appropriate form. It's a bit like placing dishes on a growing stack in the sink. If you're going to clean one, you might as well clean them all, but no one wants the job everyone else left behind.

If you do have a range of outcomes that don't rely on a chain of nested decisions, a switch statement is a better choice. We'll discuss that next.

Using a *switch* Statement

The switch statement makes it easy to list several paths from a single decision point. It's only slightly more complex than an if/else statement:

```
switch (test_expression) {
    case (matching_expression1) :
        statementA;

    case (matching_expression2):
        statementB;
        statementC;

    case (matching_expressionN):
        statementX;
        statementY;

    default:
        statementZ;
}
```

The test expression may evaluate to any integral type—char, byte, short, int—except long. It may also evaluate to an instance of their namesake classes—Character, Byte, Short, and Integer. It does not evaluate boolean or Boolean types because the if statement is sufficient to manage those. The switch structure gives you what the if statement cannot: a plain way to handle multiple outcomes, or *cases*, and a way to expand those cases over time without additional syntactic complexity.

Starting with Java SE 7, you can also use string values for the test and matching expressions. You probably won't appreciate this new feature nearly as much as your more experienced colleagues will. Let them tell you how awesome it is that we can *finally* use strings with a switch statement.

There are two kinds of labels that a switch statement allows. It can have zero or more case labels and zero or one default labels. Each case label has a value, or matching expression, whose type is any legal type for a switch expression. The case labels do *not* have to have the same type. That's the law. Having said that, creating a mix of types for a switch statement is better for an obfuscation contest or Java trivia game than it is for clear, readable code.

When the switch expression matches a case label, program control transfers immediately to that label. No two labels may share a matching value. Any

◄

The test expressions also accept a Java type called enum. We describe enums in Chapter 10, "Understanding Java Interfaces and Abstract Classes."

statements listed from that point forward execute. If no match occurs and a `default` label exists, the `default` label's statements execute. Otherwise, control falls to the end of the `switch` statement itself and continues from there.

Execution in a `switch` statement *cascades* by design. Once control passes to a matching label and its statements execute, all statements that follow in all subsequent labels will also execute. Consider the following example:

```
public static void main(String args[]) {
    switch (args[0]) {
        case "a":
            System.out.println("A");
        case "b":
            System.out.println("B");
        default:
            System.out.println("No match");
        case "c":
            System.out.println("C");
    }
}
```

If *args[0]* equals the value "a", this code will print:

```
A
B
No match
C
```

There are times this behavior works to your advantage. Let's say you want to distribute awards for an airline loyalty program. For flying 100,000 miles or more, customers get an airplane pin. For 1,000,000 miles or more, they get an airplane paperweight. For 10,000,000 miles, they get an airplane. If any customer wins a special drawing and receives 10,000,000 miles for a prize, they get all the gifts. With those rules in mind, writing a `switch` statement to handle all four cases should be simple.

But it doesn't always make sense to work this way. Sometimes you still want mutually exclusive logic of the `if/else` variety but also more than two cases to manage. At the very least, executing both a case label and the `default` label isn't what you normally want. While you could think of the `default` label as a list of statements you always want to execute at the end of the `switch`, it's far more likely you'll use it to capture cases you haven't specified.

For that reason, putting the `default` label last is not just practical advice. You will rarely, if ever, see it placed anywhere else, even though the compiler allows it. With that convention in mind, you can use break statements to jump around it, like this:

```
switch (some_integer) {
    case x:
        doSomething();
    case y:
        doSomethingElse();
        break;
    default:
        complain();
}
```

Or you can add a break statement at the end of every case. Each matching case will then execute and transfer control to the end of the switch statement, ignoring all other cases along the way. Now you have exclusive execution for each case.

THE ESSENTIALS AND BEYOND

In this chapter, we covered what the Java operators do and some of their key properties, including precedence and associativity. We discussed the concepts of absolute (or strict) and effective equality and how the latter applies specifically to object references. We also discussed two decision-making constructs—the if/else and switch statements—we can use to selectively execute code.

ADDITIONAL EXERCISES

1. Throughout the chapter there are code examples shown in a main() method body. Wrap these examples in a class so you can compile and run them. Keep them in a directory on your computer for reference.

2. Using the airline loyalty program example, write a program that prints out a prize statement for award level achieved. Use only the conditional operator.

3. Using the airline loyalty program example, write a program that prints out a prize statement for award level achieved. Use only if or if/else statements.

4. Write a program that shifts the value -32768 a distance of three to the right using both the signed and unsigned shifting operators. Print out each result.

5. Search the Internet for at least two different operator precedence and associativity tables you can print, and compare them.

(Continues)

THE ESSENTIALS AND BEYOND *(Continued)*

REVIEW QUESTIONS

1. What is the bitwise complement of an `int` whose value is 2^{31} -1?

   A. $-(2^{31} - 1)$ **B.** -2^{31}

   C. $-2^{31} + 1$ **D.** 0

2. Which option lists categories of precedence in correct order?

   A. Separators, Postfix/Prefix, Associative, Multiplicative

   B. Bitwise, Logical, Equality, Concatenate

   C. Multiplicative, Additive, Shifting, Ternary

   D. Relational, Equality, Conditional, Assignment

3. Which operator category does not have compound assignment tokens?

   A. Unary   **B.** Additive

   C. Bitwise   **D.** Multiplicative

4. True or false: A `switch` statement may have zero case labels and no `default` label. It will still compile.

5. What is the result of this expression?

   $$(3 + 4) + 5 \times 6 << 1$$

   A. 144   **B.** 67

   C. 74   **D.** 187

6. Given an integer *x* that has been assigned 1, what is the result of the statement `int y = --x++`?

   A. *y* is assigned 2; *x* will remain unchanged.

   B. *y* is assigned 1; *x* will be assigned 2.

   C. This is not a legal statement.

   D. *y* is assigned 2; *x* is equal to 2 before the statement completes, equal to 1 after the statement completes.

7. Which statement describes an effect that Java parentheses don't support?

   A. They contain zero or more parameters for method calls.

   B. They contain a boolean expression for `switch` statements.

   C. They function as a type-casting operator.

   D. They contain a truth expression for `if` statements.

(Continues)

THE ESSENTIALS AND BEYOND *(Continued)*

8. True or false: For the `Object` class, there is no difference between strict equality and effective quality, nor can there be.

9. True or false: The conditional (ternary) operator can return a result of any type.

10. True or false: All Java statements must end with a semicolon.

CHAPTER 4

Using Java Arrays

The array is a universal data structure among programming languages. With an array, you can collect many instances of one type of data in a single data structure. Once you learn the concept of an array in any language, you will know the basics for applying it in other languages.

Arrays are great for learning and have many practical uses. In Java, however, the implementation is bit funny. Arrays don't take full advantage of the object model that Java is known for. I hear some people say they are "part object, part primitive," but that's not quite right. To understand them very well, you'll want to pay close attention to how arrays are made and used.

In this chapter, we'll cover the following topics:

▶ **Understanding Java arrays**

▶ **Using a one-dimensional array**

▶ **Using a multi-dimensional array**

▶ **Using an `ArrayList` object**

Understanding Java Arrays

We have so far distinguished between primitive and object types in order to understand why and how we should treat them differently. Now as we turn our attention to arrays, we're going to get a little of both. Arrays, in some senses, blur the line between object and primitive.

An array is unquestionably an object type. It inherits from the `Object` class and, like any other subclass, supports all the methods it receives from its parent class. But an array by itself *isn't* an actual type. You can't declare an array like this:

```
[] bugs;
```

That is, an array has an `Object` class interface but no implementation of its own. It seems, in a way, closer to the kinds of classes we've been writing as test code: arrays have subclasses, yes, but nothing that modifies or extends the parent class as a fully formed subclasses would. So an array has what *type*? It depends, actually, on what you intend to put in it. An array by itself is a single structure that will hold some declared number of elements. Once you declare the array's type, you also declare the type of element it will store.

Certification Objective

To declare an array properly, you can use either a primitive or a Java class for the type:

```
String [] names;
double [] measurements;
```

Brackets, as shown in Chapter 3, "Using Java Operators and Conditional Logic," signify the array itself. In a *declaration*, the brackets establish an aspect of the type. For the two lines above, you might hear someone say "a String array of names and a double array of measurements," or you might hear them say "a names array of type String and a measurements array of type double." Either form gets the point across.

In an expression, the brackets behave as an access *operator* that contains the operand. The operand may be any expression that resolves to an integral type, except long, whose value is nonnegative and less than the declared size of the array.

The type you declare for an array defines the *elements* it may store. You must be careful, however, to understand how you refer to the array itself, which is a subclass of Object, and how you refer to an array component, which is a value of the declared component type.

```
public final class ArrayType {
    public static void main(String args[]) {
        String [] bugs = { "cricket", "beetle", "katydid" };
        String [] alias = bugs;
        System.out.println(bugs.equals(alias));
        System.out.println(bugs.toString());
        System.out.println(bugs[0].toString());
    }
}
```

```
$ javac ArrayType
$ java ArrayType
true
[Ljava.lang.String;@437dcb
cricket
```

I will cover all the ways you create arrays in the next section; ignore that aspect of our example for now. Do notice that the variable *bugs* can access the equals() method. Calling bugs.toString() returns, as all Object instances will, a report of the referent's type and memory location. The [L ... ; notation that wraps the package-qualified String class shows it's an array.

Arrays also have a built-in property called *length*, which you can access just like a field. It's just there; the Java Language Specification (JLS) defines it, so any compiler that complies with the JLS must support it somehow. The length property stores the size of the array, or the number of elements it has room for. Arrays are fixed in size upon creation. The length property is therefore always nonnegative, immutable, and read-only.

Every array has *length*. The elements are *indexed* by number. You can access any element by its numeric position, commonly called the index: The first element occupies index 0; the last one occupies the index value length-1. Figure 4.1 shows the bugs array elements by their position.

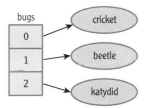

FIGURE 4.1 Elements of the bugs[] array

You can infer from Figure 4.1 that array elements do not store referents, but rather locations to referents, just like any other object reference. Thus the array itself is a referent that contains references to other referents! An array full of null values is the same size in memory as an array full of references. It is an object that is separate from the objects it collects.

The Java array is one example of a data structure that behaves like a *list*. All lists *order* their elements; it is the index value that fulfills this role in a Java array. You can think of this number as a unique identifier within the array.

Conceptually, a list identifies each element by its position, *not* by its value or its memory location. Since nothing about the element itself influences how the array identifies and orders it, you can have as many duplicate values in an array as you'd like. From the array's perspective, the index itself establishes each element's meaning.

Let's say you wanted to track four old cars that have fallen out of fashion but you like them anyway. You want to keep them in a private underground parking garage you're building. All you need to track them is a simple description of each car, including year, make and model, and the parking spot number. Even if two cars are more or less the same, they'll have different-numbered spots and that's how you'll tell them apart. This spot number could double as an array index, as shown in Figure 4.2.

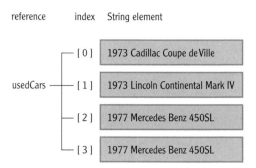

reference   index   String element

usedCars — [0]   1973 Cadillac Coupe deVille

[1]   1973 Lincoln Continental Mark IV

[2]   1977 Mercedes Benz 450SL

[3]   1977 Mercedes Benz 450SL

FIGURE 4.2 A usedCar **array with four** String **elements**

The cars at array positions 2 and 3 are identical, at least so far as our description for them goes. The element value for each is also the same. They remain distinct solely by virtue of their index, or parking spot number.

One last concept, and then we'll dive into the nuts and bolts of making arrays. Since one array is just a list of references to other objects, an array can store other arrays as its elements. We refer to this kind of array as having two *dimensions*. I will discuss declaring, populating, and accessing multi-dimensional arrays after I have covered the simpler case of one dimension.

Using a One-Dimensional Array

Certification Objective

We'll need a few examples to employ all the useful aspects an array has to offer, so the following sections cover four topics: declaring arrays, populating them, instantiating them, and using them. With one-dimensional arrays, these operations are straightforward to express and apply. I'll also note some rather subtle effects that are made possible by the array syntax defined by Java's designers.

Declaring an Array

Omitting white space seems like a small detail, but style guidelines are a big part of defining communication among Java programmers.

You can declare an array of any type by adding brackets to an existing declaration. You can declare the separators after the type or after the variable name. Either of the following forms is legal:

```
int [] numbersGuessed;
int numbersGuessed [];
```

Because the square brackets are separators that can't be used in a type or variable name, you can also omit the white space; the compiler won't complain:

```
int[] numbersGuessed;
int numbersGuessed[];
```

All these forms have the same effect. One (arguable) benefit of allowing this variety is that it's easier to declare multiple array variables at once, or declare variables together that may or may not be arrays, as follows:

```
String [] bands, players, songs;
String bands[], players[], song;
```

In the first example, I declare all three variables as String arrays. In the second example, I declare bands and players as String arrays, but song is a String only. Saving a line or two this way at the expense of more but simple declarations, I would argue, seems like a negligible benefit. Whether you like to associate brackets with the element type or the variable name is a matter of preference. It's best to choose one approach and use it consistently. Or, if you're working with code that's given to you, adopt the conventions taken in that code.

Inside a method body, you can assign an array to null if you're not going to initialize it right away:

```
void someMethod() {
    double [] plotPoints = null;
    // more code
}
```

When declaring parameters and return types for a method, it's as simple as adding brackets where you'd expect. In the return type, the separators follow the type declaration. For a method parameter, the separators may follow either type or the parameter name:

```
public float[] smoothPlotPoints(float rawData[]) { . . . };
```

Instantiating an Array

An array is a combination of types, as you've learned. There's the array itself, which is a direct subclass of Object, and the type that defines its elements. Arrays also have a size (length) that is fixed at creation time. When we construct an array, therefore, we instantiate both the element type and array's size, as in this example:

```
double [] plotPoints = new double[10];
```

This statement will create an array with a length of 10 and an index that goes from zero to nine. The elements themselves are initialized to the type-appropriate default value; in the case of a double it's 0.0. If you declared the array to contain object references, the default values would be null.

You can, by the way, construct an array with zero elements. In fact, we've done so several times already. Each time we run a Java program, we invoke a

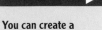

You can create a
zero-length array
yourself by using zero
in the instantiation
expression, but it's
not useful for much.

main() method. If we don't pass any arguments into the program, the JVM must construct an args array with nothing in it. You can test this yourself:

```java
public final class NoArgs {
    public static void main(String args[]) {
        if (args.length == 0)
            System.out.println("No arguments were passed in.");
    }
}
```

```
$ javac NoArgs.java
$ java NoArgs
No arguments were passed in.
```

The Java Virtual Machine creates an *args* array of zero size if no arguments are passed into a program from the command line. Many programmers prefer this to receiving a null object reference.

The wisdom of this approach is subtle. To fully test an object that is designed to contain multiple components, we normally have to consider three cases, not two:

- ▶ The array has no referent (it is null).
- ▶ The array has no elements.
- ▶ The array has one or more elements.

By eliminating the first case whenever possible, we reduce the problem to an either-or case, making our programming life just a bit less tedious.

Populating an Array with a Loop

All other things being equal, populating a 10-component array takes just as much work as initializing 10 individual variables would. *Writing the code* is less work, however, if we can use *loops* to repeat the code statements. We don't discuss loops until Chapter 5, "Using Loops in Java Code." However, it's about time we wrote something that includes everything we've discussed so far. And why not throw in a sneak preview of the next chapter, too?

```java
public final class LoopArray {
    public static void main(String args[]) {
    int [] numbers = new int[10];
    int counter = 0;
        while (counter < numbers.length) {
            numbers[counter] = counter;
```

```
        System.out.println("number[" + counter + "]: " + counter);
        counter++;
    }
  }
}
```

Use the + concat-
enation operator to
combine literal text
with program values.
Remember to allow
for spaces in the
output.

In this example, we declare and instantiate an array of 10 elements and declare a counter variable. The while statement tests whether counter is less than 10. If it is, we assign the value of counter to the corresponding array position, print it, and increment counter by one. At the end of the code block, control returns silently to the test expression that immediately follows while.

Eventually, counter will equal numbers.length. Once it does, the expression will evaluate to false and control will silently transfer to the end of the block. Here's the output for this program:

```
number[0]: 0
number[1]: 1
number[2]: 2
number[3]: 3
number[4]: 4
number[5]: 5
number[6]: 6
number[7]: 7
number[8]: 8
number[9]: 9
```

Populating an Array without a Loop

If we have values of some nonincrementing variety to put in an array such that using a loop isn't practical, we can take a different approach. We can instead populate the array at the same time we declare it. It won't matter if the arrays are class members or method variables. The way it works for each is a little different, so we'll cover them one at a time, class members first.

Recall that class members we declare but do not assign values will be initialized to a type-appropriate default by the compiler. This behavior seems like a programmer convenience, but really it complements the compiler's type-checking job. For types other than an array, you can assign your own value. How you do the same for an array relies on a use for code body separators you haven't covered yet:

```
public final class FishTank {
    String[] creatures = { "goldfish", "oscar", "guppy", "minnow" };

}
```

▶

You can add your
own main() method
to this class to test
whether the text
description of it is
accurate.

This code declares and populates the creatures array with the four elements shown, implicitly setting its length. The braces, which we normally think of as code separators, contain the element list. It's a little bit of magic that was included in the earliest versions of the Java Language Specification so that arrays had the same options for initialization as other types do.

Why is it magic? Code block separators aren't operators; they don't accept operands. Even though the FishTank class compiles, the rules you learned in Chapter 3 tell you there is no expression here to evaluate. No evaluation, no resulting value. Therefore we get nothing we could assign to the creatures array. There is in fact no legal statement in this class! The syntax must work by exception, not adherence, to the rules you've learned.

You can do the same thing inside a method body. Compile the following code; you'll get no errors:

```
public final class ArrayInitMethod {
    public static void main(String args[]) {
        int[] numbs = { 1, 2, 3,4, 5, 6 };
    }
}
```

But this magic ends with initialization. Let's say you wanted to create an array in an expression such that it evaluates to an array on the fly, like this:

```
parseArray({1, 2, 3, 4, 5, 6});
```

Assume for the sake of illustration that the parseArray() method accepts an integer array as a parameter. You can't do this in Java.

To make it work, you need a legal expression. To that end, Java added support for what it calls *anonymous arrays*. An anonymous array retains the convenience of a list but uses the new operator to complete a proper Java expression. The result isn't as clean as simply declaring a list of elements, but it's still better than having to write the array initialization and population longhand:

```
parseArray(new int[] {1, 2, 3, 4, 5, 6});
```

Writing the statement in this form preserves the rules Java programmers depend on to know that their programs are syntactically correct. The anonymous array approach also works for fields, so you can replace any occurrences of the exception syntax you may find in code with this minor edit if you wish.

Using an Array

Now let's use the arrays you've learned to declare and create. First rule: Know when the [] brackets are required and when they aren't. You already know an array reference is an Object subclass but its components belong to the type specified at declaration.

You need the separators to declare the array, either as a variable or as a method parameter. When you construct an array, you must size it, explicitly or implicitly, with a nonnegative integral value. Accessing an array component requires an integer value ranging from zero to one less than the array's length.

If you do use a negative value, or one that exceeds the array's length, the compiler won't actually notice. The JVM will, however, and will tell you about it by throwing a NegativeArraySizeException or an ArrayIndexOutOfBoundsException, respectively, and stopping the program at the scene of the crime.

◀

The full discussion on exceptions takes place in Chapter 11, "Throwing and Catching Exceptions in Java."

```
public final class NegArray {
    public static void main(String args[]) {
        int neg[] = new int[-1];
    }
}
$ javac NegArray.java
$ java NegArray
Exception in thread "main" java.lang.
NegativeArraySizeException
        at NegArray.main(NegArray.java:3)
```

Notice that the code compiles but the program bails when run. The exception report returns the program line on which the code failed. The most common out-of-bounds errors occur when a program tries to use length as an index:

```
public final class OutOfBounds {
    public static void main(String args[]) {
        int arr[] = new int[11];
        System.out.println(arr[arr.length]);
    }
}
$ javac OutOfBounds.java
$ java OutOfBounds
Exception in thread "main" java.lang.ArrayIndexOutOfBoundsException:
11
        at OutOfBounds.main(OutOfBounds.java:4)
```

Remember that arrays start at zero. The value of length will always exceed the last legal index number by one.

When passing whole arrays as method parameters, we do *not* use the [] separators:

```
public final class PassingArgs {
    public void sysPrint(String[] parms) {
        System.out.println("First argument: " + parms[0]);
```

```
    }

    public static void main(String args[]) {
        PassingArgs pa = new PassingArgs();

        if (args.length > 0)
            pa.sysPrint(args);
    }
}
```

I discuss all the details of passing parameters in Chapter 7, "Using Java Methods to Communicate."

In this example we pass the args array from the main() method directly to the sysPrint() method. We know we aren't passing a null value. The JVM makes sure args always has a length, even if it is zero. The sysPrint() method must signify that it accepts a String array, which is the type received by main(). It is sufficient to pass the array to it by name alone.

Using a *String* Object as a Character Array

I waited until Chapter 4 to discuss arrays, but as you just saw, you've been using two of them since the start. The args array in the main method is one. The other, believe it or not, is the String class. Deep down, it turns out to be nothing more than an array of characters.

Recall from Chapter 2, "Applying Data Types in Java Programming," that a String instance is an *immutable* object. Once the value has been set, you can't change a String referent in any way. You can only use the reference to refer to another String. An array, as you have learned, is immutable in size. That's how the String type manages to acquire this property.

A String really is just a char[] underneath the covers. You can in fact derive this representation from a String by asking for it, using its toCharArray() method:

```
public final class CharName {
    public static void main(String args[]) {
        String name = "Michael";
        char[] charName = name.toCharArray();
        System.out.println(charName);
        System.out.println(charName.toString());
    }
}
```

```
$ javac CharName
$ java CharName
Michael
[C@1469a69
```

The output shows that the `charName` elements match what was assigned to `name`. The open square bracket and the capital *C* in the last line signify that the printed referent is an array of characters.

The `String` class also supplies other methods to perform the nitty-gritty work of manipulating its content. As users of the `String` interface, you get the convenience of thinking in textual terms rather than in terms of the list of characters that make it up. Don't underestimate this convenience! But also remember for every method that returns an altered `String` to you, you're paying a hidden cost of making a new object. In a text-intensive program, that cost can become a significant part of your program's overall resource demand.

Using *System.arraycopy()*

When you use `String` methods such as `concat()`—the method equivalent of the + operator—or `substring()`, you're not really changing string content at the `char` level. Nonetheless, you still need an array of a different size to hold the results. For that work, and for arrays of any type, the `System.arraycopy()` method does the low-level transfer work.

As a consumer of Java classes, you'd like the class author to hide this detail for you. You'll be a provider of Java classes someday, and your users would like you to do the same for them. The `arraycopy()` method is the first one I've looked at that takes several parameters: five altogether. The method signature is as follows:

```
static void arraycopy(Object src, int srcPos, Object dest,
int destPos, int length)
```

To use it, we need two arrays (the `src` and `dest` parameters): the copy-from and copy-to starting position for each array (`srcPos` and `destPos`); and the `length`, or total number of components, we want to transfer. Using `arraycopy()`, we can write a substring test of our own:

```
public final class MySubstring {
    public static void main(String args[]) {
        char[] html = new char[] {'M','i','c','h','a','e','l'};
        char[] lastFour = new char[4];
        System.arraycopy(html, 3, lastFour, 0, lastFour.length);
        System.out.println(lastFour);
    }
}
$ javac MySubstring.java
$ java MySubstring
hael
```

▶

**Changing a method
so you can use it a
variety of ways is
called *generalizing* or
abstracting its code.**

There are two things to note here. First, our test is quite specific. It would take a bit more technical skill and know-how to generalize this code into a reusable substringing operation. When another programmer saves us that trouble, it's a big deal.

Second, to be generally useful itself, the `arraycopy()` method declares `Object` parameters when what it really needs are two arrays of the same declared type. There's nothing in the method signature for `arraycopy()` to tell you that. Either that requirement strikes you as intuitive—you've worked with Java long enough to think of such things as "common sense"—or you read the documentation. Or you write test programs that fail until you figure it out.

This schism between an open-ended method signature and more precise requirements reveals a compromise that generalized code often has to make. You need the method to allow arrays of any type as input. If the programmer doesn't make sure `src` and `dest` share the same type, however, the method will fail at runtime. It will *not* fail at compile time. The compiler, as usual, can only verify that the parameters are `Object` instances and therefore meet the requirements for `arraycopy()`.

Using Arrays of Other Types

Examining the `arraycopy()` method closely raises another issue regarding arrays and type. From time to time, it's tempting to put objects of different types into a single array because, from the programmer's perspective, their contents are logically related. Say you have a person's name, age, employee number, and date of hire. For a small program, it seems reasonable to store them as one `Object` array with `Integer`, `String`, `Integer`, and `Date` elements in it:

```
Object[] person = new Object[]
     { "Michael", new Integer(94),
     new Integer(1), new Date() };
```

An `Object` array will hold references of any type; all references have `Object` in their ancestry. The notion of implicit casting we discussed in Chapter 3 applies here for objects as well. If one type is a parent class to another type, a referent of the second type can always have the parent type for a reference.

```
Object string = new String("Some text");
```

By the same token, if we assign a `String` referent to an `Object` array index, the compiler applies implicit casting to accept the assignment.

You can even have an array of array components, which is the subject of the next section, "Understanding the `Arrays` Class." A problem arises only when you want to retrieve the component. Since components are stored in an array of Object references, accessing a component will evaluate to an Object reference. To get back to the referent's original type, you have to *cast* it explicitly, as follows:

```
String name = (String)person[0];  //ok
Integer age = (Integer)person[1]; //ok
Date start = (Date)person[2];     //oops!
```

If you cast to the wrong type, as this code suggests, the program will bail out. The compiler isn't responsible for tracking the original reference type of each array component; only the programmer is. The problem with storing objects of different types together in one array is the same as the bitset concept described in Chapter 3; in return for a certain convenience in your storage arrangement, you need code to maintain knowledge of that arrangement.

Understanding the *Arrays* Class

Java arrays are a useful but bare-bones construct. Using the String class as an example, you can see how that class's author uses character arrays to save the rest of us a lot of routine code work. The System.arraycopy() method moves content from one immutable structure to another, saving even the String class's author more than a little hassle.

For just about any other operation an experienced array user could want, there's the java.util.Arrays class. It is one example of what's called a *utility class*: a set of methods that support working with another kind of object. The Arrays class includes methods such as binarySearch(), copyOf(), fill(), and sort(). Different versions of each method support each of the primitive types, as well as object references, as parameters.

The Arrays class provides many useful utilities. I make note of it here so you'll think of it when taking inventory of methods that support array operations in the standard APIs.

Using a Multi-Dimensional Array

Arrays are objects, and of course array components can be objects. It doesn't take much time, rubbing those two facts together, to wonder if arrays can hold other arrays, and of course they can. It's a bit quirky in Java, though.

For some experienced programmers, the concept of a multi-dimensional array brings to mind a space in which each dimension has a fixed length, like a grid.

Java allows you to create such a thing, but doesn't require it, and so building an x × y array isn't as straightforward as you might expect.

Declaring a Multi-Dimensional Array

Certification Objective

Multiple array separators are all it takes to declare arrays with multiple dimensions. You can locate them with the type or variable name in the declaration, just as before:

```
int[][] vars;
int vars [][];
int[] vars [], space [][];     // also acceptable
```

This third syntax, which declares a two-dimensional array called vars and a three-dimensional array called space, is meant to be a succinct way to declare several array variables of one type. It's not fun to maintain code of this sort. When you see code of this sort posted on numerous help sites asking for an interpretation, it's a good sign that the syntax, however legal, creates more confusion than it is worth.

Even the JLS comments that this syntax is a poor choice for practice. That said, I might as well tell you now: You will come across programmers who prefer the letter of the law to its spirit. At the very least, you will certainly take exams or face technical interviews that test your command of such legalities. Be prepared.

Instantiating and Using a Multi-Dimensional Array

To create a uniform multi-dimensional array, or matrix, you can set the dimensions you want at instantiation time:

```
int [][] args = new int[4][5];
```

The result of this statement is an array args with four components, each of which refers to an array of five components. You can think of the addressable range as [0][0] through [3][4], but *don't* think of it as a structure of addresses like [0,0] or [3,4].

Using the notion of rows and columns to visualize multi-dimensional arrays in Java has a lot of appeal. It makes sense to initialize both dimensions at once to create a table of data. Just remember there are no facilities in Java that support this view of a two-dimensional array. If you want a true matrix, supply the logic in a class to support that interface, similar to the way the String class does for a char array. Or find an existing class that does it for you.

You can also initialize just an array's first dimension, and define the size of each array component in a separate statement:

```
int [][] args = new int[4][];
args[0] = new int[5];
args[1] = new int[3];
```

This technique reveals what you really get with Java: arrays of arrays that, properly managed, offer a multi-dimensional effect.

You can also use the trick that lets you assign a bracketed list of components to an array variable. Using outer braces to identify a list of arrays, and nested braces to hold the components of each component array, you can produce a makeshift table like the following:

```
public final class MDArray {
    public String[][] bits =
     { { "Michael", "Ernest", "MFE"},
       { "Ernest", "Friedman-Hill", "EFH"},
       { "Kathi", "Duggan", "KD"},
       { "Jeff", "Kellum",  "JK"} };

    public static void main(String args[]) {
        MDArray mda = new MDArray();
        System.out.println("There are " + mda.bits.length + " names:");
        System.out.println(mda.bits[0][2]);
        System.out.println(mda.bits[1][2]);
        System.out.println(mda.bits[2][2]);
        System.out.println(mda.bits[3][2]);
    }
}
```

You can use anonymous arrays as before, either with class members or for on-the-fly array creation. This approach is especially helpful if you want to fill component arrays one at a time:

```
bits[0] = new String[]
        {"Rudy", "Polanski", "RP"};
bits[1] = new String[]
        {"Rudy", "Washington", "RW"};
bits[2] = new String[]
        {"Rudy", "O'Reilly", "RO"};
```

Finding a graceful way to populate the next dimension—an array of arrays of arrays—is a challenge. Fortunately, there aren't many uses for multi-dimensional arrays that can't be managed by a simpler data structure. It's instructive to work through the challenge of using lightweight but bare-bones facilities at least once. Doing so helps you realize the other services you could use to make the work easier and less repetitive.

Doing that kind of work often enough will lead you to another benefit of object-oriented development: writing extensible code. If you don't have the method you need to make some routine task less tedious, you can write it. Methods like `System.arraycopy()` and classes like `Arrays` were developed with that motivation in mind. In a lot of cases, you can find a method like `arraycopy()`, which already does a lot of heavy lifting, and build on it.

Or, in our ongoing mission to become wide-ranging API consumers, we can browse packages and see if someone hasn't already thought of, designed, and written code that makes working with arrays even easier.

Using an *ArrayList* Object

The `ArrayList` class is a direct outcome of realizing useful, general-purpose services that can spare the everyday programmer time and effort from routine, low-level work with arrays. Like the `Arrays` class, it resides in the `java.util` package, where all classes that are known as *collections* are kept.

The `ArrayList` is a *wrapper class*, in one sense. A wrapper class is one that contains a simpler type and extends it in some fundamental way with named properties as fields and new services as methods.

Well-known wrapper classes in the `java.lang` package cover all the primitive types—`Byte`, `Character`, `Short`, `Integer`, `Long`, `Float`, `Double`, and `Boolean`. These classes let us handle their corresponding primitives as object references when that's convenient. These classes also provide methods to support the type's existing properties and add a few helpful capabilities to them.

You can also think of the relationship of `ArrayList` to an array as similar to the way `String` is related to the `char` array.

> **Subclasses also add to and extend their parent classes. The key difference is that a subclass *specializes*, or narrows, the class it extends.**

Understanding *ArrayList* Support for Array Features

The methods in the `ArrayList` class interface support many operations you already know with respect to an array:

- ▶ `isEmpty()`: Same as testing an array's length for zero. Returns `true` if the object has no elements.

- ▶ `clear()`: Removes all elements. In an array you have to clear the elements one at a time.

▶ contains(Object o): Returns true if any element matches the parameter. In any array we'd have to test the elements one at a time for effective equality.

▶ remove(Object o): Removes the first occurrence of the parameter. With an array you'd provide your own search-and-delete logic.

▶ size(): The method equivalent of an array's length property.

▶ toArray(): Returns an Object array of the elements. Similar in concept to String.toCharArray().

▶ addAll(...): A functional equivalent to System.arraycopy(). Its usage is beyond our scope, but I mention it here to illustrate a service the class programmer thinks is important.

Two aspects of ArrayList in particular make it a big deal. One, it has a mutable *capacity*. That is, through a method call you can change how many components it will hold. If you add a component to a full ArrayList object, it will resize itself. You never have to check first for an empty slot. You can also reduce an ArrayList object so its capacity and size are equal. Two, the ArrayList class implements an *interface* called List. The List interface formalizes the implicit properties of an array—the components have an order, duplicates are allowed—and gives them a *type identity*. You'll have to wait until Chapter 10, "Understanding Java Interfaces and Abstract Classes," to see why that's so great, but it will be worth it.

For now, let's review some methods in ArrayList made possible by these features:

▶ add (int index, E element): Inserts the type element at the position index

▶ ensureCapacity(int minCapacity): Resizes the ArrayList object to hold minCapacity elements

▶ removeRange(intfromIndex, inttoIndex): Removes elements from the given range; shifts trailing elements down to close the gap

▶ trimToSize(): Reduces the current capacity to equal current size

An alert reader may wonder if ArrayList methods just use System.arraycopy() to expand or trim capacity. They sure do. An array's size, after all, is still an immutable property. The ArrayList class just lets you work around it.

> **Capacity refers to the number of components a structure can hold. Size is the number of components it currently has.**

Instantiating an *ArrayList* Class

Certification Objective

Now the downside of the ArrayList class for a beginner: It's not as intuitive to use as you might hope. The class supports three constructors:

```
ArrayList()
ArrayList(Collection<? extends E> c)
ArrayList(int initialCapacity)
```

The default constructor will create space for 10 components. The third version lets you set the initial capacity. The second one is hard to interpret without a lot more information. If you just toss an array in it, you'll see it not only doesn't work, but it also spews plenty of complaints:

```
import java.util.ArrayList;

public final class ArrListCap {
    public static void main(String args[]) {
        String name = "Michael";
        ArrayList al = new ArrayList(name.toCharArray());
    }
}
```

```
$ javac ArrListCap.java
ArrListCap.java:6: error: no suitable constructor
found for ArrayList(char[])
        ArrayList al = new ArrayList(name.toCharArray());
                          ^
    constructor ArrayList.ArrayList(Collection) is not applicable
      (actual argument char[] cannot be converted to Collection
by method invocation conversion)
    constructor ArrayList.ArrayList() is not applicable
      (actual and formal argument lists differ in length)
    constructor ArrayList.ArrayList(int) is not applicable
      (actual argument char[] cannot be converted to int
by method invocation conversion)
1 error
```

Collection, like List, is a Java *interface*. It defines the methods a class must contain for its instances to be treated like a Collection type. We know arrays are Object subclasses only, so this attempt was doomed from the start.

We can instead create an ArrayList class, using one of the other constructors, and add components as you would with an array:

```
import java.util.ArrayList;

public final class ArrListCap {
    public static void main(String args[]) {
        ArrayList al = new ArrayList(25);
        al.add('M');
        al.add('i');
        al.add('c');
        al.add('h');
        al.add('a');
        al.add('e');
        al.add('l');
    }
}
```

Now we have something we can experiment with. Take this snippet as starter code and try out the other methods in the ArrayList class on your own.

Consuming the *ArrayList* API

Perhaps you did not expect it to be easy to put an array into an ArrayList object. I did, at first, because I assumed an ArrayList would want to do all sorts of things to wean me off of arrays. And in a way it does, but not without imposing some requirements of its own. It doesn't simply add every method a consumer could think to ask for.

The ArrayList, like many classes in the java.util package, is part of a larger *type system* called the Collections API. By enforcing certain rules and conditions through Java interfaces (and documentation), this type system promotes interoperability among many classes that, other than being collection oriented, don't have much to do with each other.

When you're ready to learn whole packages at a time, one of the first extended visits you should plan is with the java.util package. Learning the Collections API in particular will pay off handsomely time and again. It's not a short and shallow learning curve, but it's very well worth it. By the time you finish using this book, you'll have reviewed one or two simpler type systems that will prepare you for this journey. Until then, keep learning.

THE ESSENTIALS AND BEYOND

In this chapter, I defined the aspects of an array, the first type you've seen that lets you collect values of one type and manage them with a single object reference. We covered several ways to declare and use arrays and explored Java's support for multi-dimensional arrays. We reviewed two classes in the `java.util` package, Arrays and `ArrayList`, which support arrays by providing utility methods or expanding their native capabilities, respectively.

ADDITIONAL EXERCISES

1. Write a program to store your first name in a char array. (Just use the first eight characters if you wish). Reverse the array's order and print out the result.

2. Using the code snippet in the section "Using Arrays of Other Types," create an `Object` array. Retrieve each component from the array. Cast one to the wrong type. Compile and run the code and see what happens.

3. Write a program that requires two arguments from the command line. Transfer the two arguments to a char array big enough to hold both, including a space to separate them.

4. Using the code from Exercise 1, use the `Arrays.sort()` method on the resulting array and print it out.

5. Modify the code from the section "Instantiating an `ArrayList` Class" to your liking. Use two or three methods from the `ArrayList` class and test or print their results.

REVIEW QUESTIONS

1. True or false: You can use the `clone()` method on an array with components of type `float`.

2. Which array declaration is not legal?

    A. `int[][] scores = new int[5][];`

    B. `Object [][][] cubbies = new Object[3][0][5];`

    C. `String beans[] = new beans[6];`

    D. `java.util.Date[] dates[] = new java.util.Date[2][];`

3. True or false: Given a char array containing j, u, d, o and a `String` object containing judo, the `String` object's `length()` method will return the same value that the char array's `length` property contains.

(Continues)

THE ESSENTIALS AND BEYOND *(Continued)*

4. What is an anonymous array?

   A. An array that does not name its object reference

   B. An array that does not name its type

   C. A way to declare and initialize an array at the same time

   D. A way to initialize arrays without a loop

5. True or false: The System.arraycopy() method lets you transfer the contents of one array to any other as long as the number of components transferred doesn't exceed the target array's length.

6. Which method reports the current capacity of an ArrayList object?

   A. size()

   B. capacity()

   C. length()

   D. None of the above

7. What two properties describe a list?

   A. A list is sized and allows additional capacity.

   B. A list is ordered and allows duplicate components.

   C. A list is ordered and allows multiple dimensions.

   D. A list is sized and can hold multiple arrays.

8. True or false: Two arrays with the same content are not equal.

9. True or false: Two ArrayList objects with the same content are equal.

10. Select the true statement.

    A. You cannot create an ArrayList instance with zero capacity.

    B. You cannot trim an ArrayList to zero capacity.

    C. If you call remove(0) using an empty ArrayList object, it will compile successfully.

    D. If you call remove(0) on an empty ArrayList, it will run successfully.

CHAPTER 5

Using Loops in Java Code

In Chapter 4, "Using Java Arrays," we used the while construct to populate an array with a section of repeating code. Without the means to loop through code the way we did, a task like populating an array is still possible, just far more cumbersome to implement. Loops can make any tedious, repetitive task easier to express in code. In this chapter, we'll look at ways to use loops to make such tasks simpler and more economical.

Java supports four loop constructs. We'll look at each one, compare them, and consider how best to apply each one. We'll also look at how to break a loop when we arrive at odd conditions we can't handle nicely in repeating code.

In this chapter, we'll cover the following topics:

▶ **Applying while loops**

▶ **Applying do/while loops**

▶ **Applying for and for-each loops**

▶ **Comparing loop constructs**

▶ **Using continue and break statements**

Applying *while* Loops

Looping is a staple of everyday programming. Sooner or later, every task in processing data boils down to *iterating* over multiple data in a routine format or object type. Sometimes you know how many items you've got and can supply a hard counting limit in your logic, but just as often you need a way to repeat code until some arbitrary condition is met. The while statement handles those situations.

It is the easiest one to learn because it has the same syntax as an `if` statement:

```
while (boolean_test)
    statementA;
```

The `while` keyword introduces a test expression, contained in parentheses, that evaluates to `true` or `false`. If `true`, then `statementA` executes. If `false`, control transfers to the end of the statement and the program continues. Just as with an `if` construct, if there is more than one statement you want to execute, you use code block separators:

```
while (boolean_test) {
    statementA;
    statementB;
    // as many statements as you need
    statementN;
}
```

> A `while` statement is more or less an `if` statement that repeats, so it makes sense that they have a common syntax.

Unlike an `if` test expression, a `while` test expression *should* have the potential to evaluate to `true` more than once. Otherwise you might as well use `if`. In fact, you can just replace `if` with `while` in a statement if your test condition changes from a one-time test to a recurring one or vice versa.

If you also have an `else` clause attached to the `if` statement, however, this drop-in replacement trick doesn't apply. It's a nice idea, but it has limited potential.

Don't be lulled into thinking simple loops can create only simple problems. You can get your programs into trouble very quickly if you don't observe two potential hazards. The first has to do with expressing your test condition in a clear way, ideally one that helps express the containing method's context. The second has to do with creating an unintentional *infinite loop*.

Choosing a Useful *while* Test

The `while` statement is a bare-bones construct. As Figure 5.1 illustrates, it either executes a body of statements or it doesn't.

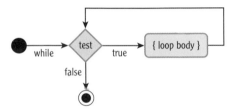

FIGURE 5.1 Flow diagram of a `while` statement

What's not evident in the construct is how the test expression changes from true to false. Without some forethought, you may not see how to do it without defeating the purpose of the loop. Consider the following piece of code:

```
public static void main(String args[]) {
    boolean officeHours = true;
    while (officeHours) {
        // meet student;
        // review paper;
        officeHours = false;
    }
}
```

This code initializes officeHours, starts the loop, executes its statements, and returns to the top to test. See the problem? This loop can execute only once. So how can we change the test condition to allow the loop multiple runs? Nesting in the while loop a condition that can change the test condition doesn't cut it, and it just clutters the code anyway, as you see here:

We avoided this problem in the last chapter by using an incrementing counter and testing for the length of the array.

```
public static void main(String args[]) {
    boolean officeHours = true;
    boolean studentsWaiting = true;
    while (officeHours) {
        // meet student
        // review paper
        if (!studentsWaiting)
            officeHours = false;
    }
}
```

In order for studentsWaiting to become false, we have to change it somewhere in the body of the while statement. To do that, we need another loop to decrement a different value for the number of waiting students, and so it goes. The logic becomes tangled in referencing its own test variable in the right way under the right conditions, and the original intent gets buried.

We need some outside help to manage a terminal condition for the loop. In Java, the usual way to handle this is by calling a method that checks a *flag* for us. Let's model the idea with *pseudocode*:

```
public class OfficeHours {
    public boolean officesOpen() {
        // if it's after 3pm or before 10am, return false
    }

    public void holdOfficeHours() {
        while (officesOpen()) {
```

```
            // meet student
            // review paper
        }
    }

    public static void main(String args[]) {
        OfficeHours oh = new OfficeHours();
        oh.holdOfficeHours();
    }
}
```

The logic and code here aren't complete, but the comments give you the idea. Once a meeting concludes, the loop calls `officesOpen()`. If the building has closed, office hours are over. I rely on some arbitrary, external condition to indicate when the test should terminate.

Notice also that whoever calls the `holdOfficeHours()` method has no idea or signal how long this call should remain open. So far we've written programs that access fields or call methods and return very quickly. What's your experience when you start a new program on your machine and nothing seems to happen? What expectations did you have when you started the program? When you're adding loops of this sort to a program, you can expect that any user of your program may have the same questions.

In most cases, we choose a `while` statement because we don't know or don't want to be held to a specific number of counts. Some value way closer to two iterations than, say, infinity iterations would be best for most cases. It's program logic that determines how long a loop might take, so it is the programmer who has to make sure infinity isn't a possible outcome.

There's nothing wrong with hard limits to a loop. The `for` *loop* is better designed for those cases and we'll discuss it shortly. But it's worth noting that no looping construct is immune from going off into forever. You always have to check that you'll reach your intended limit or that your test condition will change.

Watching Out for Infinite Loops

When using a `while` loop, make sure there's a distinction between an indefinite change and one that never occurs. A `while` loop, given a test condition that never changes, has no reason to stop. That's not something you want in most programs.

There are some designed to run this way: An HTTP server, for example, or any program that hangs around waiting for client requests, uses what's called a *service loop*. In such programs, there is a *flag condition* in the code that represents a life cycle change, like telling the program it has to restart or shut down.

A truly infinite loop is one that should have a changeable flag condition but doesn't. It's easy to write one:

```
public final class Infinite {
    public static void main(String args[]) {
        while (true)
            ;
    }
}
$ javac Infinite.java
$ ptime java Infinite
^C
real        11.474990632
user        10.915129410
sys          0.107862133
```

Notice the semicolon in the method body. This is an *empty statement*; it's a way to express "do nothing" in your code. This seemingly simple bit of code can be quite nasty. To illustrate, I've used a command available in the Solaris operating system: ptime, which breaks down the time the program used. The real time is "wall clock time," or the duration of the program from start to finish. The user and sys times show how much CPU time was consumed by the program's code and by requesting kernel services, such as allocating memory and opening files, respectively.

Most programs show a sizable gap between real time and the sum of user and sys time. The difference is called *service time*. It's the sum of time your program had to wait on the system to get around to helping it. This program spends almost 96 percent of its time on the CPU testing whether true means true! The very low sys time means it has very few reasons to stop and ask the system for any help, so it's all program logic, just about all the time.

Without any reporting, this program *appears* to do nothing. In fact, it runs its test condition as often (and as fast) as the JVM and hardware resources will allow. The only way to stop it is to kill the program.

How can this happen in your code? Take the idea of some logical test you've devised, and implement it in such a way that it looks right, so long as you don't look too hard. For logic that manages what office hours are, it's pretty easy. Let's try writing some code for the officesOpen() method described earlier:

```
public boolean officesOpen() {
    // after 10am and before 3pm, return true
    // otherwise return false
    if (hour < 1500) return true;
    if (hour > 1000) return true;
```

```
        return false;
    }
```

I want to say offices are open any hour before 3 p.m. and any hour after 10 a.m., where the field hour stores its value in military time format. The comment included with the code is a defensive statement, one that a reviewer can use to test the code's intention against its implementation. Perhaps in the name of avoiding nested logic, the programmer uses the return keyword after each decision, hoping to filter out each true case so that only the false case remains at the end.

There's a flaw in this implementation, however, that ensures officesOpen()will always return true. (Don't read further until you can explain what it is!) Any caller that uses this method in its while loop will never terminate.

The more complex a while loop's test expression gets, or the harder it is to read the implemented logic, the more vulnerable you become to this possibility. The time you spend isolating and debugging this behavior also tends to increase with the number of code lines that depend on it.

As program users, we quickly grow accustomed to letting error messages tell us something is wrong. As looping troubleshooters, we must learn to distinguish between a good kind of quiet (a busy but productive system) and a bad kind of quiet (a system happily spinning its wheels). Infinite loops will survive in your programs for as long as it takes you to recognize the difference.

In case you missed the flaw: any valid values for the hour field is either less than 1500 or more than 1000—some are both. There's no case where this implementation should return false.

Applying *do/while* Loops

Java supports an alternate form of the while statement called a do/while loop. The do/while loop inverts the while statement's flow of control, executing its code body first and its test expression second. A do/while loop therefore runs at least once. If the test evaluates to true, control returns to the top and the loop repeats. If it evaluates to false, program control escapes this statement to execute the next statement in the method. Figure 5.2 illustrates the flow.

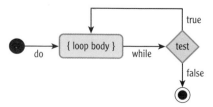

FIGURE 5.2   Flow diagram of a do/while statement

The structure of the statement is accordingly simple:

```
do {
    statementA;
    statementB;
    statementC;
} while (boolean_condition);
```

Because this form will execute its statement body at least once, it simplifies the case a while statement cannot handle on its own. A while statement will run zero times if its test evaluates to false on the first try. The only way around that without using do/while is by writing the loop statements twice, once before the test expression and once after:

```
statementA;
statementB;
statementC;
while (boolean_expression) {
    statementA;
    statementB;
    statementC;
}
```

You probably won't use the do/while statement a lot. When you do, however, it will save you from this unsightly workaround. Using our office hours example, let's say the school administration issues a new rule requiring all faculty to see at least one student a day, even if they show up late. A programmer could implement that rule in code very simply:

```
do {
    // meet student
    // review paper
} while (officesOpen());
```

What happens to the administrators, once the faculty catch up with them, could be messy, but the code looks great.

The same cautions still apply. If the test condition never evaluates to true, a do/while loop can run only once. If that's the case, all you've really produced is a trumped-up if statement. If the test condition never evaluates to false, you'll again have the much-dreaded infinite loop on your hands.

Applying *for* and For-Each Loops

A counting variable provides a concrete way to manage a loop's bounds. It's an honorable technique, and you will see often it applied in tutorials, blogs, magazine articles, and everywhere else, for the very same reason we used it in Chapter 4—it's easy to interpret:

```java
int counter = 0;
while (counter < 10) {
    //do something ten times
    counter++;
}
```

So what's wrong with it? Not anything, really. The counter variable is the simplest possible condition flag. It is incremented in the loop's statement body, but it's easy enough to understand why. It's usually placed at the bottom so it's easy to find, but it can occur wherever you need it to. The counter variable itself might be declared and initialized hundreds of lines away from the loop where it's used, but searching for it through class code should be simple enough. If doing that proves tedious, Java allows you to declare variables anywhere inside the class body, so you can move it closest to where it's used if that suits your taste.

Using *for* Loops

Certification Objective

The for loop operates on this kind of iteration, but in a tighter fashion. The syntax seems more complicated at first sight:

```java
for (initializers; test_condition; step_instructions)
    statement;
```

Or you can use this syntax:

```java
for (initializers; test_condition; step_instructions) {
    statementA;
    statementB;
    // additional statements
    statementN;
}
```

This syntax normalizes the use of counting variables (*initializers*), a test condition, and step instructions (which typically handle incrementing or decrementing). Now when we want to repeat a given step 10 times, say, the for statement puts that intention front and center:

```java
for (int counter = 0; counter < 10; counter++)
    System.out.println("Counter: " + counter);
```

This example has all the elements of our last `while` statement, but it separates the mechanics of iteration from the statements we want to iterate. Notice that we declared and initialized the `counter` variable *inside* the `for` loop: perfectly legal. This liberty lets you constrain the scope of your `counter` variable to the `for` statement. The `for` statement does not, however, have its own namespace. If you declared `counter` already in the containing method, the compiler complains if you redeclare it here.

Visually, the flow of control matches Figure 5.3.

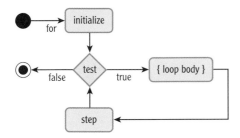

FIGURE 5.3 Flow diagram of a `for` statement

The `for` statement also allows for multiple initializations and step instructions. Just separate them with a comma, as shown in Listing 5.1.

LISTING 5.1 Multiple initializations in a `for` loop

```
public final class ForLoop {
    public static void main(String args[]) {
        for (int i = 0, j = 29; j > 0; i++, j-)
            System.out.println("i * j = " + i*j);
    }
}
$ javac ForLoop.java
$ java ForLoop
i * j = 0
i * j = 28
i * j = 54
(output elided)
i * j = 54
i * j = 28
```

The `for` statement uses semicolons to delimit its three elements. I use the term *step* to refer to any action that advances the iteration. As Figure 5.3 suggests, the step should influence the test. You can step by incrementing, decrementing, or even calling a method that could change the outcome of the test expression.

An array's *length* property provides a natural fit to a for statement. You can use it in place of a literal value for the number of elements in an array, as follows:

```
public final class ArrayLengthFor {
    public static void main(String args[]) {
        int [] squares = new int[7];
        for (int i = 0; i < squares.length; i++) {
            squares[i] = i * i;
            System.out.println("Square of " + i + " is " + squares[i]);
        }
    }
}
$ javac ArrayLengthFor.java
$ java ArrayLengthFor
Square of 0 is 0
Square of 1 is 1
Square of 2 is 4
Square of 3 is 9
Square of 4 is 16
Square of 5 is 25
Square of 6 is 36
```

Remember that arrays use an *index*; component addresses start at zero instead of one. It's common to test for a value less than length because the last component position is always length-1.

We can now address an open question from the last chapter: how to initialize a multi-dimensional array in an efficient manner. To do it, we used what's called a *nested loop*, placing one repeating body of code inside another.

Nesting Loops

You nest loop statements the same way you nest decision statements. You can also nest decisions inside of loops and loops inside of decisions. As far as the compiler is concerned, nesting to any level is fine so long as it's syntactically correct. The practical limit for nesting, ideally, is how readable the structure is to someone unfamiliar with the program logic.

Let's start with a simple example. I want to store a multiplication table of all the products for the numbers 1 through 12 using a two-dimensional array that provides 144 component positions. A nested loop is useful for this kind of work, but it's not without a kink or two.

The *outer loop* operates in the first dimension; that is, the array that holds the other arrays. The *inner loop* operates on the integer components of each array component. That's the easy part. The hard part is deciding how to relate the array positions themselves, which range from 0 to 11, to the numbers we want to store, which range from 1 to 12. In Listing 5.2, we adjust our counters by one.

LISTING 5.2 Populating a two-dimensional array

```java
public final class MultTable {
    public static void main(String args[]) {
        int products[][] = new int[12][12];
        for (int i = 0; i < products.length; i++) {
            for (int j = 0; j < products[i].length; j++) {
                products[i][j] = (i + 1) * (j + 1);
                System.out.print("i: " + (i + 1) + "  ");
                System.out.print("j: " + (j + 1) + " =");
                System.out.println(" " + products[i][j]);
            }
            System.out.println();
        }
    }
}
```

The program starts out simply enough, creating a 12×12 array. The outer loop iterates through the first array. The inner loop populates each component array. Because we want products[0][0] to hold the result of 1×1, not zero times zero, we offset the counter value by one. We also use the offset to print index values to match the user's expectations.

It may seem clumsy, but what are the alternatives? We could create a 13×13 matrix and disregard the components at position zero. Each array access would then correspond directly to its product value: products[11][11] would store 121, and so on.

Ignoring the zero index values, however, comes at a cost of 25 component spaces we'd create and never use. It's not a big deal in a small array, but it's not a small deal in a big array, either. It's a trade-off between an efficient use of space and simpler program logic for array access.

Familiarize yourself with the offset technique in the MultTable class. It's not rocket science, but whatever you store in a complex structure and however you choose to store it, you'll have to make it relate your storage scheme to your presentation scheme. This task is a significant part of any programmer's job, whether you're deciding how to represent an integer in bits or deciding how to unroll a multi-dimensional array.

Avoiding Useless and Infinite Loops

You may be less likely to create useless or infinite loops with `for` statements, but you're still free to do it. While the `for` statement normalizes the iteration setup, it doesn't make the compiler any better at detecting common mistakes. We're still concerned with making sure of the following:

- ► The test condition evaluates to `true` at least once.

- ► The loop can run multiple times.

- ► The test condition can evaluate to `false`.

All other things being equal, it's easier to spot some problems in a `for` statement. Programmers in search of adventure occasionally find ways to hide them anyway. Here are some fundamental bits of advice

Review any method call used in a step operation. A method call lets you supply complex logic for a step process without muddling the appearance of a `for` statement. That effort goes a long way to maintaining readable code. As the office-hours examples demonstrate, method calls are also great hiding places for infinity. Don't assume such a method just works; check the code.

Read every test with a relational operator carefully. It's very easy to gloss over one several times before you realize its logic is flawed; very easy. In preparing this chapter, as a matter of fact, my technical editor pointed out one problem in Listing 5.1 that I "corrected" twice before getting it right:

```
for (int i = 0, j = 29; j > 0; i++, j-)
    System.out.println("i * j = " + i*j);
```

Using this part of the code, change the operator in the test expression to less than (`<`) and equals (`==`) and see what results you get. Then explain the outcome to demonstrate your understanding. Might be as plain as day to you; might not.

Beware of unreachable code in a `for` statement. It's a less common occurrence than an infinite loop or a wrong-way relational test, and perhaps for that reason it's harder to spot. Let's look at the simplest possible example:

```
for (; false; );
```

> **Ugly for statement secret: The compiler doesn't care if you omit *all three elements* between the parentheses.**
> ▶

The compiler will notice that the test condition never evaluates to `true`. In the name of optimizing your code, it takes advantage of every literal expression that it can. It will tell you the next statement can't be reached, even if it's empty.

If you remove the second semicolon in an attempt to remove the appearance of a third statement, the compiler will complain that there's no longer a legal `for` statement. If instead you remove the `false` literal, leaving the code to look like this

```
for (;; );
```

the code will now compile. And now you've discovered the `for` statement version of an infinite loop. Which brings us to the final moral of this story: Using compiler errors to lead you to useful code is like following seagulls to dry land. You could get lucky; you could also end up sailing toward a trash barge.

Using For-Each Loops

Isn't it great when a lot of low-level, detail-oriented work is already done for you? You bet it is. When it comes to arrays and similar data structures called *Collections* types, there's some very good news. Java supports a version of the `for` loop specifically made for them, called a *for-each* loop.

The for-each loop is one kind of syntactic sugar that just seems to know how to iterate over arrays and other objects that contain data components. It works by inferring the details you would normally supply in a `for` or `while` statement. In a `for` statement, there's no distinction between an arbitrary list of values, an array, or a Collections type. You have to tell it when iteration is finished:

```
for (int i = 0; i < products.length; i++) {
    int row = products[i];
    // do something with the row variable
}
```

The for-each construct, on the other hand, knows an array when it sees one and can find the `length` value on its own. (Well, okay, you have to give it an array [or Collections type] and it knows what to do with it, but still it's pretty cool.) It can also infer the type of the array's components on its own, leaving you a lot less to write:

```
for (int row: products) {
    // do something with the row variable
}
```

Notice there is no counting variable or `length` property; it's all determined by the construct by reading properties it expects the `products` object to include. You only have to supply a variable (`row`). The construct makes sure the variable is assigned the referent of each component when its iteration comes around. The variable type has to match the array component type, of course. If the

> The for-each construct applies the *inversion-of-control* principle. It infers the information it needs from the data so you don't have to write it out.

products reference pointed to an array of `Product` referents, we'd simply change the expression to this:

```
for (Product prod: products) {
    // do something with each Product component
}
```

It won't take long to get accustomed to it. The for-each construct is far less cumbersome than a `for` loop and is designed specifically to make iterating over arrays and Collections types terse and elegant. You'll still need the `for` statement to work with primitives and objects that are neither arrays nor a Collections-compliant type.

Using the For-Each Loop with a Collections Type

Using a `for` statement with a Collections type (all of which are kept in the `java.util` package) requires more coverage of the Collections API than falls within the scope of this book. But it's hard to appreciate the full power of the for-each construct without seeing what it replaced, so we'll take a peek at it.

All Collections types subscribe to a framework of common properties and behaviors. One of those behaviors is *iterability*, or the means all Collections types have to let the caller traverse its components. The importance of iterability is its guarantee that you see each object in the collection only once in a traversal. That guarantee is something you might take for granted with an ordered list, such as an array. With other types of collections, the rules for traversing them are neither intuitive nor self-evident, so iterability is not a minor promise.

A *set*, for example, doesn't assign an order to its components. Sets are concerned with one thing: that each value in the collection is unique. Recall that a list uses its index scheme to disambiguate its components. From the list's point of view, there can be no duplicate value once a component is associated with a position in the list. Fine. But how do you traverse a set of components if there's no explicit order to them?

Iterability tells us the underlying properties of any Collections type doesn't have to matter to the caller if all they want is to see each component one time. If you call any Collections type's `iterator()` method, you'll receive an object (of type `Iterator`) that will iterate through its components for you. Depending on the type, some iterators will also *traverse* the collection.

The for-each loop understands the `Iterator` interface implicitly. A `for` statement doesn't, although it can use the `Iterator` interface explicitly, as shown here:

> We use the term *traverse* to include types that let you walk through their components backward as well as forward.

```
for (Iterator<String> iter = collect.iterator(); iter.hasNext(); ) {
    String item = iter.next();
    // do something stringy with item
}
```

Assume the `collect` variable refers to some Collections type; it doesn't matter which one. Calling the variable's `iterator()` method returns an `Iterator` reference; you can then use to iterate over `collect`'s components.

The `Iterator` interface includes two key methods: `hasNext()`, which returns `true` if there is at least one untouched object left in the Collections type, and `next()`, which returns a reference to the next available component. We have to leave the step instruction of the `for` statement empty; the `next()` method does the incrementing work behind the scenes.

In a for-each loop, by contrast, this work is understood. It looks the same for accessing a Collections type as it does for an array. The for-each equivalent to this `for` statement is as follows:

```
for (String item: collect) {
    //do stuff with the item reference
}
```

We don't need to manage the details of the `Iterator`, never mind the generics business. And while you will eventually need to learn generics, knowing you won't have to refer to it just to iterate a Collections object is a big win. Enjoy it!

The convenience of this syntactic sugar, alas, comes at the expense of a subtle trade-off. The for-each construct is a build-up of existing services in the language that removes some of the tedium of everyday coding with arrays and collections. From the compiler's point of view, it's just a `for` loop with some extra information that lets it infer some looping information.

You can think of for-each as a student in a car designed for driver training. The student controls the vehicle to the degree the instructor allows it. Similarly, a for-each gets access to a collection's components but only to the extent allowed by the underlying `for` construct.

To avoid confusion between the two constructs, the variable we use in a for-each construct gets a pseudoreference to each component. For-each iterations can't change the referents they operate on in a way that persists when the iteration completes; they can only read them. Any change you make to the reference silently drops once the iteration is over. If it were strictly a read-only copy, you'd at least expect an error.

There's also no explicit index value in a for-each construct, so you can't determine the position of any component in an array or indexed collection. If you had to traverse two arrays in parallel, for example, you'd have to use the `for` statement to manage it. The for-each construct is a wonderful thing for simple cases, as intended, but it's not a full, new feature to the language.

Comparing Loop Constructs

There isn't much variety in loop constructs. The `while` and `do/while` statements differ in one respect only, and in my experience, that difference doesn't come up very often. The for-each construct is just a smart version of the `for` statement, but it's only smart about arrays and Collections types.

Comparing these constructs boils down to knowing the best use for each form. We have already covered the following points:

▶ The `while` and `for` statements will run zero or more times.

▶ The `do/while` statement will run one or more times.

▶ The `while` and `do/while` statements work well with test expressions that change in an indefinite or program-specific manner.

▶ The `for` statement works well with step-wise and counter-based iteration, such as populating arrays or repeating some code a fixed number of times.

▶ The for-each construct is ideal for iterating one array or Collections type at a time.

Using *continue* and *break* Statements

In Chapter 3, "Using Java Operators and Conditional Logic," we used the `break` statement in a `switch` statement. Recall that a `switch` statement uses *case labels* to separate a list of statements. It will transfer control to a case label if the case's value matches the `switch` expression. This is one toned-down form of what we once called a `goto` statement.

Modern programming languages consider the `goto` statement a dangerous feature. In its original form, the `goto` statement let you transfer control from one point in your code to some arbitrary other point. In a language where the statements are numbered, like BASIC, you'd transfer control to the line number you want. Otherwise you'd use labels to name a point in the code to which you wanted to pass control. Of course it could work well, and of course it could go horribly wrong.

It is a powerful capability. Without restraint, however, it's very easy for a codebase of steadily increasing size and/or complexity to transfer control into the weeds in such a way that no programmer knows how best to retrieve it. The consensus around this danger is strong enough that no modern programming language supports a `goto` statement.

Instead, Java has what some people call *scope-based breaks.* I think it's simpler and more pointed to say you can use labels and breaks inside a method to achieve a goto-like effect. We'll discuss how you can use these to simplify your code.

Using the *continue* Statement

The continue statement works only within a loop. You can use it to bypass the remaining statements in a loop's body and begin the next iteration immediately.

Certification Objective

The number of self-evident cases for this kind of use, I must admit, usually eludes me. If I have some code in which a continue statement would save me time and effort, I take it to mean the loop at hand could have been written to factor out the need. Then I want to rewrite the loop to do exactly that. As a result, I haven't collected many cases where nothing will do a better job than a continue statement. Unfortunately for you, that means the following examples are artificial.

Let's say we wanted to ignore every multiple of 10 in a for loop. We can test whether the counter's current value is divisible by 10. If so, we just move on to the next iteration:

```java
public final class Continue {
    public static void main(String args[]) {
        for (int i = 0; i < 31; i++) {
            if ( i % 10 == 0 )
                continue;
            System.out.print(i + " ");
        }
    }
}
```

```
$ javac Continue.java
$ java Continue
1 2 3 4 5 6 7 8 9 11 12 13 14 15 16 17 18 19 21
        22 23 24 25 26 27 28 29
```

Notice that no multiple of 10 appears in the output. The continue statement simply bypasses the print() method and gets on to the next iteration.

If instead you want to execute an alternate body of statements, you can also add an else statement inside the for loop; one branch uses continue, the other runs the alternate code. Be careful, though. A loop that keeps adding branch cases quickly turns into *spaghetti code.*

In a nested loop, a continue statement acts on the loop it's in. A continue statement in an inner loop runs the next iteration of the inner loop only. What about a little more control? Say you've got some ugly triple-nested looping code

> The term *spaghetti code* describes programs that have been modified so much it is a major, time-consuming task for anyone to read them.

you can't rewrite without mortal consequences. At the same time, you need to break out from the innermost loop to the outermost loop. Can you do that?

Well, yes, if you must. It's as simple as adding a label to a `continue` statement to specify the transfer of control. We cover that approach in a few more paragraphs.

Using the *break* Statement

Certification
Objective

The `break` statement works in a `switch` statement as well as in any loop. It transfers control to the end of the current statement, making it a "fall-through" actor in a statement body. What makes it safer than a `goto`, in the eyes of Java language designers, is that it transfers control in one direction only and never outside its containing method.

It should always be easy to discern where a `break` statement transfers control. Methods that have a `switch` or loop that runs dozens or even hundreds of lines long are, unfortunately, a common case where a `break` statement is used to patch some faulty logic instead of fixing the whole. A common technique I use when troubleshooting code I've received is just to search for the word *break*. If I see it more than half a dozen times, my hourly rate goes up. Or I don't get the job, which, given the job at hand, is also okay.

Let's say the faculty from our previous office hours example staged a successful coup. They wrote some new rules and decided office hours are over as soon as it can be determined the building has closed for the day:

```java
public final class OfficeHours {
    public boolean officesOpen() {
        // if it's after 3pm or before 10am, return false
    }

    public void holdOfficeHours() {
        while (officesOpen()) {
            // meet student
            if (!officesOpen()) break;
            // review paper
            if (!officesOpen()) break;
        }
    }

    public static void main(String args[]) {
        OfficeHours oh = new OfficeHours();
        oh.holdOfficeHours();
    }
}
```

Since the holdOfficeHours() method contains just the while statement, breaking the loop causes the method to return control to the caller. In nested loops, the break statement also operates within the innermost loop that contains it.

Using Labeled Statements

In single loops it's hard to find a meaningful case for using break or continue. It's easier in simple cases to decompose a loop and manage odd cases with a separate if statement.

In a nested loop it's a different story. One day, when you've become adept in Java, you'll figure out how to untangle deeply nested loops, the hallmark of spaghetti code, altogether. Until then, however, you're going to see quite a few of them, first on exams that want to see if your head will explode and then in business applications where it was someone's challenge to bang out working code in half the time it should have taken.

One of those challenges will be how to escape some or all of the nested loops of a hopelessly complicated structure. For that, you need labels, similar to the ones you've already seen in a switch statement.

A label is just a named point in code. It can reside between any two statements that are contained by a loop. The name is followed by a colon. The label itself is *not* a statement. When control is transferred, the label does not execute; the statement that follows it does.

Let's say we want to print our MultTable output but this time stop printing after the 11th row. We can place a label at the top of the outer loop, then call break once we've printed 11×11, or 121.

```java
public final class MultTable {
    public static void main(String args[]) {
        int products[][] = new int[12][12];
        // here's the label
        goestoeleven:
        for (int i = 0; i < products.length; i++) {
            for (int j = 0; j < products[i].length; j++) {
                products[i][j] = (i + 1) * (j + 1);
                System.out.print("i: " + (i + 1) + "  ");
                System.out.print("j: " + (j + 1) + " =");
                System.out.println(" " + products[i][j]);
                if (products[i][j] == 121 ){
                    break goestoeleven;
                }
            }
        }
```

```
        System.out.println();
      }
    }
  }
```

> A no-op statement doesn't do anything. It's useful when you want to say "do nothing" explicitly.

This action may appear counterintuitive at first. The label goestoeleven appears at the top of the outer loop. When we call the label with break, control goes to the top of the loop *in order to transfer control* to the bottom. This allows us to ignore the whole if statement and proceed. Without a statement following the if, even if it's a *no-op statement*, this scheme would not compile.

THE ESSENTIALS AND BEYOND

In this chapter we covered the four loop constructs that are available in Java: while, do/while, for, and for-each. We reviewed the uses for each form and compared them to consider which is best applied to a particular task. We also discussed the break and continue statements, which help circumvent normal iteration control, and you saw a way to use labeled forms of these statements to handle code that uses nested loops.

ADDITIONAL EXERCISES

1. Write a loop that prints out a message once every million iterations. Compile and run the program. Let it run for about 10 seconds (clock time) to see how many statements get printed.

2. Write a program to calculate the sum of odd numbers from 0 to 150.

3. Using the last MultTable code presented in this chapter, change the break statement to continue. Before running it, write down what you expect to happen.

REVIEW QUESTIONS

1. True or false: The statement while (true); will produce an infinite loop.

2. Select the illegal loop expressions from the following. (Choose all that apply.)

   A. for (; false;);

   B. for (int i = -10; i < i; i++);

   C. for (;;);

   D. for (new Object(); 5 > 3; new Object());

(Continues)

THE ESSENTIALS AND BEYOND *(Continued)*

3. What is the outcome for the following code?

   ```
   do { } while (false);
   ```

   A. It will not compile.

   B. It will not run.

   C. It will run infinitely.

   D. It will run and finish.

4. How many times will the following loop execute?

   ```
   int count = 0;
   while (count <= 6) {
       count = count + 2;
   }
   ```

   A. Six

   B. Five

   C. Four

   D. Three

5. Which term describes the process of looping through a statement body?

   A. Stepping

   B. Condition testing

   C. Iterating

   D. Enumerating

6. Consider the following code and select the correct analysis:

   ```java
   public final class ForEachLoop {
       public static void main(String args[]) {
           for (String arg: args)
               System.out.println(arg);
       }
   }
   ```

   A. The class will not compile.

   B. The program will run the same with or without command-line arguments.

   C. The program will throw errors when run without command-line arguments.

   D. The program will throw an error once it runs out of command-line arguments.

(Continues)

7. Read the following code and select the correct analysis:

```java
public final class ForLoop {
    public static void main(String args[]) {
        for (int i = (2 << 30-1); true; i++)
        System.out.println(i);
        break;
    }
}
```

A. The code will not compile.

B. The code will run without error.

C. The code will run but bail out once it reaches the maximum positive value for Java integers.

D. The code will run but bail out when it reaches the break statement.

8. True or false: All other things being equal, a while statement is faster than a for statement because there's less to set up.

9. Select the option that lists the three elements of a for loop declaration in the right order.

A. Counting, testing, iterating

B. Initial step, test step, loop instruction

C. Declare, test, execute

D. Initialize, test, step instruction

10. True or false: The for-each construct will work with an array or any kind of object that contains an array.

CHAPTER 6

Encapsulating Data and Exposing Methods in Java

It's time to move past main() methods for writing programs and dig a bit deeper. This step has several elements to it, so I've broken the first big step into two chapters. This chapter covers the fundamentals of defining the interface to a class: restricting direct access to member variables and using methods to allow indirect access.

In Chapter 7, "Using Java Methods to Communicate," I'll build on this practice by designing methods that express the services a class offers.

In this chapter, we'll cover the following topics:

▶ **Encapsulating data**

▶ **Exposing data through methods**

▶ **Applying access modifiers**

▶ **Abstracting data**

Encapsulating Data

As Chapter 7 will explain, in Java we use methods to *communicate* between objects in a program. Literally, we're just passing data as parameters from one method to another, sometimes expecting a returned value, sometimes not. But learning to think in the figurative sense of communicating helps you to see your objects as actors, each playing a role or performing a service in your program. Learning to think this way takes time, but for some people it is the entire point of object-oriented programming. It contributes, among other things, to clearer design and deeper analysis when putting large programs together.

If your study of Java follows a path like mine, you may find yourself having "aha!" moments as the idea of communicating through methods kicks in. You may wonder how the code you've written before those realizations actually worked. And, if your experience is like mine, those revelations will keep coming as you take on bigger programming challenges.

This chapter is a first step toward that goal. You want to think of the data that makes up your classes as a private matter; a set of details, really, that give your Java class the means to do the work its methods support.

Understanding Data Hiding

Maybe *data hiding* is not the best term. Saying we hide data in an object is like saying we hide snacks in a vending machine or we hide circuitry in a remote control unit. It's a legitimate aspect of what's going on, of course, but the word *hide* makes it sound like some secretive nature is worth noting. Nonetheless, the term has stuck, a very large number of users accept it, and we're obliged to follow along if we want to get in the conversation with them.

What I want to convey in this chapter has more to do with *covering* data: to protect it and to promote the appearance of a single object. I also want to remove from view something I see as a detail of small consequence in a class I write. I want to retain the freedom to change it later. At the very least, I want to suggest that how I stored my data is not as important as the means to use it. I want users to focus on the service I provide with my Java class.

The rest of this chapter will show you the what and the how of encapsulation. Interpreting well-designed Java classes and writing useful and intuitive methods yourself are the practical outcomes. But I'll take a moment here to explain the motivation using accepted terms:

- ▶ Minimizing/localizing variable scope
- ▶ Cohesion
- ▶ Loose coupling
- ▶ Maintainability

I'll discuss each of these in turn.

Minimizing/localizing variable scope   Most people don't know how a remote control device works before they use it. They just press the buttons and learn from the results. Good object-oriented code follows the same model. Making visible all the elements that a useful class comprises distracts the calling programmer. We want to show them the controls, the buttons that can produce results they can observe, test, and utilize.

Consider having to explain the `ArrayList` class to someone else. You could use a simplified diagram to hit the class's high points, as I did in Chapter 4, "Using Java Arrays." Or you could show everything in one diagram, as in Figure 6.1. Chances are you'll then have two tasks: one, to explain the methods you consider relevant in an introduction; two, to explain any elements that pique your listener's curiosity. Why is there an `iterator()` and a `listIterator()` method? What does the `<E>` symbol mean? Why is the `removeRange()` method underscored? And so on.

The underscore indicates a member that has the protected access modifier.

ArrayList
modcount: int
ArrayList( ) ArrayList(Collection<? extends E> c)
+add( )   : boolean/void* +addAll( )   : boolean +clear( )   : void +clone( )   : Object +contains( )   : boolean +ensureCapacity( ) : void +get   : E +IndexOff( )   : int +isEmpty( )   : boolean +iterator( )   : Iterator<E> +lastIndexOf( ) : int +listIterator( ) : ListIterator<E> +remove( )   : boolean +removeAll( ) : boolean removeRange( ) : void +retainAll( )   : boolean +set( )   : E +size( )   : int +subList( )   : List <E> +toArray( )   : <T>T[] +trimToSize( ) : void

FIGURE 6.1 Complete diagram of the `ArrayList` class's components

The *Wikipedia* entry on cohesion is a useful introduction to the term *cohesion*: `http://en.wikipedia.org/wiki/Cohesion_(computer_science)`.

Minimizing scope isn't quite the same thing: It just means restricting access to class elements so they are visible only to other parts of the program you *know* require them. But the concept is the same with class diagrams. You're not hiding elements so much as exposing the ones that matter.

Cohesion In object-oriented programming, cohesion expresses a qualitative measure of belonging. If the methods in one class make sense as a unit or have a purpose in common, the class is said to have high cohesion. If the list of visible methods does not suggest a clear, simple purpose for using it, it is said to have low cohesion. As a qualitative measure, these values are subject to interpretation and discussion. In general, however, highly cohesive classes tend to have a small complement of methods.

Data hiding is a modest step toward high cohesion, but an essential one. Without it, a careful programmer is obliged to consider whether the type of each visible field is significant. The difference between a person's name and a street name, for example, is a matter of field naming. Whether fields are stored as String objects, StringBuilder objects, or character arrays is a technical matter. Unless you're prepared to defend that choice and how it makes the class do what it does, you shouldn't expose it.

Loose coupling One likely outcome of highly cohesive classes is looser coupling. When you refine classes to do one thing, sometimes the need for new classes falls out. Individual classes become smaller by shedding these implicit relationships, or *dependencies*, and exchanging them for explicit relationships, or *couplings*. Although *coupling* as a term describes all forms of class dependencies, in my own thinking a loose coupling is the qualitative opposite of a (tight) dependency.

If I extend one class to make another, that's the tightest dependency there is: I can't make an object of my class without first making an object of the class I extended. Sometimes that arrangement makes perfect sense. For example, if you want one parent class that every other class must inherit, such as java.lang .Object, requiring inheritance gives you that relationship.

If I want to use another type to inform my class, I use only a field of that type. There's still a relationship between the classes, but it's looser. And if the only time I use the other type is as a parameter or return type for a method, that's almost as loose as it gets. The looser (or more flexible) the relationship is, the fewer rules I have to observe to maintain it. Figure 6.2 shows these three relationships in diagram form.

The left-most diagram shows class B extending, or sublclassing, class A. The middle diagram shows a class B that contains a field of type A. The dash signifies the field is *private*, that is, not accessible outside the class. The rightmost diagram shows a class B with a method process that receives a parameter of type A, but does not keep a field of that type. The plus sign signifies the method is *public*, or accessible to anyone who has access to a B object. From left to right, the association between types A and B gets increasingly looser.

When you start writing a new program, you might assemble what you need in one file for convenience, maybe even into a single class. Over time, you add

See the Wikipedia entry on loose coupling for a primer on it: http:// en.wikipedia .org/wiki/ Loose_coupling.

Extending is one term for subclassing, or inheriting from another class. Chapter 9, "Inheriting Code and Data in Java," covers this topic in detail.

fields and methods. As useful features come to mind, you might continue adding them to this file because that's where you've always added them. And if this routine goes on long enough, you'll build a single program that just keeps doing more. We call such programs monolithic, and it's a quality we hope to avoid with object-oriented programming in the first place.

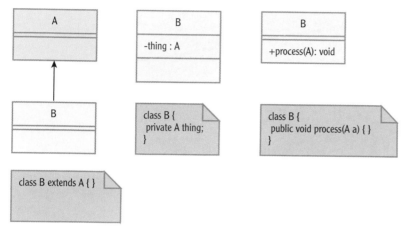

FIGURE 6.2 Degrees of coupling between two classes

Factoring all those features into cohesive, loosely coupled classes of their own is the right thing to do, but when a large body of code works well enough, change starts to look more and more risky. You might lose something you value by refactoring the program into smaller parts: good performance, a useful feature that was implemented throughout the codebase—who knows?

Experienced programmers do what they can to avoid this trap in the first place. Believe it or not, data hiding helps. By promoting localized access and cohesive classes, it encourages loose coupling from the start.

Maintainability Some programmers may tell you looser coupling means smaller classes, which means having more things to manage in a program. That's no lie. You will spend more time learning how to combine small classes into larger programs.

But the trade-off is worth it. You'll appreciate it the most when you get to troubleshooting. The first time you isolate an error to a class of, say, a hundred lines or so instead of a few thousand lines, you'll love it. And when you have to add code to a small class whose dependencies are loose and flexible, you'll love it more.

It's much easier to appreciate once you've maintained a monolithic codebase. Much like telling you to bang your head against a wall, I can't recommend you try it to understand what I'm talking about. I can only hope you can empathize with the pain and confusion of trying to keep a thousand lines of code in your head. If you can, perhaps that's motivation enough to avoid creating such stuff and to help others do the same.

It's also one reason why it's difficult to advocate for maintainable code at the outset of a project. Putting more work in now for a payoff other programmers will receive is not always a goal. If, however, you begin with this end in mind, you can learn and adopt practices that help you get there with less work.

Think data hiding. Then think encapsulation with methods. Then cohesion, factoring classes out as early in the process as you can. If you do that, loose coupling and easier maintenance will come to you.

Hiding the Data

You can hide data in a Java program with an access modifier. The access modifier `private` restricts visibility of a member to its class. A `private` field is visible to methods and constructors in the class. No other object may address it. Conversely, no member of a class can hide from a member of the same class.

I sidestepped this point in the first two chapters to describe the `Point3D` class in the simplest possible terms. Now that you know it's important to hide fields, I will write class members like this:

```java
public class Point3D {
    private int x, y, z;
}
```

Of course, without any methods to access these variables, they are hidden in the full sense of the word. You can still construct a `Point3D` object, however. The compiler will initialize x, y, and z to an `int` zero. Access modifiers don't affect visibility to the compiler or the JVM. Other objects have no idea what `Point3D` is or does other than it inherits from `java.lang.Object`.

Now you need methods that are visible to a caller. Methods that will return the value of a hidden field are called *accessor methods*, or just *get methods*. Methods that let you change the values of hidden fields are called *mutator methods*, or just *set methods*. Adding the `public` access modifier to these methods will expose them to any potential caller.

I've applied the `public` keyword to most of the classes I've shown you so far. Declaring a class `public` is not precisely the same thing as declaring a class member `public`. If a class is `public`, other objects in the same program can refer to it by name. A visible class, bear in mind, does not imply its members are *accessible*. They must also be declared `public`.

> There are two other access modifiers also more visible than the `private` keyword. For now we'll stick to using the `public` keyword.

The methods we make visible outside a class will define that class's *interface*. In a Unified Modeling Language (UML) diagram, we can signify the proper access by prefixing `private` members with a dash (or minus) and `public` members with a plus. Figure 6.3 shows the `Point3D` class with access modifiers added.

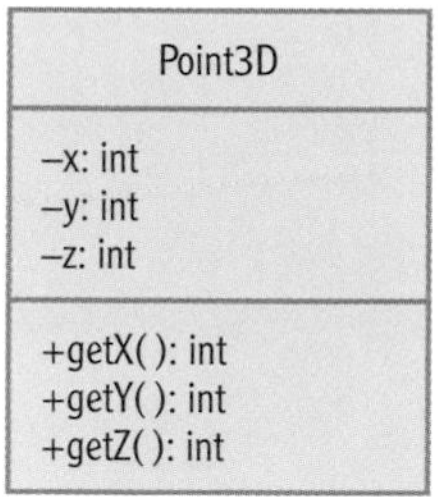

Point3D
−x: int −y: int −z: int
+getX( ): int +getY( ): int +getZ( ): int

FIGURE 6.3 Class
diagram of the `Point3D` class

The practice of hiding data is an understood practice in many shops. You may encounter many casual sketches of class diagrams in which fields are simply omitted if they are `private`, unless they are important to the meaning the diagram conveys.

It's from diagrams like this that you can form a picture of the class's cohesion and coupling. Do the methods appear to have a common purpose? Do they operate on one kind of data? Also, what dependencies (or couplings) does the class form with other types? It's no mystery that these questions become more pressing as a class grows larger, but concerns over a class's size should always be tempered by these criteria. If a class is as simple as you can make it, and it has many methods, and its utility would suffer from breaking it into smaller parts, then it may be that you have a class that is simple and cohesive—just not small.

Understanding Encapsulation

A lot of Java literature treats the term *data hiding* as a synonym of the term *encapsulation*, but there is a broader meaning to the latter. Encapsulating data means bundling it with methods that operate on it and provide indirect access to it. But that doesn't mean there has to be a one-to-one relationship between a hidden field and the method(s) that expose(s) it, such as a get and set method pair for every field.

To encapsulate data in a broader sense, we need methods that access and manipulate each field in the ways the programmer intended. If it happens that a one-to-one relationship makes sense—and it sometimes does—then an accessor method is a logical choice. But we should *not* automatically provide an accessor for every field.

Consider a class called Circle. Its data could be represented by a radius field alone. Other values a Circle user might like to retrieve, like its area and circumference, may be derived from its radius field, so there's no need to store them. There are then a couple of ways to represent a Circle object through its *method interface*, each with its own merits.

Figure 6.4 shows a simple data hiding approach on the left that makes the radius field private and its accessor method public. Anyone who wants to derive the area or circumference of a Circle object can implement the logic themselves. The chart on the right interprets encapsulation in its truest spirit, completely separating the services of the class from the data required to implement it.

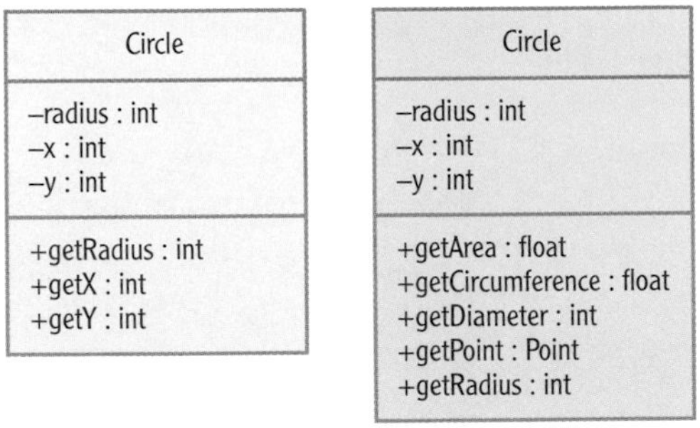

Circle
−radius : int −x : int −y : int
+getRadius : int +getX : int +getY : int

Circle
−radius : int −x : int −y : int
+getArea : float +getCircumference : float +getDiameter : int +getPoint : Point +getRadius : int

FIGURE 6.4 Two class diagram views of the Circle class

The Circle class that includes the methods getArea(), getCircumference(), and getDiameter() doesn't have any extra data, but data hiding isn't the point driving this class. It's the services the class offers that matter. Now the field is simply an *implementation detail*. Perhaps the programmer who looks at the source code will decide this approach is clever or surprising, but a caller to this interface just knows you can get all the information you need about a Circle object from its methods.

If users can get what they need through the method interface, the implementation shouldn't matter to them. For the programmer who maintains this code, it's a different matter. Through this separation of service and implementation, the class programmer has the freedom to modify the fields, or even a method's code, without changing the method interface. Whatever the reason for those changes might be, the class programmer doesn't have to worry that callers will see anything different from their view of the class.

I might be alone in suggesting *encapsulation* means more than *data hiding*. It's not just an academic point, however. *Data hiding* is a plain phrase that, without further explanation, implies that writing a bit of boilerplate code is all that's needed. To my mind, that's mistaken thinking. I'd like to make sure you avoid it. *Encapsulation*, on the other hand, implies forethought in class design as one step and realizing that design as a second step. By putting some thought into giving the users of your code more freedom, you can make it so the class lets each of them work without getting in each other's way.

Understanding Mutability

Before we add *mutators*, or methods that let the caller change an object's state, I should say more about mutable and immutable classes. Objects of an immutable class, you may recall, don't change state. What you haven't heard yet is what's good about them.

Immutable objects have two great benefits. One, they have a value that is *always true*; that is, always the same. There is never an additional cost to maintaining them and never a need to copy them. Two, they are always safe to pass as a parameter and always safe to return as a value. These properties are valuable in reducing the number of dimensions in which a state change can occur.

When programs crash, it could be for lots of reasons, but malformed logic and bad inputs cover most of the territory. When you can rule out parts of your program on the grounds they are correct and unchanging, that's a big help. One way you can do that is by reducing available mutators to the smallest useful complement. And that means asking, among other things, why each and every set method you use is necessary.

Writing a class that guarantees immutable behavior goes beyond our scope, but it's important to know they exist and do a lot to simplify large programs. Justifying your set methods before you add them is a solid beginning.

The `String` class is an immutable class, in part because of the way it's implemented (with a character array). The JVM realizes some performance benefits by fixing the size of each `String` object at construction. There are also some drawbacks, in particular when using them for parsing, concatenation, inserting or removing characters, and other character-level string operations that don't take advantage of constant values and instead add processing costs. The `StringBuilder` class is much better suited to those operations and was introduced to the core libraries for that reason.

In lieu of writing formally correct immutable classes, you can still write classes that limit mutability. The less mutable the object, the simpler it is. Which is a better approach for a `Circle` object, for example: Is it to fix its `radius` value once it's constructed and let the caller make new ones as needed? Or is it to let a caller make one `Circle` object and change it as needed? The answer depends

The term boilerplate describes routine code you have to write. Here it refers to accessor and mutator methods to accompany every field a class includes.

The term *constant* is synonymous with *immutable* but is more appropriate to primitive values.

One key benefit of immutable types is that many callers can use them at the same time without risk of corrupting their data.

on how you expect the object to be used. There's no single right answer for all applications.

As a rule, don't allow set methods in your classes until you can justify their use. In many Java classes, programmers add them as a matter of habit because it's easy and therefore seems to save time. Limited mutability is a far better prize, but it's hard to appreciate. It's like a printer that never jams; you'll like it better when you have to use a printer that throws error codes every day.

Using Final Classes

Here's another way to limit mutability: Declare your classes final. A final class cannot be extended, or *subclassed*; the compiler won't allow it. By declaring a class final, you can also imply that your class is not designed for extension by another class:

```
public final class Point3D {
    private int x = 5;
    private int y = 12;
    private int z = 13;
}

class Point4D extends Point3D {
    private int q = 42;
}
$ javac Point3D.java
Point3D.java:7: error: cannot inherit from final Point3D
class Point4D extends Point3D {
                      ^
1 error
```

In this example, I declared the class Point4D a subclass of the class Point3D, using the keyword extends. This declaration tells the compiler that the Point4D class *is-a* type of Point3D (which itself *is-a* type of Object). As you'll learn in Chapter 9, when you want to specialize an existing class and reuse its code, *inheriting* from it creates a type relationship and avoids duplication of effort.

The term *is-a* expresses one type that derives from another.

What the compiler does to support inheritance, however, has nothing to do with ensuring that subclasses are safe or reliable extensions, and there is indeed a fair amount of work to ensure those qualities. Until we learn what that work entails, it's a good idea to disallow subclassing in your own code.

Marking a class final can in fact serve a number of purposes. It may mean the author did not bother or did not want to allow inheritance. Perhaps a class contains logic that should not be altered in any way by other programmers. Perhaps it runs faster. The String class, you may have noticed, is marked final, perhaps with both reasons in mind. I'll use it for the rest of the book to signify only that my sample classes should not be considered ready for that use.

This modifier can save your average try-and-see programmer time in experimenting. It can also save the class's author a lot of time in documenting. The day will come that you have to debug some quirky bit of Java code. And you may work on it for a while before you realize that you wrote it. When that happens, you'll understand that documenting code doesn't just help other programmers. It's also a way to leave notes for your future self, who might be a very different kind of programmer by then.

Be both kind and wary of this person, your future self. He or she will go through several profound changes while learning. That person, however well meaning, also gets disoriented and forgets what they were like, kind of like an old fisherman from a small village who's suddenly grown 50 feet tall. They'll want to test their new strengths and abilities on objects that are close at hand. Old code will look like a toy and probably won't appear as fragile as it is. If the code can tell you it wasn't designed with the future giant you in mind, it may seem stifling at first, but you'll also appreciate not having it fall apart in your hands.

Exposing Data through Methods

Limiting mutability and making classes final aren't part of encapsulation. By incorporating these habits, you'll restrict yourself from using certain Java features until you better appreciate what to do with them. They do go hand in hand with an important rule of thumb: *making fields private and methods public*. This rule is (too) often interpreted to mean always use accessors (get methods) to retrieve an object's state and mutators (set methods) to change it.

Now that we know why we shouldn't do that automatically, let's discuss where it makes sense to apply it: when we want a Java class to act as a data container, and not much more. This kind of class is called a *bean*, and it has some important applications.

Certification Objective

Understanding the Bean Model

Some Java classes exist solely to expose their data as a list of *properties*. Let's say you want to write a program that reads lines from a file one at a time. Each line is a record that follows a standard format. It therefore makes sense to think of each line as one object and the format as a type, such as a Record class. All you need from this class is access to each field, which you can expose using an accessor method for each part of the record.

A Java *bean* is this kind of class, exposing each underlying field with a method pair, one accessor and one mutator. The bean model also uses a naming scheme that is spelled out so helper classes in the core libraries know how to read the method as a property type. Classes in the java.beans package provide the means to examine the method interface of a Java bean and determine its properties.

To give an example of the naming scheme, I'll write the Point3D class as a straightforward Point3DBean:

```java
public final class Point3DBean {
    private int x = 5;
    private int y = 12;
    private int z = 13;

    public int getX() {
        return x;
    }

    public void setX(int newX) {
        this.x = newX;
    }

    public int getY() {
        return y;
    }

    public void setY(int newY) {
        this.y = newY;
    }

    public int getZ() {
        return z;
    }

    public void setZ(int newZ) {
        this.z = newZ;
    }
}
```

Each field has a method pair. The accessor method returns the same value as the underlying field. The set method requires a parameter of the type and returns void. The matching names —literally, the character sequence that follows the set and get portion of each method name—does the rest. This version of the Point3DBean class has three bean properties: X, Y, and Z.

Adding the word Bean to the class name doesn't do any additional work. It just tells a knowledgeable Java programmer what purpose the class serves. Also, it's nice if the method names match the field name, but it's not required. You could have a field named x_coord and decide to name the property X instead. If you do vary the property name from a field name, however, make sure to document the variance with a comment to avoid confusion.

There are other rules that deal with capitalization (Java is case sensitive), beans with read-only properties, and other stuff, but that can wait for the day you need to learn the JavaBeans specification. Here I only wanted to explain why some classes are written this way.

For reasons not clear to me, some programmers apply this model well beyond its intended purpose. Do be wary of code where many classes seem to follow this pattern, as if every class should be considered a list of properties. Beans should *not* be taken for a default model of Java class development.

◄

The JavaBeans Component API is included with the JDK documentation under docs/ technotes/ guides/beans/ index.html.

Distinguishing Methods from Data in a Class

Now that you understand the basics of the bean model, I want you to think broadly about the purposes a method can serve. Thinking of data as an implementation detail doesn't, by itself, tell you how to write code but it does emphasize that a class's services and its composition can run along separate paths. Even in the bean model, where the relationship between fields and methods seems tight, all the methods do is define bean properties.

How do we take advantage of that? By adding meaningful code, of course, but to what end? For starters, you can add code to accomplish the following:

▶ Validate incoming parameters

▶ Restrict the range of acceptable values

▶ Induce *side effects*

I'll address each of these points in turn.

Validating Incoming Parameters

When a method receives a parameter, it has to make sure the parameter value is something it can use. In the main() method, for example, you can test the length value of the args array to see if it's nonzero. If it isn't, you can inform the user that some input was required before stopping the program.

Say you have a deposit(double amt) method in an Account class. It's used with an ATM whose console, lucky for us, doesn't allow a customer to enter a negative number. But what if the customer accidentally deposits zero dollars? It's a nonnegative value, but it's also not worth processing. The `deposit` method could return the current balance as a pseudo-update to the account, or it could just ignore that input value:

```
private double balance;

public void deposit(double amt) {
    if (amt == 0) {
        System.err.println("Zero dollar deposit!");
        return;
    }
}
```

If the parameter is instead an object reference, there are two cases like this you have to consider: one, if the reference value is `null`; and two, if it is non-`null` but also empty of data, like an `args` array with a `length` value of zero or a `String` that refers to "".

Every `public` method that accepts parameters has to defend against unusable data. If we do accept bad data, what is the worst possible outcome? It *isn't* a program crash. Program crashes aren't bad. They're inconvenient and sometimes frustrating, but they tell you something is wrong and needs attention. Bad data that goes on undetected for a long time—*that's* bad.

How long before bad data in one part of our program propagates and corrupts data in another part of our program? How long before we figure out it's happening? Once we figure it out, how do we determine its origin? That's the nightmare scenario in programming.

> I once fixed a banking program that blindly accepted bad data—and shut down several branches. You might have an account with that bank. It happens, even at big companies.

Restricting Range

Types like the `double` primitive aren't directly suitable for representing real-world objects like a dollar, so there are usually other adjustments to consider It's one thing to rule out logically invalid ranges like negative and zero deposit amounts. It's another to test both for unlikely values, such as a $2 billion deposit, and for an amount beyond two decimal places, such as $5.0014.

In traditional programming languages, it's a common task to adapt the types provided to suit a specific use. Primitive types are a tempting choice because they are register-based, faster to access, and faster to compute than their object-based equivalents. Over millions of calls, the JVM will spend less time processing primitives than references. At the same time, you have to surround the primitive type with code to make it behave like a dollar.

Once you formulate the rules that govern your datum in Java, that's when you think about designing a class, using methods to manage the data in a correct and logical manner.

Validating can weed out nonsense values much like restricting the numeric range does. I like to think of restricting range as applying a constraint, while validating protects the *sanity* of the data. Either way you're using conditional statements to test your values, following one path of execution if they're acceptable, another if they're not. Methods protect your fields. If you allow direct access instead, you have no defense against assignments that are out of range or just don't make sense.

Inducing Side Effects

Sometimes you want a method to change state in an object in a way that isn't apparent to the caller. Let's say you want to track how many times a customer makes a deposit—that is, invokes the deposit method. You could add an integer field to the Account class and increment it each time the deposit method is called. That data is not intended for the customer's eyes, so there's no reason to expose it:

```java
public final class Account {
    private int count;
    private double balance;

    public void deposit(double amount) {
        count++;
        // rest of method logic
    }

    public double getBalance() {
        return balance;
    }

    public int getCount() {
        return count;
    }

    // do we need a setBalance() to correct errors that occur?
    // what about a setCount() to roll back a failed deposit?
}
```

Every time the deposit() method is called, the count variable increments. This is an intended side effect. There are unintended ones, too, that can plague your code. Sometimes they come about because one method you use induces a change elsewhere (for example, by charging a service fee for too many deposits). Just as the plants you want to have in your garden are flowers and the ones you don't want are weeds, the side effects that you want are good and all others are bugs. Unlike weeds, bugs can be hard to spot; yet another reason to keep the mutability of your classes to a minimum.

Choosing Methods to Make Public

One more point follows from our side-effects example. With the count field, we've added information and potential state behavior to the object in a way that would be hard to handle with just private fields and public methods. As the comments in the code example suggest, how can we allow for methods that let us correct an Account object without exposing too much control?

You probably don't want the Customer object using an Account object to correct its own balance or set the number of deposits transacted in a statement period. This work is more appropriate to an AccountManager type. How do you allow an AccountManager object access to an Account object without also allowing a Customer object the same access?

There are a couple ways to think about this. One is to make the Account object something a Customer object cannot handle directly. You could use ATM and OnlineAcctManager classes to handle Account objects directly. You could then require the Customer object to use these objects to get access to their Account object. Figure 6.5 diagrams the key elements of this relationship. How you can limit access to some classes but not others is the subject of the next section.

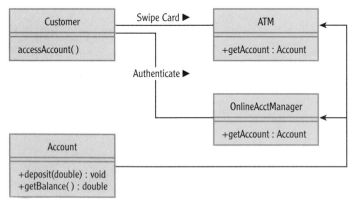

FIGURE 6.5 Possible relationship between Customer and Account classes

It's easy to say you should limit exposure. Because the goals in mind are qualitative, it's hard to come up with hard-and-fast rules for applying that principle.

A few general questions can help you qualify these decisions and give you some insight to arranging your code in the clearest manner:

- ▶ Does the method change the state of the object?
- ▶ Will the method induce a side effect?
- ▶ Does the method create new objects?
- ▶ Will the method return a reference to its containing object?

I haven't discussed the consequences of all these questions, so for now you can use them with a simple piece of advice: If your answer to these questions is yes, then ask which objects will have access to the method. If you mark that method with a `private` modifier, its only effective purpose is to help another method in the class. If you mark it with the `public` modifier, the method appears as a service anyone should be able to use. Be sure that's what you intend.

So, how do we create different levels of access for different classes? It turns out that *packages* are more than just a *namespace*. Classes that share the same package also have a shared scope. That means you can declare class members so only other classes in their package can see them. Once you apply this technique to your advantage, you'll appreciate packages on a whole new level.

Applying Access Modifiers

In Chapter 1, "Introducing the Basics of Java," you learned to store multiple classes in one file. You can actually put as many classes in one file as you like, so long as none of them are declared `public`. If you declare one of them `public`, its name must match the file's name, minus the `.java` extension. In writing code for this book, for example, I've created various files all named `stuff.java`, put them each in a different folder, one per chapter. If I find a class useful, I cut it from this file, put it in a separate namesake file, and declare it public. It's not a common scheme, but with this approach I am not committing myself to naming classes until I have a clearer picture of what they'll do.

In discussing how Java objects communicate, in fact, I am sometimes at a loss for a concrete example at the moment, and I'll start writing in abstractions like Listing 6.1.

Certification Objective

LISTING 6.1: Class relationships without a specific program context

```
final class Test {
    public static void main(String args[]) {
        FirstThis myft = new FirstThis();
```

LISTING 6.1: Class relationships without a specific program context *(continued)*

```java
        Other other = new Other();
        myft.pokeThat(other);
    }
}

final class FirstThis {
    // object-level coupling
    private ThenThat that;

    // method-level coupling with Other
    public void pokeThat(Other other) {
        that = new ThenThat(other);
        System.out.print("FirstThis to ThenThat: ");
        System.out.println("is Other there?");
        that.pokeOther();
    }
}

final class ThenThat {
    private Other other;

    // constructor-level coupling
    public ThenThat(Other other) {
        this.other = other;
    }

    public void pokeOther() {
        System.out.println("Hello, Other?");
        System.out.println(other.respond());
    }
}

final class Other {
    public String respond() {
        System.out.println("This is Other");
        return "You want something?";
    }
}
$ javac stuff.java
$ java Test
FirstThis to ThenThat: is Other there?
```

LISTING 6.1: Class relationships without a specific program context *(continued)*

```
Hello, TheOther?
This is TheOther
You want something?
```

There's a lot going on in this example, so let me point out some key features before getting back to the point at hand (which is packages). First, I added comments to point out different degrees of coupling: Use them as a first look at tight and loose relationships. The degree of intertwining you form while sketching out classes in code can quickly take on a life of its own. It's one motivation for starting with diagrams. It's easier to erase and redraw lines of association than it is to refactor even a few dozen lines of code.

Second, there is real work in naming classes well. I punted on that issue in this example, but that doesn't mean I didn't trip over myself anyway. I started out thinking I'd make This, That, and TheOther classes. I didn't think through the conflict with the this keyword; I saw how awkward it was when I needed a This variable. Oops. Starting a sentence with "the TheOther class" was another lesson in careful naming. Moral of the story: Don't commit to code before you think about naming. Communicating clearly is the goal. You won't get there by chance.

Those things said, take some time to walk through this code carefully. If you can verbalize clearly how it works, you have taken a big step. Examples like this abound in quizzes and exams, designed, it would seem, only to jellify your brain. It may not feel like fair game, but you're going to encounter code like this, and worse, you'll encounter it in your programming career. Start acclimating now.

Next, notice that all these classes can see each other, not including the private members they maintain. When you put two or more classes in the same file or the same directory, they share an *implied package*. That's good news. It means you could put each of these classes in their own file and they'd still work together. And here's the fun part: You still don't have to declare them public. Something else is afoot that keeps these classes visible to each other.

Working with Packaged Classes

Using Listing 6.1, put each class in its own file. Don't declare any class public. Compile them and run the Test class. It should all still work.

You don't have to delete the original file. Just bear in mind that you will overwrite the .class files you have each time you recompile. So long as the code remains the same, there's no difference to notice. Now, in the original `stuff.java` file, declare a package:

```
package stuff;
...
```

The code will compile as before, but you'll get errors trying to run it. If you declare a package but don't tell the compiler to produce the class files in a package-aware way, it will write them to the current directory. Now, however, the JVM won't find them:

```
$ javac stuff.java
$ java Test
Exception in thread "main" java.lang.NoClassDefFoundError:
   Test (wrong name: stuff/Test)
        at java.lang.ClassLoader.defineClass1(Native Method)
        at java.lang.ClassLoader.defineClass(ClassLoader.java:791)
<more exception information omitted>
$ java stuff.Test
Error: Could not find or load main class stuff.Test
```

If you omit the package name from the class after compiling, the error message is more information than you want right now. I clipped some of it to conserve space, but you should try it and see the full effect on your computer. If you address the class by its new package scheme, you only get a shorter error message for your trouble.

To get back to running code, tell the compiler at which location you want to create the package structure:

```
$ javac -d . stuff.java
$ ls
stuff
$ ls stuff
FirstThis.class  Other.class     Test.class      ThenThat.class
```

Simple as that! The -d option tells the compiler that the current directory, symbolized by a dot, is the start of a *classpath*. The compiler uses the package name to create a directory structure and deposits the class files accordingly. To find a packaged class, you have to pass this information using the java program with the -cp flag:

```
$ java -cp . stuff.Test
FirstThis to ThenThat: is Other there?
Hello, Other?
This is Other
You want something?
```

And we're back in business!

What happened here? Java treats a source-code file with no package declaration as a *default package* and the current directory as an implied *classpath*. Once you declare a package, you have to handle the classpath explicitly. Java's tools translate package naming to a filesystem structure in order to maintain a separate namespace for each declared package. The designers chose to remove this requirement for the simplest case (no explicit package declaration), but it's still a confusing transition.

Now try to access a class in the stuff package from a class in another package I'll call the miscellany package:

```
package miscellany;

import stuff.*;

public final class Misc {
    private FirstThis fthis;

    // add these fields if all goes well
    // private ThenThat tthat;
    // private Other other;
}
$ javac -d . -cp . Misc.java
Misc.java:6: error: FirstThis is not public in stuff;
    cannot be accessed from outside package
        private FirstThis fthis;
                   ^
1 error
```

The Misc class imports the contents of the stuff package. It compiles to its own miscellany directory and uses the classpath to locate the FirstThis class, but it doesn't matter. None of the classes in the stuff package are public, so they are, in effect, *package private*. Without at least one public class, there's no access from the outside world. What does it mean to have no access modifier keyword at all?

Using Access Modifiers with Package-Aware Classes

With explicit packaging, you gain two access modifiers. What you've observed in the previous section is the *default access* modifier, also known as *package-private*. When you want only classes in the same package to see each other's members, declare those members without an access modifier.

Packaging helps you describe internal and external class relationships in greater relief. A diagram at the package level, such as Figure 6.6, makes it easier to define class relationships between two packages.

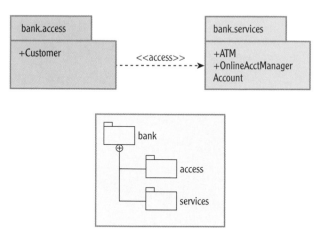

FIGURE 6.6   Package view of Customer and other classes

The bottom box shows the full package relationship. The top-level package bank holds two subpackages called access and services. The bank.access package contains a public Customer class that can see the ATM and OnlineAcctManager classes, as signified by the plus signs, but not the Account class, which has default access.

The Account class is not visible to any class outside its own package, expressing what I wanted to get across with the arrows I used in Figure 6.5. A Customer object can use an ATM or OnlineAcctManager object in principle. Now all I have to do is declare the proper import statements and set the correct classpath values. I can restrict access to the Account class itself to other classes I trust, that is, the classes I have designed to work with it the way I intended.

I used the bank package itself only for a namespace. It suggests the context of the packages and nothing more. I can add classes to it, but then I'd be treating it like a nameless, implied package, just as when I don't use package names at all. That's a condition I'm trying to get away from with named packages; it's best to leave it unpopulated, except, of course, for other package names.

Using Default Access with Class Members

Once you start working with explicit packaging, you can also apply default access to class members. Fields and methods with default access are accessible to any caller in the same package.

Since I just made the case for data hiding at length, you might ask why I would now propose increasing the visibility of class data. It's a fair question.

Declaring a package gives you a way to expose data to a limited number of classes, presumably ones you can trust, but that doesn't somehow make it a smart or safe thing to do. Let's consider an example.

Say you wanted to add an Auditor class to your bank.services package. You want the Auditor class to debit each Account object if the number of deposits made to it exceeds 10 in a statement period. This action will rely on the side effect I added, in which the deposit() method increments a count field each time it is called.

You *don't* have to remove the private declaration from the count field. A default access getCount() method gives the Auditor class the visibility it needs without adding mutability to the Account class:

```
package bank.services;

final class Account {
    private int count;
    private double balance;
    private int acctID;

    int getCount() {
        return count;
    }

    public double getBalance() {
        return balance;
    }

    void setBalance(double amt) {
// needs error checking
        balance = balance - amt;
    }
}

final class Auditor {
    private void charge(Account acct) {
        if (acct.getCount() >= 10) {
            System.out.println("Deposit limit exceeded");
            System.out.println("Fee assessed");
            acct.setBalance(acct.getBalance() - 3);
        }
    }
}
```

If you want to charge an Account object a fee for exceeding 10 deposits from outside the package, however, that's another matter.

▶

Take a look at inner and nested classes if you're curious about other approaches to tight class relationships.

Bear in mind any class in the `bank.services` package can use the `getCount()` method. If you want to make it so only the `Auditor` class can see this method, you'll have to change the packaging or use facilities in Java you haven't learned yet. Access modifiers help you limit visibility, but if you don't control the remaining classes in the package, you don't have any better protection, just fewer potential programmers hacking away at your code.

In my view, you should make an airtight case for declaring a field anything but private. Don't think better performance from accessing a field directly is a benefit, as some programmers do. You have to deluge an object with many method calls to see an appreciable difference between a method call and field access. Then consider that savings, if any, against the abuse some programmer will surely visit on that field. Also compare it against the howling you'll hear when you decide to change the field's type and programmers who depended on your class find their code now breaks. Unless you can think of an even worse consequence than this, keep your fields private.

Understanding the *protected* Access Modifier

There's one more access type I haven't covered by the `protected` keyword. It is similar to default access but includes one more thing: A `protected` class member is also visible to any *subclass* of its type, regardless of the package the subclass resides in.

I said earlier that package-private access is more reliable if you control all a package's contents. You can then decide which classes may use that access. One assumes you won't abuse the privilege. In that sense, in a package you can relax the rules for yourself and you will use that license responsibly.

Let's say you're designing a class so others can inherit from it. You want to expose certain methods to those subclasses so they can change state in the parent class. By definition, these subclasses will reside in other packages, so default access won't help them. The `protected` modifier will.

▶

We cover the details of inheritance in Chapter 9.

When would you use this extra leeway? Let's say you invited a consultant to design an `ExternalAuditor` class to complement your bank package. You decide this class should reside in a separate `client.audit` package along with other external tools. A subclass *inherits* methods from its parent, but only the ones that are visible to it. If you want an `ExternalAuditor` class to inherit certain methods from your `Auditor` class, you must declare them `protected`.

```
// final modifier removed to allow subclassing
// public modifier added to increase visibility
public class Auditor {
    // modifier changed to protected
```

```
    protected void charge(Account acct) {
        if (acct.getCount() >= 10) {
            System.out.println("Deposit limit exceeded");
            System.out.println("Fee assessed");
            acct.setBalance(acct.getBalance() - 3);
        }
    }
}
<different file>
final class ExternalAuditor extends Auditor {
    // inherits the charge() method
}
```

You should, of course, know how the protected modifier works and how to interpret it and apply it in an exam. Unless you're developing packages for other programmers to use, you may not use it much. Most of us write application code—programs—most of the time, not packages of software for others to use.

As a rule, expose class member outside their package, even to subclasses, with plenty of skepticism. (Take the lack of a diagram in this section as a hint.) It is always tempting to relax your access modifiers in the name of remaining flexible. Prefer to allow only what you need to satisfy your program's requirements. The future is not entirely unpredictable, but it doesn't have to be to foil most attempts at anticipating it.

Remember, you can always increase a class member's visibility without harming classes that depend on it. When you restrict visibility, it's a different story. You'll break someone's code somewhere. Young programmers, alas, seem inclined to believe that restrictive modifiers are like handcuffs and permissive modifiers are like blue skies. So, from me to you, old guy to new programmers, a word of wisdom: Handcuffs come off. Things fall out of the sky all the time, usually red-hot.

Relaxing access modifiers without a need is one example of future-proofing, also known as trying to write code for every eventuality. It never works.

Abstracting Data

The semantic separation between the fields that make up a class's data and the methods that make up its interface is called *abstraction*. We want a class to express some object-like concept—a dollar, a circle, or a point. The data we use to emulate that concept is storage with their own built-in services, nothing more.

A good method interface lets the programmer think in terms of an object's services and states. The human brain is far better with that idea than with having to consider all of an object's moving parts at once. Currency has everyday meaning to far more of us than floating-point values made to express dollars. We're better at thinking about shapes, on the whole, than we are about locations in three-dimensional space with integer vertices.

As you adapt to an object-oriented view of programming, you'll repeat this paradigm, assembling simple objects to make more complex ones and create more sophisticated abstractions. It is not a perfect scheme, mind you, but you're also quite a ways from seeing where this system can break down under its own weight. For now you'll have plenty to do learning the ropes.

In the next chapter, you'll learn to design methods. After that, it's a short step to thinking about the kinds of objects you need to write Java programs with objects: what you want your program to do, what objects you need to perform that work, and finally, which method names help make that work as easy on the brain as you can manage.

THE ESSENTIALS AND BEYOND

In this chapter, we made our first broad distinction between fields and methods. All other things being equal, fields should be `private`. Methods should protect fields from arbitrary change. The combination of each hidden field and the method that provides access to it is called encapsulation.

Methods should protect data, but that doesn't mean there's one way to do it. When we use methods to reveal data to access and/or mutation, as with the bean model, we're writing a class in a very literal way. When we use the method interface to express the purpose of a class instead, we think of it as creating an abstraction that separates the meaning of the class from the details of its implementation.

To get degrees of access between `public` and `private`, we showed how packages define both a namespace for classes and a scope. With packages we can take advantage of the so-called package-private modifier, which has no keyword, and the `protected` modifier.

ADDITIONAL EXERCISES

1. In Listing 6.1, the ThenThat class has a constructor that requires a parameter of type Other. Modify this class to factor out the constructor. How else can you receive an Other object and keep the class functioning the same way?

2. Write a deposit() method that accepts an amount of at least 1 dollar and no more than 250,000 dollars. Include a way to inform the user of whether the transaction fails or goes through. Put the code in an Account class so it will compile. Using a main() method, test for both valid and invalid deposits.

(Continues)

3. Declare an essentials.ch06 package for the classes you wrote in exercises 1 and 2. Recompile and run them to make sure they still work.

4. Add a Circle class to the essentials.ch06 package with methods that report its area, radius, and circumference. Include only a radius field. Add a CircleTest class to the package and use it to test the Circle class's methods.

5. Replace the radius field in the essentials.ch06.Circle class with a diameter field. Change the methods accordingly, but do not modify the CircleTest class. Recompile the Circle class, and then run the test program.

REVIEW QUESTIONS

1. If you declare a class final, you cannot do which of the following:

    A. Make an object of that type

    B. Recompile the code

    C. Subclass it

    D. Use it as a field type in another class

2. True or false: Package-private access is more lenient than protected access.

3. Which of the following statements apply to package declarations in a Java source code file? (Choose all that apply.)

    A. There has to be a top-level package name that contains no classes.

    B. You have to tell the compiler where to create the package structure in the filesystem.

    C. The classpath has to include the top-level package name.

    D. A source-code file without a package declaration is treated like a package.

4. True or false: A public class that has private fields and package-private methods is not visible to classes outside the package.

5. Which technique will most effectively limit the mutability of an object?

    A. Declare the class final.

    B. Don't provide public set methods.

    C. Let methods change the fields as little as possible.

    D. Help separate the methods from the implementation by avoiding accessors and mutators.

(Continues)

THE ESSENTIALS AND BEYOND *(Continued)*

6. How does a class in one package access a class in another package? (Choose all that apply.)

    A. The class it wants to access has to be `public`.

    B. It must import the target class by its package name.

    C. At runtime, the classpath has to point to the directory that hosts the target package.

    D. If the accessed class is `protected`, the other class has to subclass it.

7. True or false: You can use access modifiers so only some of the classes in a package see a particular package-private class.

8. Select the option that best describes an example of data abstraction:

    A. A `Dollar` class with a floating-point variable that is `private`

    B. A `Square` class with accessor and mutator methods for its width and height

    C. A `protected` `Point` class with `public` methods

    D. A `Car` class with `fuelLevel()` and `addGas()` methods

9. What risk is associated with allowing a caller to assign a value directly to another class's field?

    A. There's no validation of the correct type.

    B. There's no way to limit the range of the assignment.

    C. There's no package privacy.

    D. You can't tell if the assignment is an accessor or a mutator.

10. True or false: All packages must reside in one directory for any single computer.

CHAPTER 7

Using Java Methods to Communicate

Now that we've discussed limiting access to fields and methods in Java, we can turn our attention more generally to communicating through methods. Programmers who write Java classes for others to reuse want to design methods that indicate their purpose. Programmers who write packages of classes may write methods to indicate how one object type applies to others in the same package. And some class-private methods may even take the appearance of a class talking to itself.

In method design, every aspect of the method's *signature* counts: Its access modifier, return type, name, and parameters all communicate some aspect of the method's utility. Thoughtful design will pay for itself again and again.

In this chapter, we'll cover the following topics:

▶ **Designing methods**

▶ **Overloading methods**

▶ **Declaring methods and fields static**

▶ **Passing data among methods**

Designing Methods

Certification
Objective

Learning to communicate through well-designed methods, I'll admit now, takes a long time. In the same sense that you're taught over several years to use the words of a language, assemble them into sentences, and then arrange them in common (or novel) ways, so it is with programming. It takes time to learn, understand, apply, and improve. Don't imagine that because method signatures are short, they're easy to compose well. They take part in a much larger conversation. Designing a method isn't just about correctness—it's also about participating in that exchange.

You first learn style by mimicking what you see. For example, you compare two pieces of code that do the same work and learn by comparison what qualities you prefer. Some people prize brevity. Some value *expressiveness* (code that says what it does). Still others emphasize what they call power. Through adopting these or other virtues and applying their own preferences, serious programmers express a style.

For example, I still see Java methods like these from time to time:

```
public void LU62Xcvr() { … }
private char[] __parseFileObj(char[] strtok) { … }
public void iTakeIntArray(int[] p) { … }
```

By looking at these methods, I can guess the programmers who wrote them are (a) familiar with IBM's Logical Unit 6.2 protocol; (b) trained in C/C++ programming (probably on Windows); and (c) enamored with Hungarian notation, respectively. The technology in use influences style. The language in use influences style. Even old, outdated styles influence style.

With Java methods, it all starts with a simple form. In the abstract, it looks like this:

```
access_modifier other_modifiers returnType name(parameters) {
    // statement body
}
```

You first declare the visibility of a method, either with one of the keywords `public`, `private`, or `protected` or with no keyword, in which case you declare default (or *package-private*) access. Other modifiers refine the inherent properties of a method; I'll review those in the next section. The return type specifies what kind of result the method issues to its callers. The name and parameter list, taken together, make up the method's *signature*. The signature is what the compiler and JVM use to identify a method when it is called.

It's a simple form but with many options that allow for many diverse possibilities. Let's break them down one element at a time.

There is an optional piece to method syntax called an exception list, which we'll discuss in Chapter 11, "Throwing and Catching Exceptions in Java."

Understanding Method Modifiers

A modifier is any keyword that defines the role a method plays in a class. Given no modifiers at all, a Java method does the following:

▶ Provides default access

▶ Has a code body (with zero or more statements)

▶ May be overridden

▶ Is called with an object reference

There are other, more technical properties I haven't listed that fall outside the scope of this book.

In Chapter 6, "Encapsulating Data and Exposing Methods in Java," we covered the access modifiers: `public`, default (or *package-private*), `protected`, and `private`. There are six more modifiers that also apply to methods. Table 7.1 lists them and indicates if and where we discuss them.

TABLE 7.1 List of modifier keywords and coverage in this guide

Modifier Keyword	Where Covered
abstract	Chapter 10
final	Chapter 9
native	Not covered
static	Chapter 7
synchronized	Not covered
strictfp	Not covered

The keywords `native`, `synchronized`, and `strictfp` relate to advanced topics: integrating Java with external code libraries; using Java's built-in mechanism for managing threads in an application; and managing floating-point values in a way that keeps Java code portable across different platforms, respectively. You won't need these keywords until you encounter the topics that require them.

In Chapter 10, "Understanding Java Interfaces and Abstract Classes," I'll discuss what it means to declare a class or method with the `abstract` keyword. You already know that `final` classes can't be extended, which is similar for methods. In Chapter 9, "Inheriting Code and Data in Java," I'll show you how it applies.

You've already seen the keyword `static` a lot. The `main()` method requires it so the JVM can access it early in a program's startup routine. In this chapter, I'll discuss how and why you should use it with your own methods.

Choosing Modifiers

Now that I've deferred all but one modifier for discussion, you might wonder what else there is to talk about. The short answer is *context*. Once you settle on a method's visibility—whether it represents its class to the outside world, to its package, or merely to its own class—that decision defines a context that has some bearing on its name. Let's take a real-world context and diagram it as if we were going to transliterate it to code.

Figure 7.1 shows a hypothetical Sedan class and four *actors* that have some kind of relationship, or *use case*, with it. The diagram itself, by the way, uses UML-specified components. Those are approved, official stick figures I'm using to depict the actors. The lines are labeled to indicate each actor's visibility. The class diagram lists methods, but I've separated them by visibility to emphasize my point: Method naming begins with the intended user (that is, accessibility) in mind.

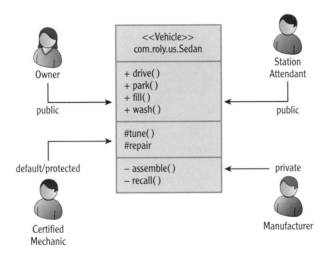

FIGURE 7.1 Car diagram with four actors

Let's say a Sedan is one kind of Vehicle that the Roly company makes in the United States. In designing it, the Manufacturer actor provides and uses the methods assemble() and recall() to operate on the vehicle. It also supplies operations for servicing the vehicle (the tune() and repair() methods), operating it (the drive() and park() methods) and performing simple maintenance (the fill() and wash() methods).

The Manufacturer might use all these methods in the production, testing, and delivery of the car, restricting the visibility of operations it reserves for "private" use. To make servicing the car less of an ordeal, it permits a Certified Mechanic some visibility into the internals of the Sedan class. An Owner or Station Attendant may also use the Sedan as the Owner (or driver) would.

The method's visibility adds to that context. It implies *who* should use it, and because you can assume a Certified Mechanic has proper skills and knowledge, the methods visible to that actor might be accordingly technical in nature, such as disconnectTensionerSpring() or advanceSparkTiming().

An actor needs the object to do something on its behalf. A use case spells out that need.

In each case, I've nonetheless applied legible method names anyone can grasp, and that's part of the idea. A method should tell you plainly what it's for. A name like LU62Xcvr isn't *bad*. So long as you're only talking to other veteran IBM programmers with System Network Architecture (SNA) experience who know that *Xcvr* is short for *transceiver*, it's fine. The same goes for a __parse() method. If your colleagues know the double underscore signifies "internal use only," they may not say anything.

The remaining modifiers are more technical in nature. If you declare a method static or final, it will have less to do with fulfilling an actor's needs and more to do with your desire to change the way the method works.

Choosing Return Types

I have two beginner rules to lay down for choosing a method's return type:

> Rule 1: If the method changes the object's state, it must return void.

> Rule 2: If the method returns an object, it should return an *interface* instead of a value.

Roll those ideas around in your mind for a second. Highlight them in this book, write them down, put them in a small shrine for Java rules above your desk—do whatever you need to commit them to memory. As you learn to write Java programs that aren't just main() methods of test code, these two rules will keep you out of trouble again and again. Both have to do with making sure each method does one thing, and does it well. Here's why.

Rule 1: If the method changes the object's state, it must return void. In short, when you write a method that performs a process, don't make it report on that process at the same time. Consider the following methods for a Sedan class:

```
public TankLevel start() { … }
public TankLevel park() { … }
public TankLevel drive() { … }
```

These methods are designed to tell you how much gas you have each time you call them. The designer thinks returning this information is a no-brainer. Without fuel, after all, it makes no sense to operate the car. Unfortunately, it's very easy to get ahead of yourself with this kind of thinking. The idea seems to be that each action should have an immediate, measurable state change, which is not wrong. The idea that each method should immediately report that change is another matter.

Assume each of these methods has numerous statements to execute, including other method calls. Callers have no idea how simple or complex the call is; they are just looking for the response they're told to expect.

The compiler has its own use for underscores and for the $ symbol. It's a good idea to avoid them both in your identifiers.

After a bit of reflection, however, some callers will wonder, When exactly was it that the state of the TankLevel object was computed? What should the caller expect? Using the park() method, a caller may feel that reporting the gas level before the car shuts off makes the most sense. Another caller may think it should report zero, confirming that the gauge shuts off when the car does. When the drive() method is used, reading the gas level before starting seems reasonable. Someone else may call the drive() method repeatedly to get the current gas level. In my experience, it's stunning how the callers assign their own meanings to some methods to get what they want from them. It is also a rule of the trade that method faults accrue to their programmer. Always.

Methods that combine the *behavior* of an object with a partial view of its *state* are problematic. When it's done, the method's context remains open to interpretation at best and misuse at worst. The temptation is the convenience of doing two things at once. The consequences come when programmers start looking more closely at the method to understand every aspect of its work. When that work proves to be two things instead of one, you run into trouble.

> Experts like Bertrand Meyer and Martin Fowler vary between calling this an absolute rule and very strong advice.

You should instead supply separate accessor methods for reporting part of the object's state. The caller can assert the context they require, before and after they invoke a state change, if that's what they need. Some test-oriented programmers may end up writing code like the following:

```
...
sedan.start();
System.out.println("Gas: " + sedan.getTankLevel());
sedan.drive();
System.out.println("Gas: " + sedan.getTankLevel());
sedan.park();
System.out.println("Gas: " + sedan.getTankLevel());
sedan.stop();
System.out.println("Gas: " + sedan.getTankLevel());
...
```

Soothing that kind of anxiety is not your problem. There's not much you can (or should) do to forestall this approach. A method interface that enables this kind of checking by making it possible with fewer lines of code only makes this wrong-headed approach more convenient.

On to Rule 2: *If the method returns an object, it should return an* interface *instead of a value.* This rule extends the idea of encapsulation I raised in Chapter 6. When you return an object reference, you want the caller to use *behavior*, not storage implementation.

Let's expand on that idea using Figure 7.2, which shows the Vehicle class from Figure 7.1 in some detail. Assume the Roly company uses this class as a general type, one that represents features that are common to all the cars it makes.

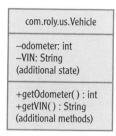

FIGURE 7.2
Vehicle class diagram

To keep it simple, I'll consider just the odometer and vehicle identification number (VIN) as state values. These are data that could apply to any Vehicle, so it makes sense to assign them to a general type. Assume for the sake of discussion that the Sedan class will *inherit* from the Vehicle class and therefore share its accessible members, including these:

```
public int getOdometer() { ... }
public String getVIN() { ... }
```

It makes sense to think of the Vehicle class as a type in its own right, one that is capable of reporting the odometer's current reading or VIN. Why not just return the object reference and let the calling programmer use it to extract the information they require? Such a method might look like this:

```
public Vehicle getStats() { ... }
```

This idea takes encapsulation to another level. By using the Vehicle class to represent features the Sedan subclass inherits from it, you *generalize* the return type. To fully appreciate this benefit, you need to learn more about *inheritance*. That full discussion doesn't take place until Chapter 9. For now, I ask you to take it on faith that this benefit is a good one.

So why not just return a Sedan type, if that class also has the methods you want to return to the caller? That would also serve the example at hand, and it's easier to understand, given the topics we have covered so far, but the Sedan class is what I'll eventually describe as a *concrete type*. It's like a "what you see is what you get" kind of class, and that's *not* a problem.

Think about it like this: You're talking about cars with your friends. One of your friends has a habit of relating everything that's being said to the Roly sedan.

Your friend knows there are other cars, but if the Roly sedan doesn't have a capability or feature you want to talk about, he doesn't have anything to say. When you want to make an observation about cars in general, that friend doesn't follow unless he can relate it back to the Roly sedan.

The point of Java's inheritance model is that, on one level, every object behaves as the Object class requires. It also behaves as every parent class requires, as Figure 7.3 shows. If you want to direct a caller's attention to what a parent type can do, *return that type*. Don't be any more specific than necessary.

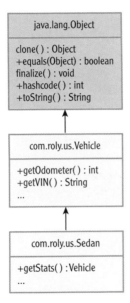

FIGURE 7.3
Method interfaces inherited
by the Sedan class

Again, I'm asking you to take this rule on faith for now. To fully understand the rationale that supports this rule, you need more, including complete information on inheritance and using parent classes as types. You'll get there soon enough.

Choosing Parameters

Choosing parameters is another key aspect of defining a method. If one method calling another is a form of communication, parameters represent the message. Along with a method's name, parameters form what we call the method's *signature*. The type, order, and number of parameters a method accepts all combine to create a unique lookup for each method in a class.

A method's parameter list can have zero or more items. The number of items can be fixed or variable. Each parameter may be a primitive type or an object reference. The list for any method can mix these types as you wish.

What matters in design is the *message*: what the method requires (or should accept) to do its job and converse efficiently with its callers. That conversation is, in part, refined by its context: the information an object contains before its methods are called. Consider the following possible methods for the Sedan class:

```
public void start(Driver drvr, Key key) { … }
public void start(Owner owner) { … }
public void start() { … }
```

There's nothing wrong with any of these methods, but a moment of reflection might tell you the message in the first two methods is possibly redundant, or at least could have been established before getting to this operation. If so, are these methods asking the caller to confirm this information, or repeat it?

You want to make a parameter list as simple as it can be, but no simpler. I still think about the System.arraycopy() method and its five parameters all the time. Five parameters are a lot to remember, but to my mind, there's just no better way of talking to that method. Fortunately, you and I don't have to use it (directly) very often. It is buried in lots of methods you will use all the time, though.

When I review a colleague's class code, I rely on a few simple categories based on each method's use of return type and parameter list. Table 7.2 shows those categories as a combination of its return and parameters.

TABLE 7.2 Defining a method by its return and parameters

Method Composition	Returns void	Returns a Type
No parameters	Procedural	Accessor
Has parameters	Mutator	Functional

The terms *procedural* and *functional* are not terms accepted by the Java community. For the sake of introduction and as terms to apply in a code review, however, I find these categories very useful. They help me describe what I think the method should do based solely on these two elements. If the method's name does not complement this categorization, it makes me wonder if the method's intent is as clear as it could be.

A get method that
is declared `static`
is an exception to
this advice. The sec-
tion on the `static`
modifier later in this
chapter will explain.

A method that takes no parameters but returns a value should return something that pertains to its object. A method that accepts a parameter but returns
nothing should modify the object. The terms *accessor* and *mutator*, which *are*
widely used, describe those roles. Accessor and mutator methods don't have to
have the prefix `get` or `set`, respectively, but most Java programmers have no
doubt what you mean when they see them.

A method that requires no information from the caller and returns none
should change its object's state. I call this kind of method *procedural*, but any
term that implies a process that leads to state change works too. A procedural
method is like a control button. You expect it to perform some kind of action, a
change in the object state you'll be able to observe in a subsequent interaction.

Finally, there are methods that accept parameters and return a value. I take
a method of this form to be one of two things. First, I guess it's a mistake, for
the reasons I gave earlier in the chapter. Any method that appears to be both a
mutator and an accessor is bound to appear ambiguous to some number of programmers and cause confusion.

Utility methods,
so-called, are often
collected together in
a class, such as the
`java.lang.Math`
class.

Second, if the method behaves like a mathematical *function*—it returns a
type that is only a computational result of operating on the supplied parameters, just like the operators you studied in Chapter 3, "Using Java Operators and
Conditional Logic"—then it's okay. Most Java programmers are taught to call
these *utility methods*, but the common term across programming languages is
functional.

I use these categories when I hear my students interpreting the term *style*
to mean something free-form, groovy, and open to what their heart is feeling.
No; style is not poetic license. There absolutely is a technical craft to it; you
can define it, and you can lock it down. We can disagree on terms, but the
discipline is not optional. Now that you know the anatomy of a method and
categories by which to understand them, what remains is assigning the best
possible name.

Naming Methods

Let's start with the hard-and-fast rules:

- ► You cannot name a method the same as a Java reserved word.
- ► The name must begin with a letter or the symbol $ or _.
- ► Subsequent characters may also be numbers.

That's it. These rules describe any *legal identifier* in Java and apply to anything you are free to name, including classes and fields. Prepare to be tested on these rules. The following examples are legal:

- ► `okidentifier`

- ► `$OK2Identifier`

- ► `_alsoOK1d3ntifi3r`

- ► `__SStillOkbutKnotsonice$`

These examples are not legal:

- ► `3DPointClass`

- ► `hollywood@vine`

- ► `*$coffee`

- ► `synchronized`

Normally I'd say there's no need to memorize Java's reserved words unless you know how to use them. Like the `synchronized` keyword, however, all of them are illegal as identifiers. I'd be embarrassed to admit how many times a method called `do()` appears in example code I type off the top of my head, if it actually happened. But I'm a professional, so it never ever does. Be careful of terms you may have acquired elsewhere, like the `goto` and `const` reserved words. The Java Language Specification (JLS) reserves these terms to make sure no one muddies Java's waters by using them.

Valid letters in Java are not just characters in the English alphabet. Java supports the Unicode character set, so there are more than 45,000 characters that can start a legal Java identifier. A few hundred more are non-Arabic numerals that may appear after the first character in a legal identifier. You don't have to worry about memorizing those for an Oracle exam.

As a matter of style, also consider these guidelines:

- ► Use lowercase letters except to start a subsequent word.

- ► Put acronyms in uppercase.

- ► Don't start identifiers with $. (The compiler also uses this symbol.)

The following are examples of conventional style:

- ► `getGrossVehicleWeight`

- ► `parseVIN`

- ► `crimeaRiver`

The `java.lang`
`.Character` class
has methods to test
whether a character can be used
in an identifier:
`isJavaIdenti-`
`fierStart()` and
`isJavaIdentifi-`
`erPart()`.

Some Java shops post their own guidelines on top of generally accepted style. The bottom line with any one codebase is consistency. When a large base of code has a clean, consistent style, it can significantly cut the burden on the reader to absorb it.

The rest of a good naming scheme, again, has everything to do with maintaining the context. What term or terms should come to mind for your caller when seeking the appropriate method in your class? Does the name you use express a clear idea? Does it suggest to someone examining your method interface that they've come to the right place?

These considerations go a long way toward conserving another programmer's time and are well worth the effort because of that. My best advice: Learn to appreciate what it is that makes classes you like to use so agreeable, and teach yourself how to follow suit. If all else fails, start with these can't-miss rules, and elaborate as needed:

> **Accessors:** Start with `get` and name a recognizable property. For a bean, using the name of the underlying field is okay.

> **Mutators:** Start with `set`; name the same property as the corresponding `get` method.

> **Procedural:** Use a verb that implies a state change or process: `start()`, `stop()`, `send()`, `receive()`, `sleep()`.

> **Functional:** Use a verb that implies a result from the parameters given: `parse()`, `multiply()`, `iterate()`.

Overloading Methods

Certification Objective

Think about the `System.out.println()` method for just a second. You haven't had reason yet to notice that it will take anything for a parameter—any primitive, any object reference:

```
class Println {
    public static void main(String args[]) {
        System.out.println("fred");
        System.out.println(true);
        System.out.println(55.55);
        System.out.println(8);
        System.out.println('a');
        System.out.println(new Object());
    }
}
$ java Println
```

```
fred
true
55.55
8
a
java.lang.Object@5a25f3
```

Regardless of type—a literal string, Boolean, integral, floating-point, or even object reference—the `println()` method knows how to print it. It's no accident, nor is it a compiler trick. The `println()` method (located in the `java.io.PrintStream` class) has 10 different versions. One version takes no parameter and prints a line return, another version accepts an object reference, and another even takes an array. The remaining seven versions cover all the primitive types except for a `short` value.

This technique is called *overloading*. Properly used, it lets the programmer define multiple ways for a caller to pass a message to the method and get a result. The caller can save the trouble of having to cast or convert a parameter to one specific type allowed by a method that isn't overloaded.

Understanding Method Signatures

Overloading relies on how the method's signature is used to locate a method in a class. You can have methods with the same name in a class, but the compiler has to identify them as unique. It does that by using the *number*, *type*, and *order of parameters* specified by a caller to match an available method. So long as two methods with the same name vary by these criteria, the compiler can tell them apart.

The following method signatures are all different, or different enough, in the eyes of the compiler:

- ▶ myMethod(Object first, int second)

- ▶ myMethod(Object first)

- ▶ myMethod(int second)

- ▶ myMethod(long first, Object second)

Remember that legal identifiers are case-sensitive, so two methods with the same name but different capitalization cannot overload each other. If you aren't accustomed to paying attention to case, you might fool yourself into thinking you've overloaded a method when you haven't:

- ▶ myMethod(Object first)

- ▶ mymethod(Object second)

The compiler won't complain because, as far as it's concerned, there's no confusion here. There are two different methods to begin with, so there's not reason to compare their parameter lists. Your only safety in this case is to proofread your code carefully, test it thoroughly, and possibly use an editor that's smart enough to warn you when you've done something like this.

Modifiers and return types are not part of the signature—these can vary all you want but only when they refer to methods with differing signatures. Parameter names have no bearing at all. The following examples are not distinguishable from each other. Different as they might appear, they are the same to the compiler:

▶ `public void myMethod(Object inky)`

▶ `private int myMethod(Object blinky)`

▶ `protected Object myMethod(Object clyde)`

Supporting Multiple Parameter Lists

You can overload a method by varying the type, number, and order of its parameters. That's the rule. There are also some conventions on top of the rule that will help you avoid confusion.

It's a bad idea, for example, to change what an overloaded method does based on the parameters provided. The name should advertise a single, consistent behavior. Overload a method only to make it easier to use. Here are some examples:

Overloading by parameter type   You can make a caller's work easier by allowing multiple types for the same parameter. The `println()` method takes this approach. It requires a `String` object in order to print, but instead of making the caller produce one, it allows every possible type—most primitives, an array, or object reference—and converts the parameter to a `String` on its own. As you can see in the previous `Object` example, the result may not be useful, but it will print.

Overloading by number of parameters   Let's say you have a method that accepts some information but could take more, if it's available. Consider a `Contact` class used in conjunction with a database. Let's say a full record includes a name, address, telephone number, and email address. You'd prefer to create partial records over waiting for all the details of a new contact. The following methods allow for differing combinations of input:

```
void addContact(String name, Phone ph, Address addr, Email
addy) {…}
void addContact(String name, Phone ph, Address addr) { … }
void addContact(String name, Phone ph) { … }
void addContact(String name) { … }
```

You could then provide additional methods to allow the caller to update individual fields once the record is established.

You can also use this technique to override default values in a class. Let's say your bank guarantees that each customer will get a receipt after each deposit. An overloaded method is one way to change this behavior should the customer decline the offer:

```
void deposit(Dollar amount, boolean receipt) { … }
void deposit(Dollar amount) { … }
```

The first example lets the caller specify a `false` value to decline the receipt. The shorter method assumes the customer wants one.

Overloading by order of parameters   Overloading by changing parameter order is the hardest of the three aspects to justify. The first two have straightforward applications we can appreciate. Different orders of the same parameters have no intuitive sense. It's a mystery to the caller what is implied by them, as these examples show:

```
void addContact(String name, Phone ph, Address addr, Email
addy) {…}
void addContact(String name, Email addy, Phone ph, Address
addr) {…}
void addContact(Email addy, String name, Address addr,
Phone p) {…}
```

Name first, phone second versus name first, email second? You'd have to work pretty hard to devise a sequence of parameters that implies one clear meaning. Getting multiple sequences to do that is much harder. Remember, the compiler just makes this feature available. It doesn't save you from going overboard with it and creating signatures with obscure meanings.

That's all overloading has to offer, but it's not a small thing. In return for varying the signature of a method a few times, you accept work your caller might otherwise have to do. Consequently, it's difficult to know in advance when overloading saves anyone time. You can always add an overloaded method without breaking the existing method interface of a class, so perhaps the best approach is conservative: Add them when other users tell you it would really help.

Allowing for a Variable Number of Parameters

You can take overloading by number of parameters a step further using Java's *varargs* feature. A varargs parameter allows for an arbitrary number of parameters so long as they share one type, just as an array does.

In fact, you could just populate an array with some values and pass it as a parameter. The varargs feature just makes it convenient to pass several literal values to a method on the fly. Underneath the hood, the compiler and JVM treats a varargs parameter list as an array.

Let's say you wanted a *functional* method that lets the caller supply a list of integers and get their mean average, like the following:

```
float mean1 = avg(1, 3, 4, 8, 45, 233, 12, 11, 29);
float mean2 = avg(5, 9, 3, 11);
float mean3 = avg(25, 25, 31, 25, 32, 21, 29, 25, 45);
```

These statements are an example of an *expressive syntax*. That is, you can infer what's supposed to happen just by reading them. It's a good way to improve code readability when you have to deal with many literal values, or even a few you want to manage on the fly. To accept a varargs parameter, create a parameter that declares its type, followed by an ellipsis (three dots), followed by the parameter name:

```
public float avg(int ... numbers) { … }
```

That's it! It's not only simple, but it will *also accept an array* in lieu of a list of values. This overloading is built in. In the method body, you treat the varargs variable like an array, as shown here:

```
public void echo (int ... numbers) {
    for (int i = 0; i < numbers.length; i++)
        System.out.print(numbers[i]+ " ");
}
```

And there's more. If the varargs type is primitive, the compiler and JVM will *box* the values for you into their object form. You can then use a for-each loop to iterate over them, as shown here:

```
public void echo (int ... numbers) {
    for (Integer i; numbers)
        System.out.print(i + " ");
}
```

Nice! You may not see a ton of opportunities to exploit this feature, but if you've written a few thousand for loops already, you'll be happy for any shortcuts you can get your hands on.

In summary, a varargs parameter has the following characteristics:

▶ Accepts zero or more elements of the same type

▶ Can occur once in a method's parameter list

> ▶ Must be the last parameter in the list
>
> ▶ Also accepts an array (including an empty one)

Chaining Overloaded Methods

Don't imagine that each overloaded `println()` method has its own code; that would be foolish. Methods by the same name should have the same behavior, of course, but that's hard to keep straight, and a bit mind-numbing, if you have to edit eight or nine methods each time you need to change the logic.

It's easier to keep the core logic in one method. Let the overloaded methods process the parameters they receive as needed. Then call the method that contains the logic all the methods need to do the intended work. With method chaining, the two `BankAccount` methods that I described earlier could look like this:

```
final class BankAccount {
    private Dollar balance;
    private boolean receipt = true;

    public void deposit(Dollar amount, boolean receipt) {
        balance.add(amount);
      // if receipt == true, print receipt
    }

    public void deposit(Dollar amount) {
        // validate and chain to base method
        deposit(amount, true);
    }
}

final class Dollar {
    private float amount;

    private void setAmount(float amt) {
        // make sure amt is a valid currency amount
        amount = amt;
    }

    float getAmount() {
        return amount;
    }
```

```
public void add(Dollar amt) {
    // validate amt
    amount += amt.getAmount();
}
}
```

Can you see why the method signatures have to be unique and why using a different return type alone isn't enough? When chaining, methods can identify their overloaded counterparts only by passing the right parameters. Even then, it's not always enough to make such calls unambiguous, but that's another conversation that has to wait until you learn more about inheritance in Chapter 9.

Declaring Methods and Fields *static*

Certification Objective

The static keyword modifies methods in a way that's quite different from how an access modifier does. Recall when I said the main() method had to be declared static. Methods that are declared static can be called without constructing an object of the class. The JVM can invoke a main() method just by knowing which class to load into memory.

Viewed another way, you have an excellent candidate for a *functional method* if you want a method that

► Won't change an object's state

► Won't report an object's state

► Will return a value based on parameters

Methods written this way offer a *utility* that, while contained in a class by necessity, doesn't provide an object-based service.

Classes that contain just these kinds of methods include

► java.lang.Math

► java.util.Collections

► java.nio.file.Files

These classes consist of methods that serve as helper tools to other classes. The Math class is like a big calculator, full of mathematical functions. In a similar manner, the other two are like a utility drawer for their respective packages, one place to keep an assortment of handy tools.

Objects themselves can still call `static` methods, including objects made from the same class. It's more common to address `static` methods by their class name, such as `Math.abs(-25)`, but it's not required.

What you can't do is use a `static` method to refer to any object's data. Once constructed, an object has what is called a *non-static context*. That attempt crosses the boundary that separates the class from its objects.

A common beginner mistake with `static` methods involves confusing them with object methods. The rules of visibility tell you a method can see all other methods in its class. It can, but it can't necessarily *call* all of them. To do that, the methods have to share a context, either class based (that is, static) or object based.

The following example illustrates a rookie mistake I see in virtually every introductory course I have taught:

```java
public final class Static {
    private String name = "Static class";
    public static void first() {
        System.out.print("first ");
    }

    public static void second() {
        System.out.print("second ");
    }

    public void third() {
        System.out.println("third");
    }

    public static void main(String args[]) {
        first();
        second();
        third();
    }
}
```

If you try compiling this class, you'll get this error message:

```
Static.java:18: error: non-static method third()
        cannot be referenced from a static context
                third();
                ^
```

Most utility classes declare `private` constructors only, so you can't construct objects from them.

The compiler, as you can see, offers one of its least helpful messages in a spot almost every new Java programmer visits. If you take this error message as advice, it seems to hint that making the third() method static will fix the problem—which it does, but then none of these methods can be used to access a non-static field like name. We've only created a different problem.

It would be nice if the compiler said, "Did you want to construct a static object in the main() method and use it to access the non-static members of the class?" because that would work. Alas, the compiler is not in the business of guessing what you want. Its only job is to tell you if what you coded is legal and correct.

If you apply the static keyword instead to a field, it has a different effect than it does for a method. It associates the field with the class rather than any one instance. All static methods *can* access any static field.

A static field's value is visible to all instances of a class at once. If we declare a class member like this, then every instance of the class shares that information:

```
private static String myHometown = "San Francisco";
```

It's not easy to come up with many uses for static fields, at least as they relate to objects. The typical example is a counter variable that's incremented every time an object gets made, like this:

```
public class Counter {
    private static int counter;

    public Counter() {
        counter++;
    }

    public int getCounter() {
        return counter;
    }

    public static void main(String args[]) {
        Counter ctr1 = new Counter();
        Counter ctr2 = new Counter();
        Counter ctr3 = new Counter();
        System.out.println(ctr1.getCounter());
    }
}
$ java Counter
3
```

The getCounter() method can access the counter variable. So can all Counter objects. It won't matter if you use ctr1, ctr2, or ctr3 with the println() statement. They'll all report 3.

Passing Data among Methods

Certification
Objective

Up to this point, I've treated methods without much concern for the differences between primitive and object types. These next sections require more careful handling—it's where beginners get confused one of two ways. The first is in misunderstanding what happens to a parameter after a called method returns. The second is getting lost in someone else's explanation that sounds simple but isn't.

Experience has taught me you can take this discussion too fast but almost never too slow, so I'm going to take it a piece at a time. When it's done you're going to see that Java methods handle all parameters the same way, but the effect it has is one thing for primitive types and another for object references.

Understanding Primitive Parameters

A primitive variable is nothing more than an alias for a literal value. When you write

```
int x = 7;
```

it's the same as saying, "x is another word for 7." When the value of x changes to 25, it becomes another word for 25. That's all a primitive type variable is: a name you assign to whatever is inside it.

When you use x as a parameter, you do *not* share it with the method you are calling; you pass along the content. The called method receives the value only, gives the thing a local name, and then operates on it.

Got it? Let's find out: What is the value of x when it is printed in the main() method here?

```
public final class Doubling {
    public void doubling(int x) {
        x = x * 2;
    }

    public static void main(String args[]) {
        int x = 7;
        Doubling dbl = new Doubling();
        dbl.doubling(x);
        System.out.println(x);
    }
}
```

What do you think, 7 or 14? Running this program will give you the answer, but that doesn't really help you unless you can verbalize the reason why. Here's a hint: If you're thinking 14, read this section again.

The variable x in the main() method is only an alias for its assigned value. The same is true for the variable x in the doubling() method. The two variables are *not* related. The doubling() method receives a literal value 7, which it assigns to its own local name, multiplies by two, and then exits. That's it. The x declared in the main() method is unaffected.

Don't move on until you are sure what's happening here. If it helps to change variable names, add println() statements as you like, and so on, by all means do so.

Understanding Reference Parameters

I'm going to repeat the last section, but this time using a MyNumber object reference that contains a field x. Here's the modified test code:

```
public final class Doubling2
{
    public void doubling(MyNumber mnd) {
        mnd.x = mnd.x * 2;
    }

    public static void main(String args[]) {
        MyNumber mnm = new MyNumber();
        Doubling2 dbl = new Doubling2();
        dbl.doubling(mnm);
        System.out.println(mnm.x);
    }
}

final class MyNumber {
    public int x = 7;
}
```

What will the main() method print now? Let's work it out.

In this program, I pass a *referent* to the doubling() method from the main() method. The variable mnm points to the reference in the main() method, and the variable mnd points to the reference in the doubling() method. Although they point to the same object, they are not related to each other. That is, an object reference is just like a primitive variable. The called method ignores the calling name and assigns its own.

What it contains, however, isn't a literal; it's a location in memory, with access to certain fields and methods. If the doubling() method mutates a value *inside*

I declared the x field in the MyNumber class public just to keep the code brief. Normally you'd encapsulate it.

the referent, the reference mnm will see the change the next time it accesses the referent. *Now* our answer is 14.

Returning Object References

An object reference provides a layer of indirection that skirts the limits of a primitive variable. A calling method can pass an object to a called method, which can change it. The calling method can see the change after the called method returns. It's (almost) that simple.

The called method still ignores the *reference* used by the calling method to pass the parameter. The difference is in the value, which is now a referent. If instead I tried to change the referent itself—for example, by trying to assign it to a different referent—the calling method would not notice.

To demonstrate this point, I'll modify the test class once more:

```
public final class Doubling3
{
    public void doubling(MyNumber mnd) {
        // assign a new referent
        mnd = new MyNumber();
        mnd.x = mnd.x * 2;
    }

    public static void main(String args[]) {
        MyNumber mynum = new MyNumber();
        Doubling3 dbl = new Doubling3();
        dbl.doubling(mynum);
        System.out.println(mynum.x);
    }
}

final class MyNumber {
    public int x = 7;
}
```

This doubling() method creates a new MyNumber object, operates on it, and then returns. You might now assume the method has replaced the referent it received with a new one and that mnm now points to it—but that's not what happens. Once the doubling() method declares a different value for the mnd variable—here, a new referent—the mnd and mnm variables no longer have a referent in common. The value of mnd.x will change to 14, and the value of mnm.x will remain 7.

Understanding Pass-by-Value

Java's behavior is the same for all cases. It's called *pass-by-value*. The difference is that a primitive type holds a literal value while an object reference holds the location of a referent. It's these intermediate values that cannot be changed by a called method.

What seems to makes understanding pass-by-value difficult is the term itself. Java programmers have argued over a correct and complete definition of this term for years, often to the point of violently agreeing with each other.

The second complication I've seen involves mock quiz questions that torture this point endlessly. While I agree it's important to test for this understanding, I don't think turning it into an exhausting time-bound puzzle proves anything, except perhaps who in a room is faster at reading a maze of twisty code. Tricky examples aside, the truth *is* simple. The value of a primitive type is always literal, like the number 5 or the keyword `false`. The value of an object reference is always a referent (or `null`). *You cannot change a variable by passing it to another method—you only ever pass its value.*

THE ESSENTIALS AND BEYOND

This chapter covers a great deal of territory about methods. Using the anatomy of a method as a guide, you learned how visibility, return type, name, and parameter list all contribute to the way a method signals how it communicates. That communication requires a context. In an object-oriented language, context is supplied by the type that contains the methods.

You also learned how method overloading works and some practices for applying it. You saw how a method can accept an indefinite number of parameters and what it means to declare a method `static`. This chapter concluded with the subject that seems to make everyone a little jumpy: what pass-by-value means when we pass primitives or objects to a method.

ADDITIONAL EXERCISES

1. Write a `LegalID` class that accepts one word on the command line and tells you whether it could be a legal identifier. Test for any word that matches a primitive type keyword.

2. Write a `Calculator` class with `multiply()` and `add()` methods. They must accept any combination of integral and `double` values. Use the `main()` method to test the methods you write.

(Continues)

3. Write a Toaster class that includes fields for its make, model, and serial number. Write a makeToaster() method that generates its own serial number for each object. Overload the method so any combination of make and/or model information is sufficient input. Use this method to construct only complete Toaster objects and return a reference to the caller. Do your best to avoid redundant code in the overloaded methods.

4. Write a VendingMachine class that includes methods for buying an item, returning coins, refilling the inventory, taking the cash out, running diagnostics on the machine, putting the machine into a maintenance state, and reporting the current state. Choose an appropriate signature for each method, including access modifiers. Don't write any method logic, but do include empty classes to reflect any parameters you want to specify as new types.

REVIEW QUESTIONS

1. Which of the following are legal identifiers for a class, method, or field? (Choose all that apply.)

   A. const

   B. $valueOf

   C. ___

   D. 3CPO

2. Given the method declaration

   ```
   private double checkWeight(Object obj)
   ```

   which of the following declarations do not overload it? (Choose all that apply.)

   A. protected int checkWeight(Object[] objects)

   B. private double checkWeight(Object obj2)

   C. public double checkWeight(Object … objects)

   D. void checkWeight(Object obj)

3. How many methods can you chain together in a single class?

   A. 15

   B. One

   C. All of them

   D. Only the overloaded ones

(Continues)

THE ESSENTIALS AND BEYOND *(Continued)*

4. Which off the following are valid method modifiers? (Choose all that apply.)

    A. synchronized

    B. void

    C. package private

    D. static

5. Which of the following are variations on a parameter list you can make to create an overloaded method?

    A. Order and accessibility

    B. Type and name

    C. Name and number

    D. Order and number

6. Which statement best describes a functional method?

    A. It contains mathematical logic.

    B. It accepts no values and returns a calculated result.

    C. It accepts values but does not change the object's state.

    D. It cannot return a primitive type.

7. Which description best matches what Table 7.2 calls a procedural method?

    A. Changes object state, doesn't return a type

    B. Calls other methods in the same class

    C. Accesses object state, doesn't return a value

    D. Changes object state based on the parameters provided

8. Which of the following parameter types are passed by value to a called method? (Choose all that apply.)

    A. Primitives

    B. References

9. True or false: A static field can be accessed only by a static method.

10. True or false: A non-static method cannot be called from a static method.

CHAPTER 8

Using Java Constructors

Constructors are the last major Java class elements you need to cover. They're a lot like methods in appearance. In fact, I'll be able to use some of the discussion in Chapter 7, "Using Java Methods to Communicate," to address what the similarities are and how you can apply them.

Unlike methods, constructors tie into the way objects get made, not just for the class they belong to, but also for classes they inherit from *and* classes that inherit from them. That subject is a chapter in itself, so here we'll confine discussion to the way constructors work for the class at hand.

In this chapter, we'll cover the following topics:

▶ **Using the default constructor**

▶ **Defining alternate constructors**

▶ **Adding parameters to constructors**

▶ **Overloading constructors**

Using the Default Constructor

**Certification
Objective**

As I mentioned back in Chapter 1, "Introducing the Basics of Java," the compiler will insert a *default constructor* into your class if you don't write one in. If you write one the way the compiler would—public visibility, no parameters, and no code—it's often called a *no-arg constructor.* It's the same code either way, but the terms help to separate the implicit and explicit options.

Either constructor has the specific role of initializing each field in its class. In Chapter 1, I claimed that Java's type-safety rules ensure that each field will get a type-appropriate default value—whether it is integral zero, floating-point zero, `false`, or `null`—if it receives no explicit assignment. The compiler uses the default constructor to apply these rules.

In Chapter 9, "Inheriting Code and Data in Java," I'll explain why the default constructor is a necessity for making objects. You do need it!

The rules for the default constructor are simple:

- ▶ Its name is the same as its class.
- ▶ It has no return type.
- ▶ It has no parameters.
- ▶ It is declared `public`.
- ▶ It has no code in its body.

If a constructor you intended to write fails the first rule, the compiler will complain that you have a bad method declaration, as shown here:

```
final class RuleOne {
    public RuleWon() {}
}
```

```
$ javac RuleOne.java
RuleOne.java:2: error: invalid method declaration;
    return type required
        public RuleWon() {}
               ^
1 error
```

Thus if you do not observe both the first and second rules, the compiler may not complain—what you have written will look like a method. If it does complain, it will probably have to do with failing to support the return type, as shown here:

```
final class RuleTwo {
    public int RuleTwo() {}
}
```

```
$ javac RuleTwo.java
RuleTwo.java:2: error: missing return statement
    public int RuleTwo() {}
                        ^
1 error
```

Those are the only two things that distinguish a constructor from a method, so far as the compiler is concerned, and they're often easy to miss.

Constructors also aren't class *members* in the same sense that fields and methods are. If you decide to name a method after the class, the compiler sees no problem:

```
public final class Class {
    public Class() {}
```

```
   public void Class() {}
}
$ javac Class.java
$
```

It's a doubly poor choice for a method name because it shadows the class name and a reserved word as well. Nonetheless, this code compiles without error.

If your constructor observes the first two rules but not the remaining three, you still have a constructor, just not a default or no-arg constructor. Like methods, constructors can be overloaded, can have narrower access, and can contain code:

```
import java.util.Date;

final class MyDate {
   private Date date;

   MyDate() {
      // Allow package caller an epoch
      // January 1, 1970 00:00:00 GMT
      date = new Date(0);
   }

   public MyDate(Date date) {
      if (date == null)
         this.date = new Date();
      else
         this.date = date;
   }
}
```

In this example, I've given the no-arg constructor default access code to construct an "epoch" date, the assigned birthday of the Unix operating system. Callers from other packages have to pass their own Date object. If they supply a null value, they get an object with the current time.

That said, I should mention here that passing an object reference into a constructor has deeper consequences than it does for a method. The usual reason for doing this is to initialize a field, as the example shows. This action implies that the calling method and the new object will share a reference, and it's worth considering whether you want to maintain a dependency of that sort. I'll review the reasons for and against this approach later in this chapter.

If you want to call another constructor in the class, you can't do it by name. See the section "Overloading Constructors" for details.

Defining Alternate Constructors

Certification
Objective It's a common inference that constructors are like methods that bear the class name and have no return type. Tread lightly with this comparison. There are useful similarities, but the differences are more important and sometimes subtle. Construction is a key player in the relationship a class has with its parent class(es). I need at least one more chapter of your time to fully define that relationship. That's Chapter 9. If you're the impatient sort, hang tight at least until then.

You also know now that a constructor isn't a class member in the same sense as a field or method. Specifically, it doesn't have quite the same scope with them. A constructor also works with fewer modifiers, so its general syntax is simpler than a method's:

```
access_modifier class_name (parameters) { statements }
```

You cannot modify a constructor with any of the following keywords:

- ► static

- ► final

- ► synchronized

- ► strictfp

- ► native

Any access modifier is acceptable. As you'll see throughout this chapter, each access modifier imparts a special meaning to a constructor.

A quick review: constructors have the following conditions:

- ► No return type

- ► Access modifiers only

- ► A separate namespace

- ► Same name as the class

Beware: Methods and fields can use their class name as a legal identifier without conflicting with a constructor or even with each other.

With those conditions in mind, I think calling a constructor a kind of method isn't completely wrong, but it's a limited comparison with more qualifications to observe than similarities to exploit.

The changes you can make with constructors—access visibility, parameter list, and code body—nonetheless allow for some interesting effects. It makes more sense to talk about the effects you want, and how to achieve them with access modifiers, than the other way around. The following sections adopt that focus.

Hiding (Replacing) the Default Constructor

A default constructor is a fine thing as long as default initialization of your fields is what you want. Remember, once you create a no-arg constructor, the default constructor goes away. So long as there is one valid, explicit constructor in a class, the compiler is satisfied and does not intervene. Replacing the default constructor is therefore synonymous with hiding the compiler's version.

The compiler will still specify default values for all member fields you don't initialize, so it's still okay to do as little work as you need to in this area. You can initialize some fields and leave others alone, as this example shows:

```
public final class MyDefault {
    private String name;
    private String location;

    public MyDefault() {
        name = "Riley Ibex";
    }
}
```

The name variable gets set to the literal String value given in the constructor. You could instead assign this value as part of the field declaration. If you do both, the constructor version wins. The location variable will be assigned the null value.

Incidentally, the short and focused nature of my examples leads me to declare fields at the top of the class structure. You don't have to do this in Java. In fact, don't. Declaring your variables close to where they are used, particularly in code that doesn't fit on a single screen, makes it easier for another programmer to refer to the type, as this example shows:

```
public final class Relates
{
    private String name;
    public String getName() { return name; }

    private String location;
    private String getLocation() { return location; }
}
```

I mention this because it's tempting to keep declarations next to an explicit constructor when you're first writing a class. It's an easy way to track types as you put the constructor together. But once a class is tested and ready for use, it's not much help to anyone who isn't debugging the constructor itself.

An explicit constructor is often self-documenting in this regard. If you're calling other constructors inside your constructor (or using literals), the type information is front and center:

```
public Relates() {
    name     = "Riley Ibex";
    location = new String("San Francisco");
}
```

It's hard to make a persuasive case in a dozen lines or fewer, but once you come across a Java class that runs hundreds of lines, or even more, you'll appreciate every means you can get of organizing the code for readability.

Limiting Constructor Access

In a Java package (or a single source file), non-public classes often participate as subordinates to the public-facing class. As I showed in a previous example, a default access constructor might initialize one or more fields to values that makes sense for the type. If the caller using the public constructor passes in nonsense or a null value, a behind-the-scenes constructor can document how the class tries to ignore those efforts and keep the program running. A constructor can also throw exceptions in response to bad input. I'll cover this technique in Chapter 11, "Throwing and Catching Exceptions in Java."

Another motivation for hiding data, encapsulating it, and even limiting access to the encapsulating methods themselves is to create an internal *context* for the class. You establish a private context in your class when you guard its fields against any mutation at all, on the premise that a caller could violate the boundaries you prescribe for an object's state.

A Java array does this by fixing its length upon construction. The String class does this by using an array *and* fixing its contents upon construction, creating an *immutable* object. While you don't always need a class to operate under constraints that are as tight, you always want to consider which methods you *must* expose to callers for the class to do its intended job and expose only that.

It's no different for constructors. Anyone can call a public constructor in a public class. That call will always allocate memory resources and will always return a new referent. Those are big consequences in an object-oriented world. If you don't plan for it a class at a time, you aren't planning at all. Start by asking when it's appropriate to make objects and how you're going to manage them.

If there's one thing programmers should be taught to dislike, it is code behavior that is surprising.

In particular, *side effects* in a constructor—operations that silently alter the object's state—can be far more confusing than it is with methods. Mixing state change with initialization is an unfair puzzle, and a programmer shouldn't have to guess if (or why) a class does it. Consider a constructor that takes an object parameter and changes it, as Listing 8.1 shows.

LISTING 8.1 Public constructor with side effects

```java
package essentials.ch08;

final class YourBuffer {
    private static int counter = 1;
    private StringBuffer buffer;

    public YourBuffer(StringBuffer buf) {
        buffer = buf;
        buf.append(counter++);
        System.out.println("YourBuffer() field: " + buffer);
    }
}

final class MyBuffer {
    private StringBuffer buffer;

    public MyBuffer() {
        buffer = new StringBuffer("starter");
    }

    public StringBuffer getBuf() {
        return buffer;
    }
}

final class TestBuffers {
    public static void main(String args[]) {
        MyBuffer mb = new MyBuffer();
        System.out.println("mb buffer: " + mb.getBuf());
        YourBuffer yb = new YourBuffer(mb.getBuf());
        System.out.println("mb buffer: " + mb.getBuf());
        yb = new YourBuffer(mb.getBuf());
        System.out.println("mb buffer: " + mb.getBuf());
    }
}
```

(Continues)

LISTING 8.1 Public constructor with side effects *(Continued)*

```
$ java -cp . essentials.ch08.TestBuffers
mb buffer: starter
YourBuffer() field: starter1
mb buffer: starter1
YourBuffer() field: starter12
mb buffer: starter12
```

Imagine that the MyBuffer and YourBuffer classes represent different storage, one of which is used to seed the other's content. In the TestBuffers class, I construct a MyBuffer object and pass its string to the YourBuffer constructor. That constructor *modifies the parameter.* The MyBuffer object gets its data changed each time the TestBuffers program uses it to construct a YourBuffer object.

You could expect a method to do this, in particular a *functional* one. In a constructor, it is unseemly behavior at best and one of the reasons you want to think carefully about passing your object data to a constructor. If there is *any* silent effect permitted by calling a public constructor, it's a matter of time before someone makes it hurt. Until you're sure your constructor doesn't induce such effects, don't make it part of the class's public interface.

Using Packages to Encapsulate Constructors

That said, there are positive reasons for using non-public constructors.

Use one class to construct another class. If you have a class that shouldn't be instantiated directly—let's say it has a context that a public caller could not piece together—then delegate the responsibility to another class in the same package.

To understand why this is important, let's review an example in detail. I need at least two public classes, one with a constructor declared public, the other with a default-access constructor. That is, I have two classes I can see but only one I can construct. The classes must share a package, but because they are all declared public, they can't share a file. That constraint implies you'll need to review multiple files at one time to understand what's going on.

This is, by the way, another (unavoidable) outcome of class dependencies: You have to learn to read two more files at the same time to piece it all together. A diagram would come in especially handy here, so let's have one. Figure 8.1 shows all the relationships I propose for the upcoming code sample using Unified Modeling Language (UML) signifiers.

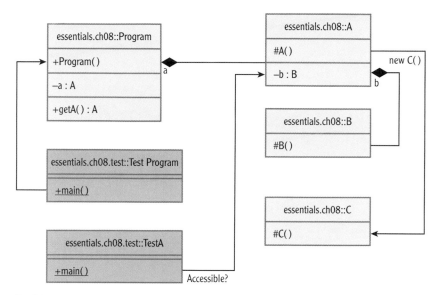

FIGURE 8.1   Using one class to construct others

The lines ending in a filled diamond signify a *composition* of elements. That is, the Program class is composed of an A object, along with whatever else, and the A class is composed of a B object, along with whatever else. The open arrowheads signify *navigability*: The TestProgram class can get to the Program class and the A class can get to the C class. (The TestA class says it gets to the A class, but that remains to be seen.)

Compilation can get tricky without a little help, so I'm keeping things simple by compiling the classes in reverse order of dependencies. Here are classes C and B:

```
package essentials.ch08;

public final class C {
   C() {
      System.out.println("C object made");
   }
}
$ javac -d . C.java
$

package essentials.ch08;

public final class B {
   B() {
```

```
        System.out.println("B object made");
    }
}

$ javac -d . B.java
$
```

Each class is declared public and has a default-access constructor that prints to the command line when an object is made. You can see them from outside the package, which is necessary to declare variables of those types.

The A class has a default-access constructor too and maintains a field of type B that it initializes in its constructor:

```
package essentials.ch08;

public final class A {
    private B b;

    A() {
        System.out.println("A object made");
        b  = new B();
    }
}
$ javac -d . A.java
$
```

The last thing I'll add to this package is a Program class with a public constructor. When called, it will construct a C object, just to demonstrate access. It also supports a makeA() method to return an A object back to any caller:

```
package essentials.ch08;

public final class Program {
    public Program() {
        System.out.println("Program object made");
        // just to show C is accessible
        C c = new C();
    }

    public A makeA() {
        return new A();
    }
}
$ javac -d . Program.java
$
```

Adding test code inside the package, by the way, is a good idea. Testing in increments and after each (substantive) change to code ensures that you're making progress and not introducing bugs to tested code. I am again streamlining that process here to stay on point. Each class you write, however, would not suffer from a `main()` method that tests the class elements. It takes longer, but the exercise also teaches you that the compiler covers only so much territory. It's fine for testing correct language use. It is inadequate for testing correct program operation.

A bug that is added to working code is called a *regression*. Testing one class at a time is called *unit testing*.

Nonetheless, I'll skip directly to the external test. I need a program in another package to construct a `Program` object and get an `A` object from it. I should also do something to prove I'm getting a live `A` object and not a `null` value.

Just before looking at code, however, I want to make sure I understand the sequence of events. It's hard and error prone to form a mental picture over several files of source code. A UML *sequence diagram* gives you a way to map the expected action. Vertical bars show the lifetime of each instance; arrows show who's calling who and who is returning what to whom. The timeline flows from top to bottom.

Figure 8.2 is a sequence diagram that specifies how a `TestProgram` class should interact with the objects in the `essentials.ch08` package.

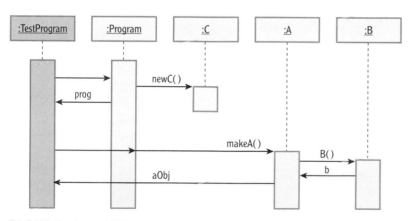

FIGURE 8.2 UML sequence diagram with the `TestProgram` class

Take a moment to see if this diagram squares with your impression of the source code shown so far. Now all that remains is to write the `TestProgram` class and see if it all works out! The `TestProgram` code is shown in Listing 8.2.

LISTING 8.2: TestProgram class code, compilation, and execution

```
package essentials.ch08.test;

import essentials.ch08.Program;
import essentials.ch08.A;

public final class TestProgram {
    public static void main(String args[]) {
        System.out.println("Testing essentials.ch08.Program\n");
        Program prog = new Program();
        A aObj = prog.makeA();
        // Prove it's an actual object
        System.out.println("A object: " + aObj);
    }
}

$ javac -d . TestProgram.java
$ java -cp . essentials.ch08.test.TestProgram
Testing essentials.ch08.Program

Program object made
C object made
A object made
B object made
A object: essentials.ch08.A@1715510
```

This program confirms our expectations. The output shows objects made from the classes C, A, and B, in respective order, and the TestProgram class receives an A object it can operate on. Now I need to show that the TestA program, specified in Figure 8.1, *doesn't* work. If it does, it means package access doesn't work as advertised. Or it means my code didn't implement it properly, which is more plausible:

```
package essentials.ch08.test;

import essentials.ch08.A;

public final class TestA {
    public static void main(String args[]) {
        // can I construct A myself?
        A a = new A();
    }
}
```

```
$ javac -d . TestA.java
TestA.java:8: error: A() is not public in A;
    cannot be accessed from outside package
      A a = new A();
            ^
1 error
```

Whew! I've successfully constructed an arrangement of classes whereby the Program class can construct default-access classes in its package and return them to a class outside the package. If you have followed along, you have taken your first step in package-level encapsulation: You've seen how it works and reviewed a minimal testing process to prove it does something useful.

Refer back to Figure 8.2 for a moment. The order in which I invoked these classes amounts to special knowledge, that is, some information that matters to the way the code runs but isn't apparent from the method interface. A programmer who deduces a simple solution to a problem, particularly after a bit of trial and error, can fool themselves into thinking the solution was evident all along, and decide it's redundant to document it. Much worse, they can imagine it doesn't or shouldn't matter. That thinking is an unsurprising consequence of spending a long time getting the code to work. When you have to maintain that code or track down a bug in it, existing tests and diagrams can save you lots of time and frustration sorting through the whole.

Writing a Proxy Construction Class

Let's say you have a package in which special knowledge is both more convoluted than our last example and not known to you. All you can see from documentation is that the classes exist. How do you convey this special knowledge to a caller from another package?

If you have a complex construction or other interactions inside a package, you can delegate that task to a specific class, which I'll call a *proxy*, and do the work on behalf of out-of-package callers.

Consider the following Helper class in a run package:

```
package essentials.ch08.run;

public final class Helper {
   Helper() {
      System.out.println("Hello there!");
   }
}
$ javac -d . Helper.java
```

As before, if you try to construct a `Helper` object from a class outside the package, like `essentials.ch08.test.HelperTest`, you'll get an error:

```
package essentials.ch08.test;

import essentials.ch08.run.Helper;

public final class HelperTest {
  public static void main(String args[]) {
    Helper help = new Helper();
  }
}
$ javac -d . HelperTest.java
HelperTest.java:7: error: Helper() is not public in Helper;
  cannot be accessed from outside package
        Helper help = new Helper();
                      ^
1 error
```

You can see the `Helper` class; you just can't access its constructor.

If you can add a class to the package that contains the `Helper` class, you're back in business. I'll write a `Proxy` class to create its own `Helper` referent and return its reference to any caller outside the package:

```
package essentials.ch08.run;

public final class Proxy {
    private Helper export = new Helper();

    public Helper getHelper() {
        return export;
    }
}
```

You can now write a `ProxyTest` program to create a `Proxy` object that can return a `Helper` reference. To demonstrate that it works, you need code similar to this:

```
package essentials.ch08.test;

import essentials.ch08.run.Proxy;
import essentials.ch08.run.Helper;

public final class ProxyTest {
    public static void main(String args[]) {
```

```
        Proxy proxy = new Proxy();
        Helper help = proxy.getHelper();
    }
}
$ javac -d . Proxy.java
$ javac -d . ProxyTest.java
$ java -cp . essentials.ch08.test.ProxyTest
Hello there!
```

The `System.out.println()` call in the `Helper` class just helps confirm that the constructor was called. You now have a technique for making one class a gatekeeper for access to another and distributing a single reference to all external callers.

A class inside the package can create multiple `Helper` objects with the default constructor.

A class like `Proxy` may also be used to manage a more complex object assembly process. It can encode so-called special knowledge into explicit program code. There are two benefits to realize. One, any callers to `Proxy` remain oblivious to any complexity. Two, and even better, you can document that special knowledge with code that makes such a process explicit. Hiding internal complexity by hiding constructors is a valuable service any package can perform.

You can use the class itself to limit its own construction. It may sound silly, but when you declare the available constructors `private`, you bar other classes from using them. The `ClosedToYall` program shows what you can (and can't) do with a `private` constructor:

```
package essentials.ch08.run;

public final class ClosedToYall {
    private ClosedToYall() {
        System.out.println("New object!");
    }

    public ClosedToYall tryMe() {
        return new ClosedToYou();
    }

    public static void main(String args[]) {
        ClosedToYall cty = new ClosedToYall();
    }
}
```

This `main()` method can construct a `ClosedToYou` object because it's a class member. Any method in the same class shares this access, but if it isn't also declared `static`, you'd need an object reference to call it. If you remove a constructor from view like this, you need some way to get to the class at all.

I used the main() method here simply because I have been using it for test code throughout the book.

You can write a separate method to invoke the constructor, return an existing object reference, or return null if that's appropriate:

```
public static ClosedToYall tryMe() {
    if ( /* the condition is right */) {
        return new ClosedToYall();
    return (ClosedToYall)null;
}
```

Requiring Parameters

Restricting access to a constructor is a useful way to manage object construction before it takes place. A constructor gives you only two options: It can return a reference to a new object, or it can throw an exception. If you want to validate the request—which seems likely if you're allowing parameters—you can either accept the incoming value or respond in a way that might terminate the program.

But let's say direct object construction is appropriate to your needs and you only want to refine its use for all callers. You could think of parameters as potential for trouble from callers that pass in values on a hit-or-miss basis. But if everyone's playing nice, or you have default values you can fall back on, using parameter lists is one way to communicate requirements to the caller.

Adding Parameters to Constructors

I covered the guidelines for parameter lists in the previous chapter. Here I'll outline particular uses for them with constructors.

Overriding Default Initialization

If you have a meaningful no-arg constructor, you can add constructors that accept parameters, and use them to set different initial states for a new object. Use the no-arg constructor for the default initial state, and use parameters to override that state.

The ArrayList class in the java.util package follows this model. It has three constructors:

```
ArrayList()
ArrayList(Collection <? extends E> c)
ArrayList(int initialCapacity)
```

The first example is its no-arg constructor. The second constructor takes a parameter that uses a Java facility called *generics*. In short, generic type definitions let the programmer constrain the type of objects used to populate the ArrayList without specifying the exact type. Generics definitions fall outside the scope of this book, but you'll see them often as you browse more Java APIs.

The third constructor lets the caller override the initialCapacity value of a default ArrayList object. You learned in Chapter 4, "Using Java Arrays," that an ArrayList object uses an array internally for its storage. If you need more room, the class will use the System.arraycopy() method to transfer its contents to a bigger array. The class itself encapsulates the resizing process so the caller doesn't have to manage it directly.

By letting the caller set initialCapacity, the ArrayList class gives a programmer the means to establish size on their own terms, potentially avoiding any behind-the-scenes array transfers.

To learn more about generics, you can start with the tutorial at http://docs.oracle.com/javase/tutorial/java/generics/.

Disallowing Default Construction

When the no-arg constructor is present, using parameters as overrides makes sense. If you remove the no-arg constructor, however, it implies that there is no meaningful default object state.

The wrapper classes—Boolean, Byte, Character, Double, Float, Integer, Long, and Short—all require parameters for their constructors. The Integer class has two:

```
public Integer(int value)
public Integer(String s)
```

The second constructor accepts a String object directly. You could pass an args value in a main() method directly to this constructor, assuming the String value is recognizable as a number. That way you don't have to perform the conversion yourself. For all these classes, a no-arg constructor isn't supplied; that defeats the purpose of wrapping a primitive value.

Or let's say you have a Contact class you use to track various people. For something like contact information, any combination of filled and empty fields might make sense, except all empty. It doesn't have to be a complicated class, as this example shows:

```
package essentials.ch08;

final class Contact {
    private String name;
    private String street;
```

```
    private String cityState;
    private String phone;
    private int ID;
    private String deptCode;

    // "disable" default constructor for now
    private Contact() {}

    // accessor methods ...
}
```

For a Contact object to make any sense, you need at least a name:

```
public Contact(String name)
```

But what if you had a more specific context you had to implement, like employee-appropriate contact information? If you're not careful, you might take the straightforward approach and modify the constructor to let a caller add more details, including department code and ID number:

```
public Contact(String name, String department, int ID)
```

This practice can go on *ad nauseam*. Requiring too many parameters can be just as bad as letting callers make objects they can't use. You also then have to guard each parameter against a null value or, worse, an empty object like the literal String "". You can anticipate type-appropriate garbage values, such as

```
Contact ctc = new Contact("", null, 0);
```

That means there's a lot of weeding out to do in the constructor.

A constructor *must* return a referent. A helper method, on the other hand, can weed out junk values and construct the object only when the caller passes in a useful value, as in this example:

```
public static Contact makeContact(String name, String dept, int ID) {
    //if the parameters are bad, return null, else...
    return new Contact(name, dept, ID);
}
```

Remember that such a method has to be declared static if you're going to declare the constructor private. Otherwise you'll have the chicken-and-egg problem I described earlier (that is, how to return an instance through a method when the class has a private constructor). You don't have to hide the constructor, but you probably don't want the caller to choose between these options.

With that in mind, you should design constructors that require parameters essential to constructing the object. Avoid constructors that implicitly accept null or empty objects. For the sake of illustration, here's one of the constructors for the GridBagConstraints class in the java.awt package:

```
public GridBagConstraints(int gridx, int gridy, int gridwidth,
    int gridheight, double weightx, double weighty, int anchor,
    int fill, Insets insets, int ipadx, int ipady)
```

Maybe once, sometime back in the 1990s, I used that constructor. Imagine if you had to read that line in a program and all the values were literals? You'd have to refer to the API and match each value to its meaning. It's not hard, but it's tedious and error prone. As a CircleMUD developer myself, even more years ago now, I occasionally saw functions written in C with more than a dozen parameters. Not fun.

The designer in this case could have reduced this list using some types, such as Grid, Weight and Pad classes. It might have looked like this:

```
public GridBagConstraints(Grid grid, Weight weight,
    int anchor, int fill, Insets insets, Pad pad)
```

Still, that doesn't remove the tedium. At best, this approach mitigates it. At worst, it replaces one kind of brain-dead work for another. If the parameter list forces callers to make two or more objects they can't use for anything else, it should be advertised as something like "expert mode"—that is, a constructor only someone with fine-grained control would use.

For the sake of comparison, here is the original constructor and my proposed remedy side by side:

```
GridBagConstraints gbc;
gbc = new GridBagContraints(0, 0, 0, 0, 0.0, 0.0, 0, 0, null, 0, 0);
Grid grid = new Grid(…);
Weight weight = new Weight(…);
Pad pad = new Pad(…);
Inset inset = new Inset(…);
gbc = new GridBagContraints(grid, weight, 0, 0, inset, pad);
```

Unless you find a way to avoid this interface altogether, you're stuck. To be fair, it was probably a consequence of prior design decisions made with the GridBag class that forced the developer's hand here.

Using Other Objects for Initialization

As you learn more about programming with objects, you will hear that classes should be *loosely coupled*. Each class should have as minimal a dependency on other classes as it can manage.

But tight coupling, so called, isn't a bad thing. In fact, it's unavoidable. The tightest possible coupling you can produce in Java is a *subclass*. You need subclasses. Without them, you can't create a *type system*, such as the Collections classes in the java.util package.

Looser coupling promotes easier reuse of individual classes. That's not always the goal, but it's good policy to prefer that in the absence of specific requirements. When you know you don't want that, don't worry about it. Just make sure you're consciously choosing against reusability.

Let's say you wanted to create an Employee class. Rather than define a Contact constructor to include employee details, which would introduce new fields into the type's state, you decide it's better to *compose* an Employee type to include Contact information. Your Employee constructor could look like this:

```
public Employee(Contact info, String department, int ID)
```

You're still telling the caller to create a Contact object in order to construct an Employee object, and some caller will try to get away with a null value. Still, if your Employee constructor requires a Contact object, enforce that rule.

You can be kind and make sure the object parameters you require aren't themselves difficult to create. If a caller can construct them on the fly, such as a literal String, then it's possible to streamline the call like this:

```
Employee emp = new Employee(new Contact("Michael E"), "Books", 28);
```

This technique is smarter than it looks. The calling class doesn't assign this String to a reference. Once we assign emp to null or another Employee referent, the String silently goes away with it.

Overloading Constructors

Certification Objective

You can also use overloaded constructors to support what I call *partial initialization*. With this technique, you provide a list of constructors that lets the caller provide as few (or as many) parameters as it has. It goes something like this:

```
public Employee(Contact ctc)
public Employee(Contact ctc, Department dept)
public Employee(Contact ctc, Department dept, Badge badge)
```

It's just like the form for overloaded methods I covered in the preceding chapter. The same rules apply: Varying the type, number, and order of parameters will give you distinct versions of the constructor. It is still a poor choice to change the parameters' order alone. Changing the type and number of parameters is a better way to communicate.

You can also use the varargs syntax to allow an indefinite number of parameters of one type:

```
public Employee(Contact ctc, Department dept, Overlord … bosses)
```

You can have one varargs element in a parameter list, and it must appear last. The compiler simply converts these arguments into an array, so you can apply a `for` or for-each statement directly to the parameter in the code body. The compiler will produce an empty array, *not* a `null` reference, if the caller supplies nothing.

For a complete view of the varargs syntax, see the discussion in Chapter 7, "Using Java Methods to Communicate."

With this approach, you allow the caller to provide the information it has. The caller should expect that one constructor choice is as good as another and that any parameters not addressed in the constructor of choice are managed underneath the covers.

Partial initialization isn't very different from the technique for overriding defaults. The appearance of multiple, telescoping constructors will simply suggest to callers that they have as much control over the process as they'd like.

Chaining Overloaded Constructors

As with overloaded methods, it's also good to centralize common code among overloaded constructors. Modifying and testing the code later is much easier to do when you know it's kept in one place.

There's one twist. Methods have their own namespace and, as it turns out, operate on a slightly different set of rules for overloading than constructors do. You can call one overloaded method from another:

```
public final class Overloaded {
    public void myMethod(int x) {
        myMethod();
    }

    public void myMethod() { }
}
$ javac Overloaded.java
$
```

You cannot do the same with constructors:

```
public final class Overloaded {
    public Overloaded(int ... values) {
        Overloaded();
    }
```

```
    public Overloaded() { }

}
$ javac Overloaded.java
Overloaded.java:7: error: cannot find symbol
          Overloaded();
              ^
  symbol:   method Overloaded()
  location: class Overloaded
1 error
```

Notice that the compiler complains that it cannot find the Overloaded()
method. Without a new keyword to signify construction, the compiler assumes
a method is the target. Adding the new keyword will call the constructor, but
the compiler assumes that I mean to create a second Overloaded object. See the
following example:

```
public final class Overloaded {
    public int [] stuff = { 4, 5, 6, 7 };

    public Overloaded(int ... values) {
        stuff = values;
        System.out.println("" + stuff[0]);
......// Won't work; calls for a new object
        new Overloaded();
    }

    public Overloaded() {
        System.out.println("" + stuff[0]);
    }

    public static void main(String args[]) {
        Overloaded ovl1 = new Overloaded(1,2,3);
        System.out.println("" + ovl1.stuff[0]);
    }
}
$ java Overloaded
1
4
1
```

In this version of the Overloaded class, I call the parameterized constructor
from the main() method. That constructor assigns its parameter to the stuff

array and calls the no-arg constructor with new. The no-arg constructor prints out the array's first element. I then print the same element in main() using the object reference.

The output makes it clear there are two objects. When the no-arg constructor is called with new, it reads the stuff array defined in the class, ignoring the caller-supplied parameters. Once the parameterized constructor returns, that object's state is lost. That's not the chaining effect I want.

The language provides a facility for chaining constructor calls using the invocation this(). Unlike a new call, which can occur anywhere in a method or constructor body, a this() call has to be the first statement of a constructor. Here's the same code, using this() to replace the new call:

```
public final class Overloaded {
    public int [] stuff = { 4, 5, 6, 7 };

    public Overloaded(int ... values) {
        this();
        stuff = values;
        System.out.println("" + stuff[0]);
        //new Overloaded();
    }

    public Overloaded() {
        System.out.println("" + stuff[0]);
    }

    public static void main(String args[]) {
        Overloaded ovl1 = new Overloaded(1,2,3);
        System.out.println("" + ovl1.stuff[0]);
    }
}
$ java Overloaded
4
1
1
```

The caller sees no difference—the value accessed through the object reference is still 1. Internally, however, the this() call will chain the constructors. Instead of sandwiching the no-arg constructor, I'm allowing it to execute first. Then I can override or complement that action as I see fit.

If you try to use a this() call anywhere but in the first statement of any constructor, the compiler complains.

Returning now to the `Employee` example that I showed earlier:

```
public Employee(Contact ctc)
public Employee(Contact ctc, Department dept)
public Employee(Contact ctc, Department dept, Badge badge)
```

I can use the `this()` call to chain them together so the constructor with the most parameters contains the logic:

```
this(ctc);
this(ctc, dept);
```

The constructor with the longest parameter list could chain to the second longest, passing along parameters the latter knows how to initialize, and then initialize the one parameter left. The code might look something like this:

```
public final class Employee {

    private Contact contact;
    private Department dept;
    private Badge badge;

    public Employee(Contact contact) {
        this.contact = contact;
    }

    public Employee(Contact ctc, Department dept) {
        this(ctc);
        this.dept = dept;
    }

    public Employee(Contact ctc, Department dept, Badge badge) {
        this(ctc, dept);
        this.badge = badge;
    }
}
```

It's a technique you don't want to take too far. When you have complex logic you don't want to cut and paste into multiple code bodies; however, it's a useful technique.

Coupling Objects with Constructors

If you must join two classes at the hip in your code, make the most of that relationship. If it makes sense to use one object as a parameter to another class's constructor, use the `this` keyword to do it.

Let's say your program creates a Contact object for the express purpose of making Employee, Manager, or Contractor objects. Instead of devising a Contact constructor to accept Employee details, you could provide a method that lets a Contact object pass itself to an Employee constructor:

```java
public final class Contact {

    private Employee emp;
    private String name;

    private Contact(String name) {
        this.name = name;
        // Use current object as a parameter
        emp = new Employee(this, "Unassigned", 63);
    }

    public static Contact makeContact(String name) {

        //
        if (name == null || name.equals(""))
            // Better to throw an exception but we don't
            // know how yet.
            return (Contact)null;
        return new Contact(name);
    }

    public boolean isEmployee() {
        return (emp != null);
    }
}
```

This version of the Contact class puts into play a number of the techniques I've described so far.

First, I provide a static method called makeContact() to return a null value if the String parameter I receive is a null or empty reference. Otherwise, the method calls the constructor and returns the new object to the caller.

The private constructor gets called only if the parameter information is good. Construction is a relatively expensive process, so catching spurious calls through a *factory method* like makeContact() helps ensure the process will return something useful.

The Contact constructor calls the Employee constructor and assigns the returned reference to the object's emp field. Once the Contact object itself is returned, the caller can use the isEmployee() method to verify its status.

You can return an empty Contact object from the makeContact() method, but that seems hostile.

In some Java frameworks you'll encounter, object construction is discouraged in favor of factory methods or similar techniques.

I'm illustrating a complex topic here, with both a small bit of code and a contrived case. In doing this, I have two goals in mind. One, I want to prepare you for questions on the Java Oracle Certified Associate (OCA) exam, which only requires that you know how constructors work. It does not require you to know how to work around their limits, as we've shown here.

My second goal is to prepare you beyond a mere recall knowledge of Java's features. Hiding constructors is a big deal in everyday practice. You need to know how to read Java code for meaning as well as validity, and you will encounter code that seems to push constructors out of sight whenever possible. You don't want to be the interviewee who says you've never seen such a thing. It's a sign that while you may know your basic Java, you aren't aware of a standard practice that has been in vogue for several years.

Creating a Singleton Object

When you *encapsulate* the constructor, you can decide when to call it and when to return a reference, either to a new object or to one you've already made. Say, for example, you wanted all callers to get a reference to the same object, like this:

```java
package essentials.c08;

public final class Singleton {
    private static Singleton ston;

    private Singleton() {
    }

    public synchronized static Singleton getInstance() {
        if (ston == null )
            ston = new Singleton();
        return ston;
    }
}
```

You could modify this code slightly to allow for a *pool* of referents too.

In any singleton class, a `getInstance()` method is usually the only visible member. When it's called, it will construct its object if and only if one hasn't been made already. Everyone who calls this method will share that referent in memory.

If there are a lot of callers, you also have to be more careful with these referents, particularly if they are *mutable*. I've added the `synchronized` keyword here to acknowledge one potential problem.

If there are two simultaneous callers to this constructor, it's *possible* that one of them gets partway through a method, then gets held up by the JVM. Then the JVM lets the other caller go all the way through. When the first caller is allowed to resume, if it's already past the `ston == null` check, it will then make another object, and you'll make another object. The `synchronized` keyword will keep that from happening.

If that's too much information for now, don't worry about it. It's beyond the scope of this book and the OCA exam. But I'd be remiss if I showed you an incomplete singleton technique.

THE ESSENTIALS AND BEYOND

In this chapter, you learned the basics of Java class constructors—and quite a bit more. I described what a default constructor is and the compiler's rules for defining it. I also described reasons and use cases for adding alternate constructors to a class and how a caller can interpret your intentions based on the ones you supply. I also covered some common defensive strategies that are used with constructors, including proxy, factory, and singleton techniques, which mitigate some of the consequences of keeping your constructors public.

ADDITIONAL EXERCISES

1. Write two classes, Push and Pull. Give each one a `main()` method that prints out the name of the containing class. Call the `main()` method in one class from the other class's `main()` method.

2. Write a ThreeParts class that creates three instances of itself. Supply the methods `first()`, `second()`, and `third()` and declare them `static`. Make each method return one of the three instances.

3. Test a parameterized constructor from the classes `ArrayList`, `StringBuilder`, and `Date`. Use negative numbers, `null` references, or empty objects, as appropriate, and observe the response you get from each.

4. The `Integer.valueOf()` method is a factory method: You give it a primitive integer, it returns an `Integer` object containing that value. Give it the number 7 as a parameter, but make two `Integer` objects with it. Make a third `Integer` object with the value −20. Will the objects be equal? What kind of equality do you get, if any? How can you demonstrate it?

(Continues)

THE ESSENTIALS AND BEYOND *(Continued)*

REVIEW QUESTIONS

1. Which statement applies exclusively to the default constructor?

   A. It has no return type.

   B. It has the same name as its class.

   C. It is `public`.

   D. It is written by the compiler.

2. Which modifier(s) may not be applied to a constructor? (Choose all that apply.)

   A. `static`

   B. `synchronized`

   C. `protected`

   D. `native`

3. True or false: You must include a default constructor in the code if the compiler does not include one.

4. What does the keyword `this` refer to?

   A. The current class

   B. The current object

   C. The current method

   D. The current constructor

5. True or false: You can call the default constructor written by the compiler using `this()`.

6. What can a constructor do that a method can't do?

   A. Return an object reference

   B. Call a constructor using `this()`

   C. Allocate memory

   D. Use overloading

(Continues)

7. Which statement correctly describes a property or limitation of object construction?

    A. You can use the new keyword in any method or constructor.

    B. You can use this() as the first statement in any method or constructor.

    C. You cannot use the new keyword with a private constructor unless there is at least one method declared static.

    D. All you need to construct an object from another package is a constructor declared public.

8. True or false: You can access a private constructor with a main() method.

9. Declaring a constructor private but allowing it to be accessed through a static method is an example of which of the following?

    A. Coupling

    B. Encapsulation

    C. Factoring

    D. Proxying

10. Who can call a default-access constructor? (Choose all that apply.)

    A. Any class that resides in the same package

    B. Any class that imports the same packages

    C. Any class that resides in the same file

    D. Any main() method that constructs the class

Inheriting Code and Data in Java

You've come a long way already in this book. In this chapter and the next two, you get the payoff: learning how to inherit code, create so-called *pure types*, and examine a *type system*. As I cover each of these topics, you'll get your first look at moving from writing programs that happen to be Java classes to writing classes that can be used to build multiple programs.

It's a challenging step to move from writing code you need right now to writing code you can reuse. It is a practice that takes time to master. You'll start in this chapter by understanding how you can extend code that's already been written.

In this chapter, I'll cover the following topics:

▶ **Extending a class**

▶ **Using the super keyword**

▶ **Overriding a method**

▶ **Casting objects**

▶ **Implementing polymorphic behavior**

Extending a Class

Certification Objective

Ten to 15 years ago, the author of a Java primer would probably have made a big splash over the benefits of inheriting code—best thing since sliced bread and all that. Say you happen across a complicated but useful class. You want to build on it, but also keep the existing code intact. In Java, all you have to do is apply the extends keyword, like this:

```
public final class MyAction extends Thread {
    // add your program code here
}
```

The Thread class lives in the java .lang package.

When you use the keyword `extends` and name a Java class like `Thread`, the `MyAction` class *becomes* a version of the `Thread` class. In that sense, your average author from long ago could then exclaim how powerful a feature inheritance is—using the word *power*, in this case, as a synonym for *convenience*. By creating objects of type `MyAction`, you can invoke any visible method the `Thread` class contains as if it belongs to the subclass, which it does.

This property of the language is a powerful lure. Most people are tempted (and taught) to apply it well before they understand all the trade-offs of its use, and while those trade-offs do not foretell the death of any program, they do not go away easily either. In this chapter, then, I will focus on when and when not to use inheritance. It does you no good to learn about the problems you can create for yourself after you've written an important program. Years of practice have taught us all that thinking "inheritance first" can create as many problems as it's been used to solve.

Understanding What Inheritance Provides

What does inheritance give you? For one, it makes all the accessible members of the *parent class* available to the *child class*. This set includes all fields and methods declared `public` or `protected`. If the child class resides in the same package as the parent, it will also see the parent's default-access members.

A subclass does *not* inherit, nor does it have any special access to, the `private` members of the parent class. It also does not inherit methods and fields that are declared `static`, but the reasons why are different. Members that are declared `private` are internal elements of a class, available only to objects of that kind. A `static` member can be made accessible to anyone, but it is rooted in the class that declared it.

It seems like you could emulate inheritance, if you wanted to, by wrapping every available method of a class that you declared as a field. For example, if the `MyAction` class declared a `Thread` member instead of extending the class, it could include a `run()` method that simply calls the `run()` method of the `Thread` field, like this:

```
public final class MyAction {
    private Thread thr = new Thread();
    public void run() {
        thr.run();
    }
```

```
    public void start() {
       thr.start();
    }
    // wrap remaining methods of Thread
}
```

This MyAction class uses a thr reference to invoke the Thread class's run() and start() methods. I could go on to wrap every other accessible method, but even if I did, this version of the MyAction class wouldn't work quite the same as a Thread subclass. It's that difference I want you to learn from this chapter.

First, there is a difference in access rights. The protected keyword provides default access that also includes subclasses in other packages. If you want to wrap a number of methods from a class in a different package, you won't have access to any methods that are declared protected. If you extend that same class, access to all protected methods is included. You may have wondered, "Why bother?" when you first came across the protected keyword, but without it, a parent class cannot share its members with subclasses outside its package.

Second, when you extend the Thread class, the compiler and the JVM can infer its type as a part of the MyAction class. With a wrapping technique, you can hide (or encapsulate) one class's relationship to other classes. Two wrapper classes can have exactly the same data and methods, and the compiler will never assume they are related. A class that extends the Thread class, however, is always that type of object. That means if you have a method that requires a Thread parameter, you can pass it a MyAction object instead, and the compiler will always accept it.

This distinction in relationships is important enough that you will diagram the two in different ways. Figure 9.1 illustrates an *inheritance* relationship on the left and a *composition* relationship on the right.

The run() method in the Thread class has no code, so it won't do anything observable if you call it.

You can also refer to inheritance as an *is-a* relationship and composition as a *has-a* relationship.

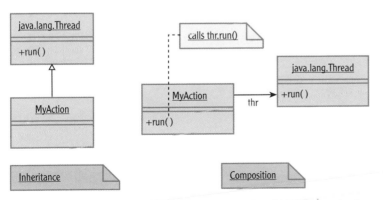

FIGURE 9.1 Extending and incorporating the Thread class in the MyAction class

In the Unified Modeling Language (UML), an unfilled arrowhead with a solid line pointing from one class to another, implies inheritance. The pointing class captures the attributes of the pointed-to class. In UML terms, the pointing class, which we call a child, *specializes* the one we call a parent. Unfortunately for beginners, UML defines this relationship from the bottom up and instead calls it a generalization. That is, the child class is generalized by its parent. Since UML is concerned with code modeling, not implementation, it describes class relationships in terms that favor a designer's point of view.

Extending the Parent Class

Once you add code and data to a new subclass, you apply the full meaning of extending the parent. In composition, you add code and data to create a new class that is specific to your needs. When you extend a class, you're doing the same thing but with a specific type for a base. In this example, we're creating a type that *specializes* the Thread class.

Specializing simply means that you add members to the MyAction class to further refine or elaborate on its Thread capability. If you decide a MyAction class should walk as well as run, you can just add a method called walk():

```
public final class MyAction extends Thread {
    public void walk() {
        // "walk" the code instead of running it
    }
}
```

This is a purely figurative example, of course. The run() method in the Thread class doesn't do anything "fast," it just executes code that's been supplied to it. But the idea of adding fields and methods to a subclass is important. When you add new operations to a child class, you express how it differs from its parent and expresses a new type.

Some subclasses don't do this at all, opting instead to *change the behavior* provided by the parent class. This is done by *overriding* one or more parent methods. It's loosely similar to method overloading. In method overloading, you change the parameter list of an existing method to supply an alternate version of it. In overriding, a child class overrides an inherited method by duplicating its method name and parameter list, then changing the code. I'll review method overriding in detail later in this chapter.

Removing the *final* Keyword

When you define a class with the final modifier, you declare it ineligible for subclassing. Remove the modifier, recompile the code, and voilà! You can then use the extends keyword and inherit from that class. I've used this modifier since Chapter 2, "Applying Data Types in Java Programming," to signify that the classes I've written aren't intended as parent types. It doesn't mean they're unsafe, or ineligible, or somehow incomplete. It's my way of saying that a class shouldn't allow inheritance unless it has been designed to support it. The absence of the final keyword, in my view, should signal that it's *safe*, not just legal, to inherit from the class at hand. If you leave the final modifier off of your class declarations, I'd go further and say you're *promoting* your class as a parent type. Inheritance is such a powerful facility that, if I had designed the language, I'd have made it necessary to declare a class eligible as a parent.

Here's one reason why: A subclass can't access any parent class private member, including constructors. That means inheritance isn't absolute; it relies on exposing at least one constructor to its subclasses. You can therefore break an existing child class just by changing visibility in the parent class. The simplest example of this condition looks like this:

```
public class Parent {
    public Parent() {}
}
final class Child extends Parent { }
```

This Parent class is just a shell that the Child class extends. Let's say, for the sake of illustration, that you're using both classes in some program. For some reason, you decide the access modifier of the Parent() constructor should be private. Then you recompile the Parent class. Then you try to compile the Child class and find out it won't.

You had a working Child class, you didn't touch it, and now it's broken. It won't help, by the way, to avoid recompiling the Child class; you'll just see the problem at runtime instead of compile time. What happened? The error message ("Parent() has private access in Parent") won't help unless you already know what's going on. The short answer is that a subclass depends on its parent class for construction. You cannot *encapsulate* the Parent class in a way that protects the Child class from such changes.

This outcome illustrates one reason for using the final modifier. You can use it to mean, as I usually do, that the class members are not yet stable enough that making subclasses will be safe.

Observing the Equality Contract

A less obvious reason for using the final keyword has to do with what's called the *equality contract*, which is related to the semantic difference between the == operator and the equals() method.

In Chapter 3, "Using Java Operators and Conditional Logic," you learned that the equals() method in the Object class wraps the == operator. You also learned that subclasses like String alter this method to provide a more permissive test, one that compares the content of two String referents. The strict test, whether two references point to the same referent, is the strictest possible case for that test.

To change a method in a subclass, you have to *override* it. You'll learn how to do that later in this chapter. Changing the equals() method is just one step. As the documentation will tell you, there are five requirements you should observe if you want to change the way equality works for your class. And while it's always safe to leave the equals() method as it is, it's usually too strict to be useful.

A non-final class that changes the equals() method but doesn't observe the remaining criteria might be brittle. Its subclasses will inherit that brittleness without knowing about it and will assume that the equals() method is both reliable and useful. And that's another reason to use the final keyword: to signify that a class does not fulfill the equality contract and probably shouldn't be subclassed until it does.

It's worth noting there are several benefits in using the final modifier too. For one, the compiler can convert a final class to bytecode in a way that improves its performance traits over non-final classes. You should not expect another programmer to infer your intentions when using this modifier. Take time to add comments to your code and remove any doubts.

> The rules for over-riding the equals() method are documented at http:// docs.oracle .com/javase/7/ docs/api/java/ lang/Object .html#equals(java .lang.Object).

Observing Java's Single Inheritance Rule

There's one more thing to consider when choosing inheritance or composition to implement a new class. Java lets you inherit from one parent class only. Every class in Java has only one direct is-a relationship.

Languages like C++ allow programmers to inherit from multiple classes as they see fit. Like any powerful feature in any language, multiple inheritance is easy to misuse if you don't think through its consequences before you apply it. Java's designers felt the potential harm of this feature outweighed its benefits and chose to disallow it.

If you do choose to extend another class, know that you are fixing the ancestry of the new class to its parent *and* its super-parents, if any. A new class will always inherit something from the Object class, but the most important relationship should be with its most immediate parent.

Ask yourself if a class you want to extend fulfills all of the following criteria:

- ▶ It implements the equality contract.

- ▶ It provides one or more methods that will save the subclass a lot of work.

- ▶ You will add to or modify the inherited code and data to specialize its operations.

If all of these tenets hold, you can justify inheritance over composition. If they don't, ask yourself if you're just counting on inheritance to save you time. This convenience always seems attractive in the early stages of writing a program but often loses its charm once the first few problems with coordinating your objects set in. When in doubt, remember that it's usually easier to change your mind and switch to subclassing than it is to switch to composition.

Understanding How Inheritance Works

Every class in Java inherits from the Object class, but how is that enforced? How can you observe the relationship between a class and the Object class? More to the point, how can you observe the relationship between any class and its parent class or subclasses?

In Java, it's the constructor that manages this relationship. Every time you write a new Java class, the compiler tests whether you may inherit from the parent you have claimed. It does this by ensuring that each constructor can call a valid constructor in the parent class. You can demonstrate this linkage by making the parent constructor do something observable, as shown in Listing 9.1.

LISTING 9.1: Demonstrating inheritance among three related classes

```
public class Grandparent {
   public Grandparent() {
      System.err.println("Construct Grandparent");
   }
}

class Parent extends Grandparent {
   public Parent() {
      System.err.println("Construct Parent");
   }
}
```

(Continues)

LISTING 9.1: Demonstrating inheritance among three related classes *(Continued)*

```java
final class Child extends Parent {
    public Child() {
        System.err.println("Construct Child");
    }

    public static void main(String args[]) {
        // Create one Child object; the rest
      // takes care of itself.
        Child ch = new Child();
    }
}
$ javac Grandparent.java
$ ls *class
Child.class    Grandparent.class    Parent.class
$ java Child
Construct Grandparent
Construct Parent
Construct Child
```

Notice in Listing 9.1 that each class inherits from the class before it. To allow this, I removed the final keyword from the Grandparent and Parent class definitions. I also added to each class a no-arg constructor that will print a message when it's called. The Child class contains a main() method that constructs only a Child object.

The output shows that before the Child object is constructed, a Parent object is constructed, and before that, a Grandparent object is constructed. If you could modify the Object class code to follow suit, you'd see its output first. Thus the construction of any object *requires* the construction of its parent objects first.

In one sense, this process demonstrates that a Child class is a Parent type, which is a Grandparent type (which is an Object type). It also shows that an accessible constructor is essential to permitting inheritance. In another sense, it explains why a variable of any parent type can refer to a Child referent.

Although it confuses our terms to say a Child class is composed of its parent classes, technically it's not that far off the mark. Composition and inheritance are not opposing techniques in Java, although they are often presented as such. They are complementary techniques—two ways of achieving the same goal, which is to reuse existing code.

The parent-first construction model suggests that inheritance occurs by layering new class members on top of the ones declared by parent classes. The compiler and JVM validate and construct the parent classes first. When they arrive at the Child class, they can then ascertain if that class either reuses or *overrides* the inherited members. I will expand on that point later in the chapter, in the section "Overriding a Method."

Listing 9.2 shows how one class can defeat subclassing without using the final keyword.

LISTING 9.2: A broken inheritance relationship

```
public class Paternity {
    public Paternity() {}
}

class Parent extends Paternity {
    public Parent(int xy) {}
}

class Child extends Parent {}

class Lab {
    Parent sample = new Parent(25);
}
$ javac Paternity.java
Paternity.java:11: error: constructor Parent in class Parent
    cannot be applied to given types;
class Child extends Parent {}
^
    required: int
    found: no arguments
    reason: actual and formal argument lists differ in length
1 error
```

In Listing 9.2, the Paternity class has one no-arg constructor. The Parent class subclasses Paternity and supplies a constructor that requires an integer. The Child class extends Parent. The Lab class declares and constructs a Parent member.

The Lab class, which constructs a Parent instance, appears to work fine. The Child class throws an error. The output is trying to tell us the Child constructor must also provide an integer. The chain of inheritance breaks because the Child class does not adhere to the same rules as any class that, like the Lab class, passes the Parent class what it needs to construct.

There are only two ways to manage this problem. You can remove the extends declaration from the Child class and use composition with the Parent class, just as the Lab class does. Or, you can pass a parameter to the Parent class through a Child constructor. If only you knew how.

Using the *super* Keyword

Certification Objective

When you use the final keyword, you intend to prevent inheritance. If you're not careful, requiring parameters in a parent class's constructor can have the same effect. Now that you know Java uses constructors to confirm inheritance, you need a way to pass information through them from any subclass to its parent class. The super keyword, treated as a constructor call, supports this need.

Passing Parameters to a Parent Constructor

Does the constructor linkage I described in the preceding section seem like a bit of magic? It's not anything of the sort. It's just another bit of behind-the-scenes work in Java. The compiler happens to inserts a super() call in every constructor. You won't see it in source code, but if you learn to read the bytecode a compiler produces, you will. It is always the first call made in a constructor's statement body. Like other implicit class elements in Java, you're not required to include it, but you can. The compiler won't like it only if you try to move it around, however, as shown in Listing 9.3.

LISTING 9.3: Using the super() call in a constructor

```
public class NewParent {
}

class GoodChild extends NewParent {
   public GoodChild() {
      super();
      int x = 1;
   }
}

class BadChild extends NewParent {
   public BadChild() {
      int x = 1;
      super();
   }
}
$ javac NewParent.java
NewParent.java:14: error: call to super must be first statement
   in constructor
```

LISTING 9.3: Using the `super()` call in a constructor *(Continued)*

```
        super();
            ^
    1 error
```

In Listing 9.3, the GoodChild and BadChild classes each extend the NewParent class. Their constructors do the same work but in different order. The compiler's error message is plain enough; we can trace the line number (14) back to the use of super() in the BadChild class. The GoodChild class shows we can make the call explicit so long as it adheres to the rule.

The super() invocation calls the no-arg constructor in the NewParent class, whether it's supplied by the compiler or the programmer. If a parameter is required by the parent class, making the call explicit wouldn't help; you would also have to supply parameters just as you would with a method.

If you rewrite the Child class in Listing 9.2 with this advice in mind, you can compile it without complaint. Here's the new version of that Child class and the results of compilation:

```
class Child extends Parent {
    public Child() {
        super(0);
    }
}
$ javac Paternity.java
$
```

As always, the compiler doesn't know or care if the value you supply is meaningful to the parent class. It only cares that the value's type passes legal muster.

Choosing a Parent Constructor

If a parent class has multiple constructors, each subclass can use the appropriate super() call to select the constructor it wants to use. It's just like calling a specific constructor using the new keyword and the correct parameters. Listing 9.4 shows an Option class with overloaded constructors and subclasses that use different ones.

LISTING 9.4: Class with multiple constructors and subclasses

```
public class Options {
    private String str = "default";

    public Options() {}
```

(Continues)

LISTING 9.4: Class with multiple constructors and subclasses *(Continued)*

```java
        public Options(String str) {
            this.str = str;
        }

        public Options(char [] chars) {
            this.str = new String(chars);
        }
    }

    class Default extends Options {}

    class OptionB extends Options {
        public OptionB() {
            super("OptionB");
        }
    }

    class OptionC extends Options {
        private static char[] name =
            { 'O', 'p', 't', 'i', 'o', 'n', 'C' };

        public OptionC() {
            super(name);
        }
    }
```

The `Options` class has three constructors. Their net result is to assign the member `str` the value `"default"` unless a `String` or character array parameter is passed in. The `Default` class uses the no-arg constructor, while the `OptionB` and `OptionC` classes pass in the text of their class names using different types.

You can use overloaded constructors to spare the caller the effort of converting their data to a type required by one constructor. There may be other good cases as well. A class that varies its constructors' behavior with different parameters is still a bad idea, just as it is with overloaded methods.

Overriding a Method

Certification
Objective

In Chapter 7, "Using Java Methods to Communicate," you learned the rules of overloading. You can write the same method (or constructor) with different parameter lists, giving the caller more flexible ways to communicate. Allowing for multiple parameter types is one reason to support overloading, but you might also want to let the caller provide varying amounts of information. I didn't show this second case with the constructor example earlier, but it works the same way as it would with methods.

Method overriding is similar in appearance to overloading, but its action and purpose are quite different. On first view, it appears to have the same effect as wrapping a method call from another class, as shown in Listing 9.5.

LISTING 9.5: Wrapping a String class method

```
public final class StringWrap {
    private String str = "wrapper";

    public String toUpperCase() {
        return str.toUpperCase();
    }

      public static void main(String args[]) {
        StringWrap sw = new StringWrap();
        System.out.println(sw.toUpperCase());
          }
}

$ javac StringWrap.java
$ java StringWrap
WRAPPER
```

In the StringWrap class, I duplicated the signature of the String.toUpperCase() method and wrapped a call to it, passing its work off as my own. I could also have decorated its behavior with additional logic or even changed it altogether. Whatever I do, I want my toUpperCase() method to look the same. I want it to be familiar to programmers who know the String class, and I want them to have similar expectations for using this method.

In a subclass, you only have to redeclare a member you inherited. The compiler silently *overrides* or replaces the inherited member from the parent class with your version. It doesn't matter which parent class the method appears in, but you will override the one in the most immediate parent class. Overriding is how you change the behavior of the equals() method in the Object class or any other member along the way.

There are a couple rules to follow, some required and some that are just good advice. For one, *you must match the signature of the inherited method*. If you

Most member variables are encapsulated, so they aren't visible to subclasses.

don't—if you get the parameter list wrong, for example—you will overload the method instead. There's no rule that says you have to overload a method in the same class. There's nothing wrong with overloading an inherited method, but it can be a frustrating thing to track down.

Also, *you may not restrict the visibility of an inherited method*. That is, you cannot override an inherited `public` method and declare it to have `protected`, default, or `private` access. The compiler will not interpret this modifier change as an attempt at overloading; it will simply reject it. You can, however, change the visibility from a more restrictive to a more open modifier.

> **This visibility rule does *not* apply to member variables.**

Using the *@Override* Annotation

There is a third rule that isn't required but goes a long way to clarifying your code: *Use the @Override annotation*. The compiler accepts correct method over-riding and overloading silently, so it's not necessarily clear which technique you've applied, as shown in Listing 9.6.

LISTING 9.6: Mistaking method overloading for method overriding

```java
public class MyMethod {
    String str = "Philadephia";
    public void engage(String str) {
        System.out.println(str);
    }
}

final class Override extends MyMethod {
    // @Override
    public String engage() {
        return this.str;
    }

    public static void main(String args[]) {
        Override sc = new Override();
        // the method you intended to override:
        // sc.engage("Philadephia");
        System.out.println(sc.engage());
    }
}
$ javac MyMethod.java
$ java Override
Philadephia
```

The MyMethod class has an engage() method that accepts a String parameter to print. The Override class also has an engage() method, but it returns a reference to the String variable it inherited from the MyMethod class.

For the sake of argument, let's say the MyMethod class is located in a different file. It's late and you're tired. You're pretty sure you remember the engage() method's signature, so you write the Override class as a test and persuade yourself from the output that your version of the engage() method is an override. You call it a day, and maybe a couple days later you pick up where you left off.

It could be a long time before you figure out you've actually overloaded the engage() method instead of overriding it. If you forget why you wrote the Override class to begin with, it would be hard to deduce that your output was a fluke, aided by an object field you normally would not make visible.

Of course you could cut through the problem by looking up the MyMethod class code and seeing your mistake. It would be quicker, however, just to apply the @Override annotation to the failed override and let the compiler tell you what's up. If you uncomment that line in Listing 9.6, you'll see this output:

```
$ javac MyMethod.java
MyOverride.java:9: error: method does not override or
    implement a method from a supertype
    @Override
    ^
1 error
```

Apply this annotation any time you want to override a method and you will turn the compiler's gift for complaining to your advantage.

Modifying or Replacing an Inherited Method

Sometimes you only want to add to the code you receive from a parent method. Or, possibly, there are cases in which a parent's method code is more appropriate than yours. In either event, you can use the super keyword as an object reference to the parent implementation. Listing 9.7 shows code that will use the Object class's toString() method if a user passes the null value to the constructor.

LISTING 9.7: Using the super keyword to access a parent method

```
public final class SuperTest {
    private String str;

    public SuperTest(String str) {
        this.str = str;
```
(Continues)

LISTING 9.7: Using the super keyword to access a parent method *(Continued)*

```java
        }

        @Override
        public String toString() {
            if (this.str == null) {
                System.err.print("Null value: called Object.
toString(): ");
                return super.toString();
            }
            return this.str;
        }

        public static void main(String args[]) {
            SuperTest sm1 = new SuperTest(null);
            SuperTest sm2 = new SuperTest("");
            SuperTest sm3 = new SuperTest("hello");
            System.out.println(sm1);
            System.out.println(sm2);
            System.out.println(sm3);
        }
    }
$ javac SuperTest.java
$ java SuperTest
Null value: called Object.toString(): SuperTest@437dcb

hello
```

> **Remember, there is a difference between a reference that points to an empty object and a reference that points to null.**

The toString() method in the SuperTest class tests the member variable str. If it is equal to null, the method calls the parent version of the toString() method. Otherwise it returns the value of its member variable. I also added a System.err.print() method to explain what caused the call to the parent method.

> **It's good advice to override the toString() method in all cases. Almost anything is better than the Object class's implementation.**

You *can't* call the parent's parent method using this technique (or any other in Java). Just as in real life, sometimes the methods your parent class has don't look as good as the ones it inherited. Still, there's no way around your immediate parent. In the Java language, this relationship is a condition your subclass must observe, not a problem it can solve.

To completely replace a method you've inherited, just redeclare it and write your own logic. The compiler requires your override to observe only the parameters and return type supplied. Although it does not enforce the meaning or the effect originally intended by the method, it's expected that you won't deviate from what other programmers expect the method to achieve. It's your obligation to support those expectations.

This requirement may sound like an obvious bit of wisdom. However, in an object-oriented language, *naming matters*. Names convey semantic meaning. If you pick good names and remain consistent with their interpretation, a calling programmer can learn those meanings and apply them to any number of related classes without researching them for each case.

If you preserve these meanings well as you go about implementing methods, you can achieve what's called a *polymorphic effect* among your related classes. This effect is a very big deal when it's done well. I'll address the basics of polymorphic effect in the final section of this chapter.

Prohibiting Method Overrides

Maybe your method logic has been implemented to perfection for all time and satisfies all cases in the known universe. Or maybe its operation depends completely on the object state of its host class, so much so that it would break in strange ways if it were overridden. Whatever the case might be, you sometimes have to protect certain methods from change. You have three options, each with differing effects.

Reduce your method's visibility. You can make a method visible only to its class, only to its package, or only to its package and subclasses, whichever makes sense. This approach limits the range of subclasses that can modify it. This approach prohibits overriding only in the sense of making the parent method logic inaccessible outside the scope you allow.

If a subclass declares a method that has the same signature as a parent's `private` method, the compiler *will* allow it. It's not an override, however; the parent method is still inaccessible. It's a consequence of the rules for each class's namespace. The names of `private` members in a parent class are not restricted from any subclass's namespace.

Associate your method with its class. If you declare a method `static`, the method is bound to its host class and cannot be inherited. If the method is designed to behave like a function—a method that returns some result but does not affect object state—using the `static` modifier is a good choice. If the method is supposed to change object state, using the `static` modifier defeats that purpose.

The `static` members of a class load before objects can be constructed and therefore cannot refer to them.

If a subclass declares a method with the same signature as a parent's `static` method, minus the modifier, the compiler will not allow it. An accessible `static` method in the parent class does affect the namespace of the subclass. This approach prohibits overriding by way of visibility. The parent method is bound to its class but it is not hidden. You cannot override a `static` method in a subclass.

Declare your method closed to overriding. Finally, you can just apply the `final` modifier to a method, even if its class is declared `final` too. If you want to open a class to inheritance but protect certain methods from overriding, declare those methods `final`. It is the clearest, most direct approach and has no strange conditions or side effects. Unlike the first two options, declaring a method `final` renders the method name off limits to all subclasses for all cases.

Casting Objects

Certification Objective

In Listing 9.1, I showed an inheritance relationship among the `Grandparent`, `Parent`, and `Child` classes. The code demonstrates how the order of construction plays a role in forming any new referent. It's as if the parent referents provide a core on which the child referents rely, as shown in Figure 9.2.

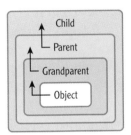

FIGURE 9.2
Conceptual view of a
subclassed referent

In a real sense, all four of these types shown occupy the area in memory that stores the referent. You can demonstrate this idea by using any parent type to refer to the actual object. Modify the `main()` method in Listing 9.1 as shown here:

```
public static void main(String args[]) {
    Child ch = new Child();
    Parent pt = ch;
    Grandparent gp = ch;
    Object ob = ch;
}
```

In this example there is one `Child` referent in memory associated with four different reference types. This method will compile, indicating all these types are legal references to a `Child` referent. It does *not* mean an `Object` reference can invoke a method that has been defined by a subclass. The `Object` reference only understands its own class interface. What the Object reference can access are the Object-specific attributes of the referent, which I will now start calling a *concrete referent*.

The same holds true for the Grandparent and Parent references. What they can see of the concrete referent is restricted to their own interfaces, including the ones they have inherited.

You can also construct a new concrete referent with a parent reference:

```
public static void main(String args[]) {
    Child ch = new Child();
    Parent pt = new Child();
    Grandparent gp = new Child();
    Object ob = new Child();
}
```

In this example I assigned a new Child referent to each reference type. Other than being different instances, these referents are all the same. What's different is the access you have to each one, which is now limited by the reference type as well as accessibility modifiers.

Why would you want to do this? More to the point, why would the Java language promote this kind of flexibility? One answer is that subclasses let us specialize the state and behavior of an existing class, but we still need the ability to address many specific classes in one general way. In Java, you can do that by addressing an object by any type it has inherited.

With that in mind, you're going to need two operations to help you keep your references and their referents straight. You need a way to test whether a referent conforms to a specific type. The instanceof operator provides that test. You also will need a way to assign a more specific reference to an existing referent. The casting operator provides that service.

To *cast* an object, you provide the name of a class in parentheses next to an expression that evaluates to an object referent, like this:

```
Child ch2 = (Child)pt;
Child ch3 = (Child)gp;
Child ch4 = (Child)ob;
```

Here I've cast each of the references from the previous code snippet to the Child class, then assigned the results to Child references. Casting tells the compiler to examine the reference and ensure that the operation results in a type that is legal for the assigned variable.

Casting works in both directions, but it's not required to cast "up." Assigning an int value to a long variable requires no additional instruction because there is no possible loss of precision. In a similar sense, when assigning an Object

Review Chapter 3, "Using Java Operators and Conditional Logic," to understand casting for primitive types.

reference to a `Child` referent, it's always safe. Although an `Object` reference cannot access all the concrete referent's members, they're not going anywhere. They just require a more specific interface to get to them.

Casting "down," on the other hand, tests whether the reference type can access every member available through the casting type. As the code snippet shows, this rule means casting statements often appear redundant, but the programmers must acknowledge to the compiler, when casting down, that it might not work.

Believe it or not, casting up can fail too. After all, you can't just assign a `String` reference to a `Child` referent, as if Java supported magic type conversion:

```
// Won't work!
String str = (String)ch1;
```

When you cast up in your code, the compiler completes the type check by examining the declared referent. When you cast down, there are certain run-time operations that can only be resolved as the code runs. Since the compiler can't guarantee its type checking when you cast down, it requires you to spell out the test.

Sometimes you want to test a concrete referent for its actual type before you try casting to it. Older Java code in particular is full of examples like this:

```
Child ch5 = null;
if (pt instanceof Child)
    ch5 = (Child)pt;
```

The `instanceof` operator takes an object reference and a class type as operands and performs a Boolean test. Code like this can protect a program from crashing. If you tried casting blind and the variable `pt` did not point to a `Child` referent, the JVM would have to throw an exception. A defensive test like this avoids that outcome.

But let's say you have a `Parent` class that has been extended by several subclasses, such as `Child1`, `Child2`, and `Child3`. Also, let's say the `Parent` class is used as a parameter in a method, like this:

```
public void checkStatus(Parent p) { … }
```

You could pass any subclass of `Parent` into this method with no worries. In other words, you can always cast up implicitly. The compiler can always confirm it. What if, however, you wanted to check the passed-in parameter and see if it is actually a specific subclass? You'd also use the `instanceof` operator to test that, as in this example:

```
public void checkStatus(Parent p) {
    if (p instanceof Child1) return;
    // otherwise do something with p
}
```

If a type you use as a parameter inspires many subclasses, they will all be legal parameters for that method. If for some reason that method's code has to sort through those subclasses and behave differently for some of them, you can end up writing a lot of defensive (testing) code before you get to do anything constructive. It can get out of hand pretty quickly if you're not careful.

Implementing Polymorphic Behavior

Method names are important. The method names of one class, taken individually or as a whole, communicate an idea or intent to the calling programmer. The more methods a class has, the harder it becomes to interpret that intent. When designing a class with `public` methods, therefore, you should consider how many there are as well as what their names signify.

These factors are even more important once you allow inheritance in a class. In my experience, you don't let programmers inherit your classes; you dare them. Java programmers will start creating subclasses the minute they learn the `extends` keyword. It's easy to use, and the compiler doesn't monitor the quality of inheritance the programmer achieves.

Once you support it and have good method names to boot, you have great potential you can tap. To say more about that potential, I need to flip the thought process I used to introduce this chapter. To get you started, I used a `Grandfather` class that was extended by a `Parent` class that was extended by a `Child` class. This represents our sense in the natural world of how inheritance is supposed to work.

Organizing Objects by Type

This kind of ancestry is actually backward thinking in an object-oriented-type system. Think about it this way: In the natural world, is your child a kind of grandparent? Odds are it's too early to tell. But every grandparent is, or was, a child. You could even say a grandparent is a child who grew up to have children who also grew up to have children. That's an example of the perspective we need to develop a proper type system: A `Grandparent` class should specialize a `Child` class, not the other way around.

Here's another example, this one in geometry. There are rectangles and squares. A rectangle is a shape whose opposing sides have the same length. So is a square, but it is also true that all its sides have the same length.

A less well-known case involves ellipses and circles. An ellipse (oval) is a set of all points in a plane that are equidistant from two other points. It's like having

In Chapter 10, "Understanding Java Interfaces and Abstract Classes," you'll learn to avoid using the `instanceof` operator by using the `enum` type and `switch` statements.

Certification
Objective

In my view, it's just good defense to declare classes `final`. Allow for inheritance once the class fully supports it, but not a moment sooner.

two radii that, added together, represent one distance to a set of other points. A circle is the same, but for a circle, the two center points happen to be in the same location.

So a square is a special case of a rectangle, and a circle is a special case of an ellipse. All four of them are shapes, and all four of them have an area they contain. All four have different ways to calculate their area. With just that much information, you can at least imagine how an object-oriented drawing program might organize these ideas into related classes.

Using Method Names to Effect Polymorphism

Let's say that all children play. So do their parents, and so do their grandparents—they just have different kinds of games, and perhaps they don't play nearly as much. But let's say children play the most kinds of games and have the most "general" play behavior. It would make sense, in terms of objects, to place a Child class at the top of a type system and add a play() method to it. The Parent class can then inherit the play() method and override the Child class's logic. The Grandparent class can inherit from the Parent class, also making appropriate changes to its behavior.

To give the idea one more dimension, Figure 9.3 depicts this relationship using Father and Mother classes, which are extended by Grandfather and Grandmother classes, respectively. Each class has or inherits the play() method. I have repeated the method name in the figure to emphasize that each class will override it.

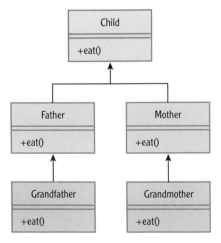

FIGURE 9.3 A type system of classes

Because these classes are related by inheritance, they share a *type* of behavior, not just the method name. Any other class can have a method by the same name. Classes that are related by type, however, enjoy a special facility called the *polymorphic* effect. Through polymorphism, you can invoke the `play()` method in a `Grandfather` object *using a `Child` reference*, and it will still behave like a `Grandfather` object.

No matter how you refer to a `Grandfather` referent—using a `Father`, `Child`, or even an `Object` reference—calling the `play()` method from it executes the behavior of that referent. So if you want all your `Child` objects to play at once, regardless of their concrete type, polymorphism guarantees an elegant way to express that intention.

Listing 9.8 shows an implementation of all five classes using various inheritance-based effects that you have studied so far, including member inheritance, overriding, and restricting member visibility to subclasses.

LISTING 9.8: Polymorphic effect using the `Child` class and its subclasses

```java
class Child {
    private int fun = 10;

    public void play() {
        fun *= 2;
        System.out.println(report());
    }

    private String report() {
        return "I had fun!";
    }
}

class Father extends Child {
    private short fun = 4;

    @Override public void play() {
        fun += 2;
        log("play");
    }

    private void log(String str) {
        System.out.println("Achieved fun level: " + fun);
    }
}
```

(Continues)

LISTING 9.8: Polymorphic effect using the Child class and its subclasses *(Continued)*

```java
class Mother extends Child {
    private short fun = 2;

    @Override public void play() {
        fun++;
        remember();
    }

    protected void remember() {
        System.out.println("Great time for all!");
    }
}

class Grandfather extends Father {
    private byte fun = -10;

    @Override public void play() {
        fun++;
        System.out.println(mutter());
    }

    private String mutter() {
        return "Oy it's hot.";
    }
}

class Grandmother extends Mother {
    private byte fun = 1;

    @Override public void play() {
        fun += 3;
        remember();
    }
}

class FunTest {
    public static void main(String args[]) {
        Child[] kids = new Child[] {
            new Child(), new Mother(),
            new Father(), new Child(),
            new Grandfather(), new Grandmother()
        };
```

LISTING 9.8: Polymorphic effect using the `Child` class and its subclasses *(Continued)*

```
        for (Child kid : kids) {
            kid.play();
        }
    }
}
$ java FunTest
I had fun!
Great time for all!
Achieved fun level: 6
I had fun!
Oy it's hot.
Great time for all!
```

In the `FunTest` class, I declare and populate a simple array of `Child` references with various concrete types. In the for-each loop, I then call the `play()` method on each element. As the output shows, each concrete type reports the way it ought to.

The implementations supporting the `play()` method in each class are a little different. Each level of subclass, for example, uses a different primitive type to store the `fun` value. Also notice that the `Grandmother` class uses a `remember()` method it inherits from the `Mother` class. Each class encapsulates these support features as details of its implementation. Our test class only cares that it can invoke the `play()` method.

Naming behavior in a clear but common way gives polymorphic behavior its power. Once you have it, it becomes possible to invoke the same behavior on a variety of objects at one time and let each object execute as it should. To do this well, it's essential to consider what type and behavior belong at the top of the scheme and which types represent specializations of that general behavior and design accordingly. It takes time to develop that skill, of course. Now, however, you have just enough information to track this kind of design through packages in the JDK and see why certain method names pop up again and again.

THE ESSENTIALS AND BEYOND

In this chapter, we examined how inheritance works in Java and how it is different from creating a class by composition. You saw through the construction process how a Java object is made from a subclass. I described key expectations, such as the equality contract, that every class should either fulfill or document as unsupported if it allows inheritance.

(Continues)

THE ESSENTIALS AND BEYOND *(Continued)*

Subclasses can specialize themselves by adding new methods and/or overriding inherited ones. They can also be referred to by variables of a parent type. I used the term *concrete referent* to distinguish between the object itself and the type of any legal reference for it. The casting and `instanceof` operators give us a way to test the concrete type of any referent and to get back to it. Finally, we took a look at what polymorphic behavior is, how to design for it, and how to implement it.

ADDITIONAL EXERCISES

1. Write a test program to show that an array of type `char` inherits from the `Object` class.

2. Write a class called `BadCast` that casts a character array referent to a `String` reference. Also include a statement to construct a `String` object using the array. Compile and observe the results.

3. Modify the `Options` class in Listing 9.4 so that a `null` parameter, if passed into any valid constructor, is ignored and the member variable's default value is preserved.

4. Write a class called `OverTest` that contains the methods `priv()`, `stat()`, and `fin()`. Declare these methods as `private`, `static`, and `final`, respectively. Next write a class called `ChildTest` that overrides each method. Compile the class and observe the error message for each case.

5. Write a `Rectangle` class that includes members for `width` and `length`. Include a method called `area()` that calculates and returns the area. Next, write a `Square` subclass; make sure the length and width parameters are the same; also, override the `area()` method with the specific equation for calculating a square's area.

REVIEW QUESTIONS

1. Which of the following statements identify a difference between inheritance and composition? (Choose all that apply.)

   A. Only inherited members are type-safe.

   B. Only subclasses can access `protected` members.

   C. Only inherited methods can be overridden.

   D. Only inherited methods can be overloaded.

(Continues)

2. Which of the following correctly describes inheritance?

    A. You cannot overload a `final` method.

    B. You cannot reuse the name of a parent class's `static` method.

    C. You cannot override a parent class's `private` method.

    D. You cannot declare a method `final` and `static`.

3. True or false: You can declare a `main()` method as `final` and it will compile.

4. Does the operation (`obj instanceof Object`) always return true? The member `obj` could be declared as any object type. Choose only the most specific correct option.

    A. Yes, it always returns a `true` value.

    B. No, it could return a `false` value.

    C. It depends on the type of the `obj` member.

    D. It depends on the value of the `obj` member.

5. What does the `@Override` annotation do for a method?

    A. It tells the compiler to issue a warning if the method doesn't perform an override.

    B. It verifies that overriding is legal for the method.

    C. It determines whether the method's signature matches a method in the parent class.

    D. It disables overloading for the method.

6. True or false: A class with only `private` constructors cannot have subclasses.

7. Assume you have a member variable obj that is not assigned the `null` value. Can you call `obj.super.toString()`?

    A. Yes, it will work even if the `obj` reference has an `Object` referent.

    B. No. The super keyword is not a class member.

    C. It works if the `toString()` method called is an override of the `Object` class.

    D. You cannot call it from a `static` method like `main()`, but a non-static method is okay.

    (Continues)

THE ESSENTIALS AND BEYOND *(Continued)*

8. How can you express a polymorphic effect in Java?

   A. You need classes related by inheritance that use method overriding to create local effects.

   B. You need classes with the same method names that are implemented the same way; you don't need a shared type.

   C. You need classes all in one package to inherit from the same class.

   D. You only have to override methods. Polymorphism is in the eye of the beholder.

9. Assume you are preparing a system of types for a human resources application. Which class name would you use as the best parent to the other types?

   A. Director

   B. Executive

   C. Employee

   D. Manager

10. True or false: You can use the @Override annotation on a method that is declared final.

Understanding Java Interfaces and Abstract Classes

This book now arrives at the *coup de grace* of object-oriented programming: making use of abstract types. It can be a hard topic to get a handle on, but the payoff is huge. Once you're able to think about method naming first and then decide how you're going to make your methods work second, you're ready for abstract types. It's a tall order. Believe me, I know it. And so, in this chapter I'm going to use one extended example to tell a kind of story, with some side examples to make individual points along the way. Abstract typing is a design process, and design means working out relationships over multiple revisions. I'll therefore spend less time touching on every compiler rule—although they're still important—and more time on the power of writing programs by thinking about design first, implementation second.

In this chapter, we'll cover the following topics:

▶ **Understanding abstract types**

▶ **Using abstract classes**

▶ **Using interfaces**

▶ **Using the enum type**

▶ **Distinguishing between abstract and concrete references**

Understanding Abstract Types

In object-oriented programming, abstract types help answer a what-if question that arises when you need a *type system*. A type system describes any number of classes that use the polymorphic effect to share behavior, not just member names. Inheritance is the simplest way to achieve this effect, but it also creates dependencies and requirements that are sometimes too confining for your needs. With abstract types, you can create a type system that is more flexible and more dynamic than subclassing allows.

Let's say you want to name some behavior (that is, a method) that you know you will implement differently for most subclasses. Let's also say the behavior you have in mind, unlike the `Child` class's `play()` method from Chapter 9, "Inheriting Code and Data in Java," has no default logic or meaning of its own. The method name you have in mind merely characterizes the logic you'll need, and that's all a name can do.

If you're writing a customer interface for a banking system, it's easy to imagine you'll need general behaviors such as `deposit()`, `withdrawal()`, `transfer()`, and `getBalance()`. It's also clear these behaviors will have to work under one set of rules for a checking account, another for a retirement savings account, and still another for a certificate of deposit. So what's a useful, general class name that takes all those products into consideration? `Account`? `BankAccount`? `Product`? `FinancialInstrument`? Whatever it is, you'd be smart to build a consensus on that key name early in the development process. If it's going to sit at the top of a type system, other programmers and designers will have to stare at it a lot.

You still haven't considered how the code will work—that's a long way off in design. You just know that all the different products one bank offers ought to fit together into a type system somehow and that the way you're going to make these things appear related to each other is by inheritance, as we discussed in Chapter 9.

So let's put this idea in real-world terms, but let's use something less controversial than banking for our chapter-long example. Let's say I'm running a lawn care business. I've got six employees I can assign to six clients at one time. The general instructions for doing the work are always the same:

- ▶ Clear the lawn of any debris.
- ▶ Mow and edge the lawn.
- ▶ Gather the clippings.
- ▶ Water the lawn.

Of course, there's no such thing as an abstract lawn or a general kind of lawn. There may be one type that's common or popular, but that doesn't mean it's a suitable prototype for all other lawns. Even if I wanted to maintain a "standard lawn" on which to train new hires, what would that be? What I do instead is define what should be done to care for any lawn and then work out the details for each different type you encounter.

The conditions under which those operations are performed will vary from site to site. Some lawns are big, some are small. Some may have a small bit of debris to clear, some may have a lot. Some lawns may require no detail work, like edging or weeding, at all, while others may have grass racing down every crack in the sidewalk and driveway. The degree of work required for each task is made evident by the site itself. I therefore have to rely on my employees to apply my steps as it suits the conditions they find.

To promote the same idea of polymorphic behavior in Java, you communicate intention through the names you choose for your methods. The class name can help too, by expressing some collective meaning for those methods. Often a quick sketch of the operations will suggest the need for an organizing concept, as shown in Figure 10.1.

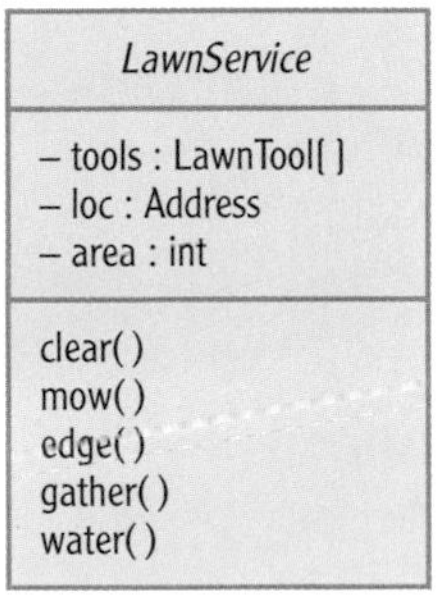

```
LawnService
------------------------
– tools : LawnTool[ ]
– loc : Address
– area : int
------------------------
clear( )
mow( )
edge( )
gather( )
water( )
```

FIGURE 10.1 Sketch
of the LawnService interface

All I've done in Figure 10.1 is mock up each discrete operation as a method and provide the concept name LawnService. I've given all of two minutes of thought to possible members and type names. It's not a true class diagram. I haven't applied Unified Modeling Language (UML) signifiers formally, much less correctly. I've only sketched out something that could be polished into a proper design later.

Now, assuming I have clients I want to remember and continue to please, I should offer to each site a concrete form of my services that matches their conditions and needs. Instead of capturing all the details for all jobs in one concept called LawnService, I can divide them into concrete services as shown in Figure 10.2.

I have applied one detail in particular to this diagram. I show the name LawnService in italics. This treatment implies that the LawnService collective is an *abstraction*, something that defines behaviors without necessarily providing them. As I am sure you can guess, I will translate each of these components to a Java class, but the italics help me signify a distinction between an abstract type and the various concrete types, including HackItBack, ShowItOff, TouchItUp, and KnockItDown.

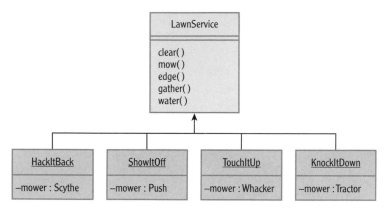

FIGURE 10.2 Different LawnService jobs

I've also given each of the four services depicted here some detail to set them apart. The mower reference is represented by a different type for each class, suggesting the tool most appropriate to perform the job. In a proper diagram, you generally would not bother to illustrate that each type can have its own style of implementation. That's not just implied; it's expected. All each type has to do is support the declared methods. How they do it is commonly described as an implementation detail.

The term *implementation detail* doesn't mean writing code is easy or trivial, just that it doesn't (and shouldn't) alter the design.

The subclass names I've chosen are colloquial by design. I want to suggest that these are intended as internal references—that is, classes that are not designed to communicate directly with clients. I only want my clients to call and ask for a LawnService job. Once I have categorized the job by reviewing the details of their site, *I'll decide which concrete type is appropriate* and send the right employee with the right resources for the job.

Every client expects a LawnService job, and they will each get the service they've ordered. The actual product will emphasize some operations and downplay others, according to their site. As an example, Figure 10.3 depicts a use case that links a LawnService request to a HackItBack job. The note included in the diagram helps define the kind of work that such a job entails.

Bear in mind that I'm using UML artifacts rather casually. Applying UML is an exacting discipline in large-scale application development.

I think it's important for my business image that I use only the term LawnService with my clients. They just have one lawn, after all, and they don't need to know how I categorize it, nor do they need to learn the internal vocabulary of my business. I also don't want to let out the idea that the client should have to make line-item decisions on which tools or resources are necessary. It's my job to ascertain the client's needs and return the right *kind* of service. Clients don't need to study services they can't use. I don't need them to hear terms like *hack* or *knock it down* and get the wrong idea.

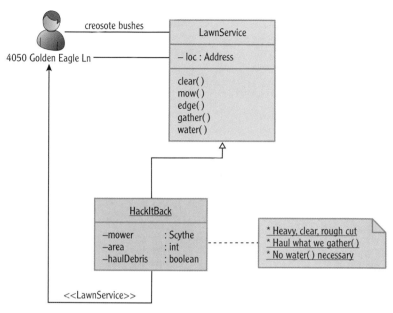

FIGURE 10.3 Use case for the HackItBack job

With just that much consideration, I've started to form a type system with a public interface and some number of encapsulated concrete types. I know what the business logic looks like, so now I want to separate the high-level operations of the business from the concrete details of the work. Now all I need is a class model that will help me maintain that separation.

Or that's the dream, anyway. Before you can realize it in Java, you need to know how the language lets you create and express abstract types and what rules you must observe to use them.

Using Abstract Classes

An abstract method includes most of the usual things a regular method has: modifiers (including the abstract modifier), a return type, a name, and a parameter list. What it cannot include is a method body (also called the *implementation*). An abstract method looks like this example:

Certification Objective

```
public abstract void testMe();
```

You can declare as many methods abstract as you like in one class. The compiler uses the modifier to enforce the absence of a statement body. If you forget the semicolon separator and add curly braces instead, the compiler will complain. By using this modifier, you also implicitly declare that the class that contains it is incomplete. Any class may be declared abstract, but if it has abstract methods, it *must* be declared abstract.

Why does that matter? Because classes declared abstract cannot be constructed. This kind of class lets you establish a type that provides methods, with some or all of them implemented, without allowing objects to be made from it. I suppose you could say it is the opposite of classes that are implicitly *concrete*—that is, made to produce objects.

To use an abstract class, you have to subclass it, even if it has no abstract methods. If it does, and you want to make a concrete subclass, then you must implement all methods declared abstract in the parent. If you don't, you'll make another abstract class. Also, the compiler will complain about it unless you declare it to be one.

You can cheat the intention of an abstract method by overriding it and implementing an empty code body. If you're worried only about getting past the compiler, that's all you need to do. Usually, however, abstract classes are written in such a way that they depend on their abstract methods to do something useful. Consider the following example:

You'll see how enforcing an implementation is possible in the section "Understanding the Template Method Pattern" later in this chapter.

```
abstract class PokerNight {
    private int white = 1;
    private int red = 5;
    private int blue = 25;
    private int black;

    public int startingValue() {
        int total = 0;
        total += (25 * white);
        total += (20 * red);
        total += (15 * blue);
        total += (10 * blackValue());
        return total;
    }

    public abstract int blackValue();
}
```

The PokerNight class uses the method startingValue() to determine how many chips each player gets to start. It sets the number of chips each player receives and their values, except for the black chips. Depending on the game, you might want to value them each at 50 cents, 1 dollar, or more. All you have to do is subclass the PokerNight class and override the blackValue() method to return the desired amount:

```
class MyPokerNight extends PokerNight {
    @Override
    public int blackValue() {
        return 100;
    }

    public static void main(String args[]) {
        MyPokerNight mpn = new MyPokerNight();
        float buyin = mpn.startingValue()/100;
        System.out.println("Buy-in = " + buyin);
    }
}
$ java MyPokerNight
Buy-in = 15.0
```

Many abstract classes do something like this. They integrate their abstract method(s) into the logic of their concrete methods. A programmer can use this approach to supply missing values or logic and customize the abstract class. "Stubbing out" abstract methods just so they satisfy the compiler can foul this intent. Ten black chips that are worth 0, for example, won't add much life to a poker game.

Of course you should also check that you can't actually construct a PokerNight object. You should see an error like this:

```
PokerNight.java:5: error: PokerNight is abstract;
cannot be instantiated
        PokerNight pn = new PokerNight();
                        ^
1 error
```

Because you can't instantiate an abstract class, you can't use it in another class as a field, except as a reference type for its subclasses. Any time you extend one and implement its methods, you end up with a *concrete class* from which you can make objects. Listing 10.1 shows the Concrete class extending the Abstract class:

Abstract classes *do* have constructors; they're needed by subclasses to complete the construction process.

LISTING 10.1: Extending and implementing an abstract class

```
public abstract class DeclareAbstract {
    public abstract void testMe();
}
```

(Continues)

LISTING 10.1: Extending and implementing an abstract class *(Continued)*

```java
final class Concrete extends DeclareAbstract {
    @Override
    public void testMe() {
        System.out.println("Tested");
    }

    public static void main(String args[]) {
        DeclareAbstract dab = new Concrete();
        dab.testMe();
    }
}
$ javac DeclareAbstract.java
$ java Concrete
Tested
```

The Concrete class and testMe() method both drop the abstract modifier. In the main() method, I refer to the Concrete object with the DeclareAbstract variable dab, just to show that the same kind of relationship exists between parent and child type as discussed in Chapter 9. In fact, this use of types makes it clear that you *cannot* invoke code that belongs to the reference type. The reference defines which members of the referent are accessible, but they always belong to the referent.

> **Fields cannot be declared abstract.**

As before, I could have implemented the testMe() method just by replacing the semicolon separator with curly braces. This override honors the letter of the contract but ignores the intent of it. If any problems arise from this code, you can catch them only by testing the program at runtime. A lazy implementation of an abstract class is bound to haunt you sooner or later; honor these contracts as fully as possible.

It stands to reason that you should not be able to declare an abstract class or method as final. It's a self-defeating combination. If you could, you'd be able to make classes and methods that are incomplete and unavailable for subclassing and overriding. Fortunately, the compiler checks for this combination and disallows it. You cannot apply the static modifier to an abstract method for similar reasons: Binding an incomplete method to its class serves no useful purpose.

By understanding the rationale behind the compiler's checks, you'll better prepare yourself for exam questions that test your understanding of each modifier. Anywhere in this text where I recite a rule but don't demonstrate it with test code, you should write the test yourself. It's good practice, but more importantly, you'll teach yourself the compiler's exact responses. Some compiler complaints seem to bear no relationship to the code that raises them, so it's well worth your time to learn these correlations. To get you started on that exercise, I've listed some key rules for the abstract modifier here.

The rules for an `abstract` class in Java are as follows:

- ▶ It must include the `abstract` modifier in its declaration.
- ▶ It cannot be declared `final`.
- ▶ It can have constructors.

In addition, here are the rules for an `abstract` method in Java:

- ▶ It must include the `abstract` modifier in its declaration.
- ▶ It cannot be declared `final` or `static`.
- ▶ It can be overloaded.
- ▶ It must be overridden in a concrete subclass.

Understanding the Template Method Pattern

Here's the thing about abstract methods and classes: You're probably not going to use them very often. There are a couple of reasons why.

Reason one is that a class is abstract only as a matter of degree. It can have zero or more methods in it that are declared `abstract`. The remainder of the class is still concrete in some sense; it can have state as expressed by its fields and behavior as expressed by its implemented methods. Although you can't call an abstract class constructor with a reference, its subclasses must, either through the implicit construction process or by using the `super()` call.

Chapter 9 discusses the use of `super()` to call an accessible constructor in the parent class.

An abstract class, therefore, is not a *pure type*, one that defines operations but has no behavior of its own. You can make a class purely abstract by declaring all of its methods that way. Unless you need to include a constructor, however, there's a better way to do that: Write a Java interface. I'll discuss those in the later, in the section "Using Interfaces."

A pure type is one that has no mutable state or code implementation.

Reason two is that there is a use case that suits the hybrid form of abstract classes very well. It just doesn't come up very often, particularly in entry-level programming work. A design pattern called the Template Method pattern, when implemented in Java, exploits the abstract class's part-concrete, part-abstract makeup. Before I put abstract classes to rest, I want to make sure you have at least one good motivation for remembering them and even applying them one day. If you're going to learn only one way to use an abstract class, you could do much worse than committing the Template Method pattern to memory.

You can learn more about this pattern at http://en.wikipedia.org/wiki/Template Method_pattern.

Learning design patterns on the whole is an advanced skill and well beyond the scope of this book, but I'm not trying to introduce the discipline as a whole here. Taken one at a time, design patterns are code techniques that prove themselves useful in a variety of situations. To take this subject area seriously, you'd want to learn the theory that drives their use and the practical trade-offs you make when applying one. Short of that, there's no reason you can't think of any one pattern as a simple recipe for getting work done that you'd otherwise have to discover by trial and error.

It turns out the LawnService example you've been following could resolve a particular issue with keeping its business operations consistent using the Template Method pattern. The next section explains how.

Applying the Template Method Pattern

The formal requirements of the Template Method pattern are something you should eventually learn, but they aren't necessary in the moment, so I'll just describe the challenge the pattern can address. Say you want to encapsulate the sequence of method calls associated with the LawnService concept. (See Figure 10.1 for a refresher.) It's important to preserve the order of these operations. Keeping to a particular sequence makes training new hires easier and gives repeat customers a sense of consistency they like.

Certain aspects of each job setup are fixed. Every employee, for example, carries a hose to use for watering. If there's no need for it on a particular job type, you can override the default water() code with an empty statement body and ignore the hose. Other aspects of each job vary with the type of service required —what equipment to bring for cutting and edging, for example, or whether a truck is needed to haul clippings away. These needs derive from the kind of lawn, the total area to cut, and so on.

The Template Method pattern describes a way to modify the individual steps of each procedure without disturbing the sequence. First, you define a final method that describes the procedure as a series of Java statements. You can then declare as abstract the methods that can't be implemented until you have all the concrete details you need. Listing 10.2 shows a skeletal example that will compile.

LISTING 10.2: Foundation of a Template Method pattern

```
public abstract class LawnService {
    // fields have been defined
    private String address;

    // Subclass must invoke super(String)
    protected LawnService(String addr) {
        address = addr;
    }
```

LISTING 10.2: Foundation of a Template Method pattern *(Continued)*

```
        public void clear() { // implemented
        }

        public void edge()  { // implemented
        }

        public void water() { // implemented
        }

        public final void execute() {
          clear();
          mow();
          edge();
          gather();
          water();
        }

        public abstract void mow();
        public abstract void gather();
    }
```

The execute() method invokes the operations in their intended order and is declared final so it can't be overridden. The subclasses (or jobs, as I refer to them in the discussion of Figure 10.2) must implement the methods mow() and gather() to become concrete classes They can override the methods clear(), edge(), and water(), if appropriate, or rely on the parent's implementation.

I also added a constructor that requires a String parameter. An Address class that could validate the location (and maybe even map it!) would be cool, but for a quick class sketch like this, a String placeholder is tolerable. This constructor obliges the subclass to inform the parent through a super() call. The address variable is included just so the code will compile; I'll have to replace that once I get serious about developing this class properly.

Nothing in Listing 10.2 will keep a subclass from passing in the null value or an empty String. Since it's all my code and it's only half-formed so far, I'm on my own honor system to observe the spirit of the code. If other programmers are going to write subclasses, my code has to take enforcement up a notch and keep them honest, but also it has to be resilient to honest mistakes.

Enforcing a Pattern

There are some techniques to support the methods mow() and gather() so a subclass doesn't just implement them with empty bodies. Since it doesn't take much to get past the compiler, your best bet is to help the code fail as quickly or as visibly as you can. If the mow() method returns a value the gather() method relies on, you could validate the received value and throw an exception when it's inappropriate or out of range. You'll learn how to throw exceptions in the next chapter.

You could also change a state condition in the object, using perhaps a private field called internalError, so the execute() method can acknowledge the flag but also complete without crashing. At the same time, it's not usually worth the time it takes to keep code running in the face of every possible abuse others can visit upon it. Somewhere between checking the input to every method and adding flags for every possibly malady, there's a happy medium. The Template Method pattern isn't the only use for an abstract class, but it's a pretty good one. Some packages in the core libraries will use abstract methods to deal with low-level variations—such as filesystem, operating system, or even hardware elements—they can't express as a general case. The pixel is an excellent example. A pixel is defined by each operating system's windowing software. Some cross-platform graphics libraries manage it by declaring their pixel-getting methods abstract, then using code in a platform-specific library to implement their properties, similar to our PokerNight example.

You should think to use an abstract class when you want to create some bigger picture that needs to be completed. You should also think of it when you want to declare a fixed procedure in a way that lets another programmer change the implementation of the steps. You won't find many other novel uses for abstract methods and classes, but these two conditions cover a lot of ground.

Using Interfaces

Certification
Objective

We're now ready to discuss Java's version of a completely abstract type, the interface. An interface has no mutable data, no implemented methods, and no constructors. The first two restrictions imply the third. Given a type that has no data you can change and no methods you can invoke, there's not much point in trying to make an object from it.

All a Java interface can do is declare abstract methods and immutable data. It doesn't seem like much fun, but it is a very powerful tool. Java interfaces add an additional aspect to the what-if case I presented at the beginning of the chapter.

> **Methods in an interface are implicitly public and abstract. Including the keywords is considered redundant and is discouraged.**

It goes like this: What if I wanted to describe *how* to care for a lawn by listing the essential steps *any* lawn service should include? I don't want to impose a procedure, as the Template Method pattern lets me do, or provide any implementations at all. I just want to describe the steps required, expressed as methods.

Here is a `LawnServices` interface that declares the operations I have used before. Now, however, there's no code and no data, just a type that declares certain methods without implementing them or even suggesting how they should relate to each other:

```
public interface LawnServices {
    void clear();
    void edge();
    void water();
    void mow();
    void gather();
}
```

There's no way to enforce order of invocation, to encapsulate them, or to do almost anything else I've been doing with methods in the last few chapters. What I can do with an interface, however, is name the methods for *any* lawn service I care to implement and declare a common type for them. A Java interface is nothing more than a definition of methods that can be treated as a type.

Let's say my lawn service is just crushing the competition. Other operators must now capitulate to my grass-mowing, clipping-gathering, edge-trimming juggernaut of a business. I'm prepared to buy them all out, but first I want to make sure I can adapt their business operations to mine. I *don't* want to impose the details of my operations on theirs; acquiring a business and then disrupting it with unfamiliar, mandated practices is a time-honored way to lose existing customers. I just want to make sure I can incorporate the services they provide and manage them on my own terms. This case is where a *pure type*, one that allows only a definition of behavior, comes in handy.

A Java interface is a so-called *pure type*. A good one names a list of methods that communicate a cohesive service. When you want to incorporate the methods of an interface into your class, you *implement* it by providing a method body for each of its members. A class that implements an interface implicitly declares that it *includes the type of the interface* in its definition.

Since my `LawnService` concept has already taken shape and I am happy with it, I want to keep using it. I want to apply it to other new types without forcing inheritance. So here's a really neat thing about Java interfaces: I can just redeclare the operations of my abstract class in an interface and then declare that the abstract class implements it, like this:

```
public abstract class LawnService implements LawnServices {...}
```

I've just added a new type to the `LawnService` definition without changing a thing. You can do that with all or part of an existing class interface. I will even claim here that good interfaces aren't usually conceived out of thin air. Instead, they are factored out of well-designed classes by people who realize the broader applications of that design.

My LawnService class is now a *type* of the LawnServices interface. What have I gained? My class can now share a type with any other class that also implements the LawnServices interface. Let's say one business I'm about to buy is Joe's Cut 'n' Blow Express. I tell him I need to see his business code so I can test it for adaptation to my interface. Joe uses a single top-level class that looks like this:

```
public final class MowAndBlow {
    public void cut() { }
    public void blow() { }
    public void go() { }
}
```

Assume the methods shown here are fully implemented. Unlike me, Joe likes to improvise a lot while on the job, so there's no enforced sequence to his operations. The class is also marked final, so I can't just extend the MowAndBlow class. I don't want to anyway; I don't want to find out down the road that the class is unsuitable for extending. Using the LawnServices interface, however, I can just wrap Joe's methods with mine, as shown in Listing 10.3.

LISTING 10.3: The MowAndBlow class implementing the LawnServices interface

```
public final class MowAndBlow implements LawnServices {
    // Joe's methods
    public void cut() { }
    public void blow() { }
    public void go() { }

    // methods to implement
    @Override public void clear() {}

    @Override public void edge() {}

    @Override public void water() {}

    @Override public void mow() {
        this.cut();
    }

    @Override public void gather() {
        this.blow();
        this.go();
    }
}
```

Wrapping the cut() method with my mow() method seems like the right thing to do. So does rolling the blow() and go() methods together into my gather() method. There could be other things to fit in the methods that are currently empty, but at least I can persuade the compiler that the MowAndBlow class is now a LawnServices type of thing.

That's all it takes to fold the MowAndBlow class into my LawnServices type. I don't have to modify the existing code or remove the final modifier. I also don't require the MowAndBlow class to extend another class. I have expanded my type system without using inheritance, overloading constructors, or mucking with package access. I can't do much about concealing Joe's public methods, but for initial testing it's not a primary concern.

Let this fact seep in for a bit. Just by implementing an interface, you can confer an additional type on an existing class. You get the power of type-sharing that works around Java's single-inheritance rule. You also get the flexibility of composition. That's a sweet deal. There are better and subtler ways to exploit this feature, but this is your first look. Refinements can wait while you absorb the primary lesson.

In addition, a class can implement more than one interface by declaring them all in a comma-delimited list:

Many interface methods do no harm if you give them empty implementations.

```
import java.io.Serializable;
import java.util.List;
class GimmeEverything implements Serializable, List { }
```

You must then implement all the methods they declare. You don't have to integrate these methods with each other or with the existing methods of your class. However, as a class becomes an aggregation of interfaces, it also tends to lose focus. The infinite possibilities of implementing interfaces might be interesting to imagine, but in practice it can be tedious and distracting to try.

You can include fields in an interface definition too, like this:

Many Java programmers, if not most, consider it bad form to include implied modifiers in an interface declaration.

```
public interface Deck {
    int COUNT = 52;
}
```

An interface field is the closest thing Java has to a *constant*, an immutable value that serves as a kind of dictionary term for a program. Interface fields are implicitly public, final, and static, so you have to declare their values up front. You can then use the field name as a mnemonic device to clarify program code:

```
class Test {
    public static void main(String args[]) {
        System.out.println("Total cards in a deck: " + Deck.COUNT);
    }
}
```

In the old days of Java, it was common to see long lists of these immutable values in an interface. If you see it in recently written code, make a habit of wincing at it. There is a much better way to do this kind of work now, but you should know what the old style looks like:

```
interface Position {
    int PITCHER = 1;
    int CATCHER = 2;
    int FIRST_BASE = 3;
    // … more values
    int RIGHT_FIELD = 9;
}
```

This technique approximates a traditional programming structure called an *enumeration*. Enumerations are useful when you have a list of items with a well-known order that you want to represent in code in a more readable way. Consider the numeric field positions for a baseball team as an example. Fans of the game know them by their number as well as their name. You can say "six to four to three" to baseball fans, and they will understand you to mean a double play that involved the third baseman (sixth position), the second baseman (fourth position) for one out, and the first baseman (third position) for another out. You could write a double play into a baseball computer game using those numbers, and your average baseball-loving Java programmer will understand it. Unfortunately, programmers who don't know or care for baseball will have no idea what's going on without some more help.

By using mnemonics in an enumeration, you can make the same thing clearer to more code readers. Instead of numbers, you can express something like Position.THIRD_BASE to Position.SECOND_BASE to Position.FIRST_BASE. This approach makes the meaning explicit in the code. The mnemonics are still supported by their underlying integer representation. It's a bulkier expression, but it pays off in readability.

This same technique is attractive for lots of uses, but it gets hairy if the list itself isn't stable. Say, for example, you wanted to change the numbering of field positions to make the shortstop sixth and the third baseman fifth. And you wanted to insert a position for the designated hitter even though he doesn't play on defense.

Any code that relies on the original numbering wouldn't necessarily break— that would actually be pretty nice. Because the underlying integers are legal types, you'd more likely have broken code that works oddly. The enumeration merely assigns the integers themselves a name. If you don't care about baseball but maintain baseball game software, you might not figure out what's wrong, at least not until a user complains that their designated hitter just tagged out a runner at shortstop.

As a result, programmers who use traditional enumerations have few attractive options. One option is to freeze an enumeration once it's written and resort to writing a new one if the elements have to change. Another option is to add elements only at the end of an existing enumeration. If you do that often enough, the underlying numeric representation can appear more arbitrary with each change.

To get past these and other limits, Java first introduced a specific type, called the enum, in Java 5. It's a very useful thing, and I want to make sure you see why. That discussion is coming up later in this chapter.

Planning for Variation

Before we talk about the enum type, let's return to the LawnServices example and create a use case for it. My testing so far shows I can absorb Joe's business application logic into my own by yoking both systems under a common interface. Doing it that way saves me a lot of fuss. In production code, it might take more careful testing and possibly some ugly workarounds to complete the integration, but a good interface design will help me isolate and mitigate any trouble spots. I can now visualize my class relationships as shown in Figure 10.4.

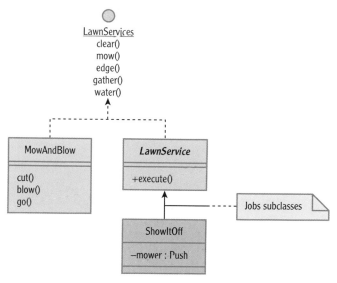

FIGURE 10.4 LawnServices interface incorporating dissimilar classes

In this figure, I've added the `LawnServices` interface and factored my common operations into it. There's no need to repeat those methods in the implementing classes. The association shown by the dashed line, called a *realization* in UML, implies that. Instead, I can just add to each class the details that distinguish it from the other realizations.

If I decided the interface should include more operations, I could add them, but then I'd have to add an implementation into each existing subclass. If I decided a certain operation was redundant or interfered with the interface's *cohesiveness*, I could remove it, but then I would probably break more than a few implementing classes.

With interfaces, your best approach is to keep them simple and commit to them for the long run. Correcting for oversights down the road only gets harder as more classes implement your interface. There's no Java programming frustration quite so intense as having your code break because someone you don't even know changed an interface you depend on, and code you haven't modified in months now just won't work.

Reviewing Polymorphism

Looking again at Figure 10.4, notice that the `LawnService` class is still marked `abstract` and the `MowAndBlow` class is still marked `final`. Those are incompatible differences, but it doesn't matter. Neither class relies on the other. They just share a common type in the `LawnServices` interface.

You can take advantage of this shared relationship another way. The `LawnServices` interface hides the differences among my concrete classes—it's a prime candidate for use as a reference type, as a field, return type, or parameter. That means you can create methods that can use any object whose class implements the `LawnServices` interface.

Let's say I want to track all the jobs I can complete in one day. I estimate an average of two jobs per day per employee. After I absorb Joe's business, I've got 10 employees—that's 20 jobs a day. To keep things simple, I can use a regular Java array and track each job by its index number.

Are you curious what one of the exercises for this chapter might be?

```
interface Jobs {
   int MAX = 20;
}

LawnServices[] jobs; //populated elsewhere

public LawnServices jobTracker(int index) {
   if (index < Jobs.MAX)
      return jobs[index];
}
...
```

The full power of polymorphism becomes apparent once you use it to communicate behaviors that have been implemented by the concrete object that has been conveyed in the communication. This form lends itself to code that doesn't require the programmer to consider the variation of every possible concrete type to understand what's supposed to happen. It also hides a lot of detail; such a terse appearance can be a little frustrating while you're first learning how this all works. Give yourself time to acclimate to it. I'm sure once you have a chance to appreciate the resulting simplicity, you'll be happy to contribute to it.

Using the *enum* Type

Java introduced the enum type in version 1.5. Up to that point, a programmer had to use an interface populated with integers and good variable names to emulate an *enumerated type*. The idea's simple enough: Name some elements of a common group, like the positions of a baseball team. Give each position a unique number in that enumeration.

The variable names you choose serve as mnemonic devices in your program code. The numeric values give you a way to communicate by type. It's a useful arrangement that's used heavily in languages like C and C++ to make code easier to read.

Java programmers at one time emulated this structure with interfaces. Now we can do much better. The enum type not only resolves certain limits inherent in representing names with an underlying number; it also provides an entire type scheme. Each enumerated value is itself an *object* of the type that declares it, not just a name.

This form makes it very easy to implement simple constructs of a well-known collection in which the items are unique and may have a natural order to them. Consider this rewrite of the Position interface I described earlier as an enum type:

The Wikipedia article on enumerated types describes its uses and limits: `http://en.wikipedia.org/wiki/Enumerated_type`.

```
public enum Position {
    PITCHER,
    CATCHER,
    FIRST_BASE,
    SECOND_BASE,
    SHORTSTOP,
    THIRD_BASE,
    LEFT_FIELD,
    CENTER_FIELD,
    RIGHT_FIELD
}
```

That's everything. Each of the listed elements *is* a Position type, not a name with some other underlying value.

An enum element has a variety of additional useful properties. Because it is an instance of the enum type, you can write methods that declare the type as a return type or a parameter; the range of acceptable values is *inherently limited to the enumerated elements*. Unlike an interface, which gives you a way to address any class that implements it, an enum type lets you limit the acceptable values of one type. You can always add an element to a Java enumeration without breaking any class that already uses it. Removing an element will not break all users of the type. It will, of course, affect any program that relied on that deleted element.

You can print the name of an element just by passing it to the System.out .println() method, as shown in Listing 10.4.

LISTING 10.4: Using an enum element as a parameter

```
class Report {
    public void printPos(Position pos) {
        System.out.println(pos);
    }
    public static void main(String args[]) {
        Report r = new Report();
        r.printPos(Position.CATCHER);
    }
}
$ javac Report.java
$ java Report
CATCHER
```

Notice the printPos() method accepts a Position type as a parameter. The element Position.CATCHER is one element of that type. You can treat that element as a constant, but you can also treat it like an Object subclass when using it for a parameter. When the toString() method is called on an enum element, it will return a String object that matches its name.

Using this feature, let's say I wanted to encode the different lawn jobs I've named. I now want to make more readable code by using these internal names while still keeping them separate from how I communicate with a client. This work is trivial for an enum type:

```
enum Job {
    HACKITBACK,
    SHOWITOFF,
    TOUCHITUP,
    KNOCKITDOWN,
    MOWANDBLOW}
```

Now that I have named each job type in code, there's a great deal more I can do. Figure 10.3 illustrated the case for selecting a job type the client needs, based on site conditions, but returning a LawnService reference to the caller.

I'll use the LawnServices interface as a drop-in replacement for the LawnService class. That way, I can also include concrete types that use the same operations but don't extend the LawnService class. That means I can include the MowAndBlow type with the LawnService subclasses I have.

Now I can write a method that returns a concrete reference, selected by processing an incoming parameter, but in the form of the interface type:

```
public LawnServices getLawnServices (Job job) { }
```

Notice how the power of an enum type kicks in when I implement this method. I can use it as an argument to a switch statement. Because the elements are constants, I can use them as case labels just as they are. I don't even need to give their fully qualified name because it is made plain by the argument to the switch test. My getLawnServices() method looks like this:

The compiler will actually complain if you use fully qualified case labels with an enum.

```
public LawnServices getLawnServices(Job job) {
    switch(job) {
    case HACKITBACK:
        return new HackItBack();
    case SHOWITOFF:
        return new ShowItOff();
    case TOUCHITUP:
        return new TouchItUp();
    case KNOCKITDOWN:
        return new KnockItDown();
    case MOWANDBLOW:
        return new MowAndBlow();
    case default:
        return null;
    }
}
```

Each case label uses a return statement, so there is no cascading effect and no need for break statements. All the elements listed in the Job enumeration have a case label, so there is also no need for a default label. It's considered best practice to have one, so I included it. And now we have a method that creates the right object for each job but always returns the same interface.

To test it, you'll need a few more pieces. Rather than implement all the methods I've described so far, however, it will be less work if you declare just one of

This arrangement resembles a scheme called a *Factory Pattern*, in which a method returns a subclass of the expected type, based on the input.

the methods given in the `LawnServices` interface. When you get that one working properly, add the others. For example, you could start with just this much:

```
interface LawnService {
    void testing();
}
```

Then you can write a dummy class for each job to show that the objects will get created:

```
class HackItBack implements LawnServices {
    @Override public void testing() {
        System.out.println("HackItBack: testing()");
    }
}

class ShowItOff implements LawnServices {
    @Override public void testing() {
        System.out.println("ShowItOff: testing()");
    }
}

class TouchItUp implements LawnServices {
    @Override public void testing() {
        System.out.println("TouchItUp: testing()");
    }
}

class KnockItDown implements LawnServices {
    @Override public void testing() {
        System.out.println("KnockItDown: testing()");
    }
}

class MowAndBlow implements LawnServices {
    @Override public void testing() {
        System.out.println("MowAndBlow: testing()");
    }
}
```

Each class can implement the `testing()` method with a self-identifying message—that's enough to show the right method has been invoked. All that's needed now is a class to contain the `getLawnServices()` method and then a `main()` method to test it. But wait, there's more!

You can also use the enhanced for loop with any enum type. The compiler inserts a values() method into each one so it can return an array of its elements. Iterating through one is short work:

```
public class Switcheroo {
    // Insert getLawnServices() method here
    public static void main(String args[]) {
        Switcheroo scope = new Switcheroo();
        for (Job job : Job.values())
            scope.getLawnServices(job).testing();
    }
}
$ javac JobTest.java
$ java JobTest
HackItBack: testing()
ShowItOff: testing()
TouchItUp: testing()
KnockItDown: testing()
MowAndBlow: testing()
```

The last thing I have done, both to reduce the code required and to show you a tiny trick about method invocation, is invoke the testing() method directly after calling the getLawnServices() method. The latter method evaluates to an object of type LawnServices. It's not required that you declare a reference and assign the result to it. You can just chain a method that is accessible from that type, using dot notation as you can see.

You now have enough of a framework that you can add concrete classes whenever you want. The existing design ensures that every type-conforming subclass will "just work" once it is added to the framework. If you later want to incorporate a top-level class of another business into it, the process is straightforward:

1. Implement the LawnServices interface in the new class.

2. Add an element for the modified class in the Job enum.

3. Add a case for the modified class in the getLawnServices() method.

4. Test thoroughly.

This arrangement shows the benefits of object-oriented design. There's a bit more theory that informs this kind of development, but this result is what you want: a way to expand the number of concrete classes without having to change the way the framework supports them. To add new job types, you only have to modify the Job enumeration and the getLawnServices() method. And, therefore, those are the only framework components that require testing.

It takes a while to learn to think this way, but as I said at the beginning of the chapter, the rewards are substantial.

Distinguishing between Abstract and Concrete References

Certification Objective

Imagine, for example, that I want to know how many square feet of lawn my business covers in a day, perhaps for advertising or other bragging rights. Rather than add this requirement to an existing interface, I could write a new one called Coverage:

```
interface Coverage {
    int getCoverage() ;
}
```

Why bother? Because it's easier, especially in programs with many lawns to manage, to use a Coverage reference and imply exactly what I'm after. It's the difference between using a reference type that has only one method I can call and a reference type that lets me call any number of methods:

```
Coverage cov = new TouchItUp();
Object obj = cov;
LawnService svc = cov;
LawnServices isvc = cov;
```

Each reference type implies my intentions with the referent. The Coverage interface leaves no room to guess. I can call getCoverage(), get an integer, and get on with it. Using abstract reference types this way isn't just a question of demonstrating that you can do it. When you can narrow the context of a piece of code by employing a precise type, you're making it easier for other programmers to understand your intent.

Using a general type, like the interface LawnServices, helps when you want to create collections. It also helps when defining return and parameter types for a method because it opens the door to future implementations. When you use concrete types, you limit the possibilities to subclasses. Consider the following example method:

```
public LawnServices getScope(Coverage cov) { … }
```

You know that the return value and parameter have to refer to concrete objects. You also know it doesn't matter to the caller what the names of those objects are. Callers need to know the interface of the parameter and return types, and that's all. The method tells them everything they need to know—that is, which method calls are available when receiving a Coverage object and when returning a LawnServices object.

There's no hard science to designing methods with abstract types in mind, and it goes a bit beyond the required scope for this book. I'm not elaborating with examples for that reason, just planting seeds for the future. But now that you've come this far, it's worth telling you what the next step for thinking in Java looks like.

THE ESSENTIALS AND BEYOND

In this chapter, you learned and applied three key types: the abstract class, the interface, and the enum. Each form provides capabilities that can't be satisfied with concrete classes alone. Each one promotes the use of abstraction to separate the meaning of class interfaces, which move to the top of the type system, from the implementation details, which move to the bottom.

This separation associates behavior with the method interfaces that you design and operations with the concrete classes that you implement. By working in this manner, you can ultimately minimize how much code any future changes or additions may affect.

ADDITIONAL EXERCISES

1. Write an enum type for the days of the week. Add two methods to it (yes, it's allowed): a static method to print the elements and a main() method that calls the static method so you can test it.

2. Write a class called NullJob that implements a LawnService interface with just the testing() method. Include a constructor that prints a message indicating a NullJob object has been made.

3. Write an empty class called Ball. Write an interface called Catcher with a receive() method that takes a Ball parameter. Write a Pitcher class with a method called partner() that takes a Catcher parameter and assigns it to a member variable. Write a Player class that implements the Catcher interface. Finally, write a Test class with a main() method that creates Pitcher and Player objects. Pass the Player reference to the Pitcher object's partner() method.

   When that is all done and compiled, add a pitch() method to the Pitcher class so it will throw a Ball object to the Player.

(Continues)

THE ESSENTIALS AND BEYOND *(Continued)*

REVIEW QUESTIONS

1. Which option identifies a difference between an `execute()` method declared in an interface and an abstract method named `execute()`?

    A. An abstract method can have default access.

    B. An interface method has `public` access.

    C. An abstract method can be overloaded.

2. True or false: An interface method cannot be declared with protected access.

3. Which of the following interfaces are declared in the `java.lang` package? (Choose all that apply.)

    A. `Serializable`

    B. `Runnable`

    C. `Readable`

    D. `List`

4. True or false: All interfaces are instances of the `Object` class.

5. Which of the following declarations is legal?

    A. `private abstract testMe();`

    B. `public abstract testMe(Object obj) ;`

    C. `private final static void testMe() {}`

    D. `protected abstract null testMe() ;`

6. Which of the following reference types would be legal parameters for a method declared `public String getAddress(Location loc) {}` ?

    A. Any subclass of `Location`, if `Location` is a class

    B. Any subclass of the `String` class

    C. Any implementation of `Location`, if `Location` is an enum

    D. Any implementation of `Location`, if `Location` is an interface

7. True or false: You can make an interface's methods visible only within their package.

(Continues)

THE ESSENTIALS AND BEYOND *(Continued)*

8. Assume you have an enumeration called Cards in which the first declared element is ACE_SPADES. What is the result of System.out.println(Cards .ACE_SPADES)?

   A. 0

   B. 1

   C. null

   D. ACE_SPADES

9. True or false: You can declare an interface method abstract.

10. If you declare an interface Tag with no methods, what is required to implement the interface?

   A. You only have to declare implements Tag.

   B. Same as A, but the class must also be concrete.

   C. You cannot implement an interface with no methods.

   D. Same as A, but the class must also be abstract.

CHAPTER 11

Throwing and Catching Exceptions in Java

Perhaps the most important aspect of writing a complete and useful Java program is dealing with exceptions to its intended execution. To paraphrase an old piece of wisdom, a program runs well for just one reason, but it can fail for all sorts of reasons. Writing a solid program has to do with good design and focusing on correct results. Protecting a program from failure has to do with checking every operation that could go sideways and providing a remedy. I'll discuss how the exception system works in the Java language and the tools at your disposal to implement it.

In this chapter, we'll cover the following topics:

▶ **Understanding the role exceptions play**

▶ **Using a try-catch block**

▶ **Understanding exception types**

▶ **Calling methods that throw exceptions**

▶ **Recognizing common exception types**

Understanding the Role Exceptions Play

Let's start with a simple premise: Any program can fail for just about any reason. Some reasons you might introduce yourself, such as code that depends on conditions you can't enforce. For example, if you make an assumption about the size of an array you can't directly control, your program runs the risk of counting on array elements that don't exist, as shown in Listing 11.1.

LISTING 11.1: Java program that generates an exception

```
void main(String args[]) {
    for (int i = 0; i < 3; i++)
        System.out.println(args[i]);
    }
}
$ java BadArrayCall 1 2
1
2
Exception in thread "main" java.lang.
ArrayIndexOutOfBoundsException: 2
        at BadArrayCall.main(arrayexc.java:4)
```

The for loop in the ArrayException program assumes that the args array will have at least three elements in it. The compiler cannot possibly check for this condition because the length of the args array isn't set until a user executes the program. The way to fix it is plain. Until then, however, the JVM has to *throw* an exception to indicate the problem.

Other kinds of exceptions are harder to fathom at first. They may relate to conditions you can't control or simply don't understand the first time you see them. You might have program code to open a file that no longer exists; there is a java.io.FileNotFoundException class to cover that eventuality. What is less obvious is which classes throw it and when. (Here's a hint: The File class doesn't use it at all.)

Still other exceptions are so completely removed from your own environment that all you can do is wonder what they mean. If you've used several web applications that are Java-based, chances are you've seen one or two long stack traces dumped in your browser, suggesting something went wrong on the server. You can't do anything about these at all.

Exceptions can and do occur all the time, even in solid program code. You can remove some exceptions by correcting the code, but eradicating them altogether isn't a viable option. Any program that draws on system resources, local and remote filesystems, networks, and other outside services have to acknowledge those requests sometimes fail. There is only one remedy for that: Embrace failure and incorporate it into your code.

Understanding Exceptions

Certification Objective

Exceptions make up the second most prolific type system in the Java core libraries following the supertype java.lang.Object. It begins with the class java.lang .Throwable, which extends Object and implements the java.io.Serializable interface. The Serializable interface lets the JVM convert implementing classes to a stream of bytes that, unlike the `toString()` method, will retain elements of the class's structure.

As you can see in Figure 11.1, two key classes extend the `Throwable` class: `Error` and `Exception`. In the section "Understanding Exception Types," I'll discuss the purpose of these two classes in detail.

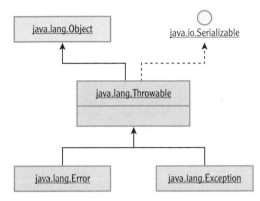

FIGURE 11.1   `Throwable` **class relationships**

The idea of a `Throwable` object is a novel one. Once a Java program encounters a problem that disrupts its normal flow of execution, the JVM captures certain information about the program state and creates an object to hold it. The JVM then *throws* this object, as in outside the execution path. If there is nothing in the program to *catch* it, the JVM receives it back, prints some of this information, and terminates the program run.

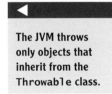

The JVM throws only objects that inherit from the `Throwable` class.

The `Throwable` class itself is concrete but doesn't have many practical direct uses. As a parent to both the `Exception` and `Error` classes, it provides a method interface and a default implementation for each method. A diagram of its key constructors and methods is shown in Figure 11.2. A UML class diagram supplies one compartment for all *operations*. A strictly-correct diagram would not separate methods and constructors, which I have added solely for visual appeal.

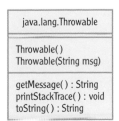

FIGURE 11.2
A diagram of the
`Throwable` **class**

The key data that a `Throwable` object holds is a *stack trace,* a list of methods that were open and waiting on called methods to return when the exception was thrown. The more methods that are open at the time, the deeper the stack. Listing 11.2 shows a program that produces a deeper stack.

LISTING 11.2: A program that throws a stack trace

```
final class StackedThrow {
    public void callOne(String bits[]) {
        callTwo(bits);
    }

    public void callTwo(String bits[]) {
        callThree(bits);
    }

    public void callThree(String bits[]) {
        System.out.println(bits[0]);
    }

    public static void main(String args[]) {
        StackedThrow st = new StackedThrow();
        st.callOne(args);
    }
}
$ java StackedThrow
Exception in thread "main" java.lang.
ArrayIndexOutOfBoundsException: 0
        at StackedThrow.callThree(arrayexc.java:18)
        at StackedThrow.callTwo(arrayexc.java:14)
        at StackedThrow.callOne(arrayexc.java:10)
        at StackedThrow.main(arrayexc.java:23)
```

Stack traces are written in inverted form. The method that began the trace appears at the bottom; the last method appears at the top. I've named the methods in Listing 11.2 to highlight this scheme.

You wouldn't expect to see a trace this simple in working code because they're easy to repair. The traces you will see tend to be much harder to untangle. They involve calls from one class to another across different packages written by other programmers and often result from some misunderstanding that winds through several methods before causing a problem.

A `Throwable` object might also contain a message, in the form of a `String` object, that describes the exception's cause. These are nice to have when you get them, especially if they help isolate the source of the problem. If the problem isn't caused by buggy code or by a failure to acquire a system resource, chances are it's a parameter with a bad value. If an exception message can tell you where it's best to start looking, it can save a lot of time.

Handling Exceptions

An exception seems like a surprising thing when you encounter it, and *surprising* is a nasty word in programming. Even if your programs don't behave as you'd like, they should fail in predictable and expected ways to the same degree they produce correct and reliable results. In Java, that responsibility means handling the exceptions that come your way.

What Java does with its exception type system, first and foremost, is identify and name well-known errors in program code execution. If you refer to the API of any package in the core libraries, you'll see Exception subclasses (and possibly Error subclasses too) listed as part of the package's contents.

For the sake of discussion, I'll refer to code that can throw exceptions as risky code. The term *risky code* does *not* include incorrect code, such as attempts to read past the length of an array or cast a value to a type to which it doesn't conform. Bugs of this sort are called *unchecked exceptions*, which is a dry but diplomatic term meaning "something you did in your code the JVM can't do much to prevent." The ArrayIndexOutOfBoundsException class is one example.

Checked exceptions represent a class of conditions that fall outside of your program's normal flow of control, as I described earlier. It is nonetheless a necessary part of programming in any language to understand that programs never operate in a foolproof environment. Networks, for one, are notoriously failure-prone resources. They may fail only momentarily and recover very quickly, but sooner or later your program code will encounter one those failures. Checked exceptions ensure that you'll be able to identify that failure; the exception facility in Java gives you a way to acknowledge and address those failures if and when they occur.

As a practical matter, the distinction between these types can be reduced to this: The compiler makes you deal with checked exceptions when they appear in code. It doesn't make you deal with unchecked exceptions. That's how the term *checking* originates in all of this.

When exceptions do get thrown, the ideal robust program will respond with the following goals in mind:

Save the data or program state.   There may be no effective way to store the current results of a program or even indicate what progress was made. Indeed, to realize this first goal, you must plan for failure and devise a strategy to minimize the loss of information. It seems a lot of people don't like thinking about how their code fails while they're trying to figure out how to succeed, but it's not optional.

All unchecked exceptions extend the RuntimeException class, which itself subclasses the Exception class.

Software that is worth the money its programmers were paid will account for the reasonable and predictable paths it can take. That's all there is to it.

Inform the user.   In the best of all worlds, a program user restarts after a crash and everything Just Works. That's a great feature in software we all use, but it sure doesn't happen by itself. A program user has to know where to find the results and whether they are reliable for use in a subsequent session. Information to the user should always consider whether they have the knowledge and experience to interpret the message. If you've handled buggy code before, you know most software doesn't do this well.

Recover and continue execution.   I like saying that for software to succeed, it has to be resilient to error. Of course, I am dead wrong about that. Successful software only has to raise its users' tolerance for failure above its capacity for failure. Still, I want programmers to write resilient programs. Let others think about gaming the user. Writing code that recovers from exceptions and continues past them—and in the best of worlds, makes them transparent to the user—isn't very hard to do, but it can get awkward and cumbersome.

To achieve some or all of these goals, a programmer must act on two fronts. One, eliminate any unchecked exceptions that can occur. This work isn't always easy or self-evident. It helps to know a few key Exception classes ahead of time. I'll address that part later in this chapter, in the section "Recognizing Common Exception Types."

Two, *catch* any checked exceptions that are thrown by the code. In a way, this work can be a little easier because the compiler will complain when you haven't done it. The work can also be tedious, especially if you let the compiler lead you around by the nose, pointing out each checked exception you haven't addressed. I discuss how to do this work in the next section.

Using a *try-catch* Block

Certification Objective

Java's catching mechanism is composed of three blocks, a try block, one or more catch blocks, and a finally block. You can put any legal statements in the try block, but it's expected that one more of those statements could throw an exception. A catch block can name one or more exception classes like parameters. Here's a trivial example:

```
public void tryCode() {
    System.out.println("Outside try block");
    try {
        System.out.println("Inside try block");
```

```
        int x = 5;
    }
    catch (Exception ex) {
        ex.printStackTrace();
    }
    // Won't compile
    System.out.println(x);
}
```

The `tryCode()` method contains a `try` block that prints a message, then declares and initializes the integer x. The `catch` block declares it will receive an `Exception` object, which like any other type, also supports any subclasses. If an exception is thrown, the variable ex refers to the object.

In this example, I call the `printStackTrace()` method using this reference. Although it appears in Java code all the time, it is about the least useful way to handle an exception. All it does is dump the stack trace, just like the JVM. The program doesn't terminate on the spot; that's the only difference.

◀

The least useful catch block, by a wide margin, is an empty one.

You should also note that a `try` block has its own *scope* within the method. Any variable, like x, that is declared inside a `try` block is lost once the block completes. Such variables do not carry over to the `catch` block. They are also not visible to the whole method unless they are declared at method scope.

Catching an Exception

To catch an actual exception, you must include at least one statement in the `try` block that throws. The section "Calling Methods That Throw Exceptions" later in this chapter has more detail on this point. For now, I'll provide example code to show how the mechanism works. Let's say we want a program that hangs around for 5 seconds before it quits. The `Thread` class has a `sleep()` method that takes a number of milliseconds for an argument. You might be tempted to write it like this:

```
final class Sleeper {
    public static void main(String args[]) {
        Thread.sleep(5000);
    }
}
```

This code, however, will not compile. If you try, you'll get this error:

```
Sleeper.java:3: error: unreported exception InterruptedException;
    must be caught or declared to be thrown
                Thread.sleep(5000);
                    ^
1 error
```

The compiler complains that you haven't handled the `InterruptedException` class, which means it's required when calling the `Thread.sleep()` method. I'll rewrite the class accordingly:

```
final class Sleeper {
    public static void main(String args[]) {
        try {
            System.out.println("Entering sleep()");
            Thread.sleep(5000);
            System.out.println("Exited sleep()");
        }
        catch (InterruptedException iex) {
            System.out.println("Sleeper.main: " + iex);
        }
    }
}
$ java Sleeper
Entering sleep()
<five second pause>
Exited sleep()
```

I've added methods in the `try` block to print before and after calling the `sleep()` method. I've also changed the `catch` block to print the name of the current class and invoke the `InterruptedException` object's `toString()` method. This program doesn't induce the exception it catches, which may make the `try`/`catch` block seem unnecessary to the untrained eye. Nonetheless, the compiler requires us to observe every exception thrown by any method we call.

Throwing an Exception

But what's the point of implementing a catch block if you can't see how it works? Fortunately that's not a hard problem to solve. Remember that exceptions are just classes, so you can create one if you have access to its constructor. The JVM can throw any object that is a subclass of the `Throwable` class; as it turns out, so can you.

Replace the code in the body of the `try` block in the current example with this statement:

See Chapter 3,
"Using Java
Operators and
Conditional Logic,"
for a review of deci-
sion constructs.

▶

```
throw new InterruptedException("Thrown by hand");
```

If you run the program now, you'll see this output:

```
Sleeper.main: java.lang.InterruptedException: Thrown by hand
```

If instead you insert a `throw` statement before the other statements, the compiler will complain that the other statements are unreachable. This error occurs because throwing an exception is a transfer of control, similar to what takes place with a `return` statement, except control transfers directly to a `catch` block, as shown in Figure 11.3. Any subsequent statements in the `try` block are ignored.

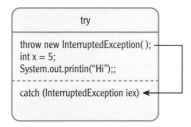

FIGURE 11.3 Throwing an exception in a `try` block

The compiler can't evaluate which statement in a `try` block will raise an exception at runtime. It knows which methods *could* throw an exception—that is what checked exceptions are for. A `throw` statement, however, leaves no room for doubt. As with a `return` statement, no statement that follows in the code block may execute. The compiler is required to complain and insist the matter be corrected before it can compile the offending class.

The compiler also complains if you declare a `catch` block with an exception that cannot be thrown in the `try` block. You'll see this error if you remove both the `Thread.sleep()` method call and the `throw` statement. The `Exception` class itself is not subject to this rule; even with an empty try block, you can declare catching an Exception object and it will compile..

Using Multiple Catch Blocks

There's one more aspect to consider with a thrown exception. The JVM will transfer control to the first `catch` block that *matches the exception's type*.

The statements in one `try` block can throw more than one kind of exception. When that's the case, you can write separate `catch` statements to handle each one. Because the JVM matches the exception by type, `catch` blocks that define the narrowest range of exceptions must come first. Supertype exceptions must come later, as shown in Figure 11.4.

Notice in Figure 11.4 that the two unrelated exceptions, `InterruptedException` and `FileNotFoundException`, could be listed in either order, so long as the first type doesn't claim exception objects of the second type. If you place a more general type first, the compiler tells you that exceptions of the narrower types are already caught, as shown in Listing 11.3.

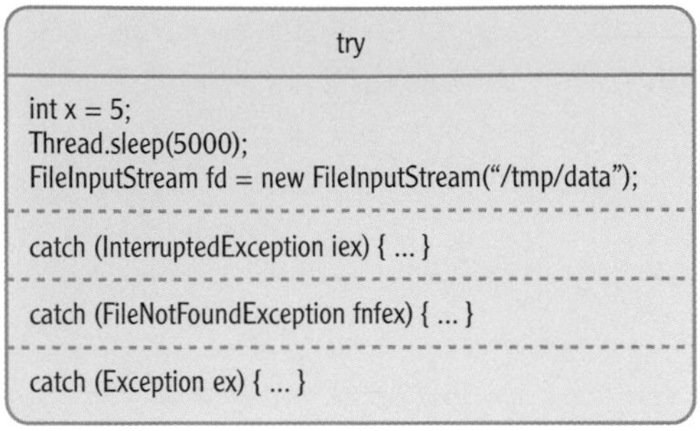

FIGURE 11.4 A try block with multiple catch statements

LISTING 11.3: Program with catch blocks listed out of order

```
// needed for FileNotFoundException reference
import java.io.*;

final class BadCatch {
    public static void main(String args[]) {
        try {
            System.out.println("Whichever");
            Thread.sleep(5000);
            FileInputStream fd = new FileInputStream("/tmp/
dummy");
        }
        catch (InterruptedException iex) {
            System.out.println("BadCatch.main: " + iex);
        }
        catch (Exception ex) {}
        catch (FileNotFoundException fnfex) {
            System.out.println("BadCatch.main: " + fnfex);
        }
    }
}
$ javac BadCatch.java
arrayexc.java:13: error: exception FileNotFoundException has
    already been caught
        catch (FileNotFoundException fnfex) {
        ^
1 error
```

In this arrangement, the catch block for Exception receives control for any exception thrown that isn't an InterruptedException object. Any subsequent catch blocks are unreachable code.

There's another unfortunate outcome in this example. One of the catch blocks has no code. I purposely did this to save space on the page and avoid distracting you from the main point—but this outcome is quite common with catch blocks. It's easy to dismiss them as unimportant code in the moment and tell yourself you'll return to it later.

Resist this urge. If you don't intend to think through all the consequences of running your code, you don't intend to write a complete program (also my excuse here). It's as simple as that. Remember the goals:

▶ Save data or program state.

▶ Inform the user.

▶ Provide ongoing execution.

Don't worry too much about it, though. You'll fall short of these goals, even when they're not hard to implement. Every programmer does. It's often a question of the time available to complete a program. Sometimes, the awkward style that exception code foists on the programmer is discouraging. The extra indentation takes up space; long class names for exceptions make that problem worse. Coding multiple catch blocks can be repetitive and error prone. Writing tests to cover every catch block without modifying the try block is also a tedious exercise.

This work can take on a life of its own that, under time pressure, doesn't seem justified by the time required to do it well. In this matter, I can only say your conscience is your guide. It wouldn't hurt, though, to collaborate with other programmers and establish some incentives. I know one company that uses a catch jar; if someone spots an empty or trivial catch block you wrote, you have to put some money in the jar (and fix the block).

Fortunately, the Java SE 7 platform has added a couple of features to make writing exception code a little easier. One of those features is multi-catch statement syntax. It lets you declare multiple exception types for a single catch block so they can use the same code. I can now revise the current example like this:

Inspecting others' programs is called *code review*. It's not just an exercise in proofreading; it's also a valuable learning tool.

```
catch (FileNotFoundException | InterruptedException mx) {
    System.out.println("BadCatch.main: " + mx);
}
```

Proper syntax requires you to separate exception classes from each other with a pipe and use a single variable to represent them. Now it's possible to write one catch block for all exceptions that can use the same logic.

Using a *finally* Block

Let's say you have a try block with several statements in it, which altogether can throw any one of several exceptions. You decide to write a catch block for each possible exception. One hard thing to sort out in this situation is how to get all the possible execution paths to transfer control to one place. In my example, there are three ways to leave the `try` block:

- ▶ Normal execution.
- ▶ Throw an `InterruptionException` object.
- ▶ Throw a `FileNotFoundException` object.

And there are four possible paths that can follow from them:

- ▶ Bypass all `catch` blocks.
- ▶ Catch an `InterruptedException` object.
- ▶ Catch a `FileNotFoundException` object.
- ▶ Catch an `Exception` object.

The compiler will always let you catch an `Exception` object as a guard against bad logic.

When a `catch` block executes, it has two possible paths. It can execute normally, after which control bypasses the remaining blocks and processing continues in the host method. Or the `catch` block could also throw an exception. It's just more Java code, after all, and just as vulnerable to bad logic (or a deliberate use of the `throw` statement) as any other code block. When a `catch` block throws an exception, however, there's not a lot you can do to manage that new `Throwable` thing that isn't awkward and cumbersome.

If you want to ensure that all possible paths of execution will transfer control to a single point, add a `finally` block to the end of your `try-catch` block scheme. A `finally` block is guaranteed to execute following any path of execution that results from a `try-catch` sequence, except when the JVM terminates the program or a call to the `System.exit()` method occurs along the way. Those two cases aside, it doesn't matter if your code happens to cascade through a series of thrown exceptions: The JVM will return control, sooner or later, to the `finally` block.

A common use for the `finally` block is to release or close out system resources that were allocated along the way. Classes in the `java.io` and `java.net` packages do a lot of this. When you open files or network sockets, or even launch external processes (using the `Runtime.getRuntime().exec()` method), you acquire resources through the operating system that are bound to your program.

If a Java program dies "the right way," most operating systems will figure out what happened and restore such resources back to their own pools. It is an egregious error to rely on that behavior taking place, however, and it's as sincere a request for creating trouble for the system as a program can make. If you open a network socket or other system resource, you're obliged to close it. The API will absolutely provide a method for that purpose. The same goes for any system resource you request.

At the same time, resources external to your program that you have allocated can fail for lots of reasons you don't control. That's where a `finally` block's guarantee makes its money. If for some reason those conditions force your JVM to throw an exception, the `finally` block is your chance to release those resources before your program goes away. Listing 11.4 shows an example program that creates a test file (which it has to clean up) and tries a couple of remote network services.

LISTING 11.4: Using a `finally` block to restore system state

```java
import java.io.File;
import java.net.Socket;
import java.io.IOException;
import java.net.UnknownHostException;

final class TestResources {

    private File file;
    private Socket socket;

    void getFile(String fname) {
        try {
            file = new File("newData");
            if (file.createNewFile()) {
                System.out.println("New file");
            } else {
                System.out.println("Existing file");
            }
        } catch (IOException iox) {
            System.err.println("Problem getting file " + fname);
            // could encounter the same IO problem
            file = new File("test");
        } finally {
            // clean up test file
            if (file != null) {
                file.deleteOnExit();
            }
        }
    }
```

(Continues)

LISTING 11.4: Using a `finally` block to restore system state *(Continued)*

```java
    void getConnected(String host, int port) {
        try {
            socket = new Socket(host, port);
        } catch (UnknownHostException ex) {
            System.err.println("No service at " + host + ":" +
port);
        } catch (IOException ex) {
            System.err.println("Connection attempt failed");
        } finally {
            System.err.println("Closing down");
            try {
                if (socket != null) {
                    socket.close();
                }
                System.out.println("Socket resource closed");
            } catch (IOException ex) {
                System.err.println("Oh well, I tried.");
            }
        }
    }

    public static void main(String args[]) {
        TestResources tr = new TestResources();
        // does this file exist?
        tr.getFile("plugh");
        // test various sites and ports
        tr.getConnected("localhost", 80);
        // bad host
        tr.getConnected("plugh", 1234);
        // bad port
        tr.getConnected("localhost", 99999);
    }
}
$ java TestResources
New file
Connection attempt failed
Socket resource closed
Closing down
No service at plugh:1234
Closing down
Socket resource closed
Socket resource closed
Closing down
```

(Continues)

LISTING 11.4: Using a `finally` block to restore system state *(Continued)*

```
Exception in thread "main" java.lang.IllegalArgumentException:
    port out of range:99999
  at java.net.InetSocketAddress.<init>(InetSocketAddress.
java:118)
  at java.net.Socket.<init>(Socket.java:189)
  at TestResources.getConnected(TestResources.java:33)
  at TestResources.main(TestResources.java:60)
```

The first thing you might notice is that exception handling can add a lot of lines of code. Here I've implemented the blocks in a straightforward way. The more deliberate your style, the bulkier it gets, but it's too soon to discuss ways to tone it down. Get accustomed to the "added weight" for now. Somewhere lower on your list of things to learn, you can add "find a cleaner way to implement `try` blocks."

Following the `main()` method, you'll notice I create a `TestResources` object, exercising the `getFile()` method once and the `getConnected()` method three times. In the first case, the `finally` block in the `getFile()` method makes sure the test file gets deleted; that's just good manners.

In the latter case, I am testing for success and failure of both checked and unchecked exceptions. Your results might vary. If you have a service open at port 80 of your own system, for example, the first connection attempt might succeed. The second one will fail, unless you happen to locate a system named `plugh` on your local network that's running a service on port 1234. The third attempt will always fail: The highest-numbered port on a system is 65535.

Notice the `finally` block in the `getConnected()` method includes another `try/catch` block! That's legal, of course, and necessary if you invoke a risky call inside. And it gets a bit crowded in the file too. There's nothing to be done for that except to find a style that helps you manage the clutter without making the code harder to read. Again, worry about that later.

At last, you can see that my final test raises an unchecked exception. Spurious inputs like that are the kind of thing you can throw right back at the user if it doesn't make sense to do anything else. There's no reason to believe most programs are obliged to protect users against their own bad input—if in fact it's coming from the user. There might instead be a configuration file in the mix, and for that situation, it would be nice if the program reported that the file's content must be wrong.

If you just want to make sure some concluding bit of logic runs for all cases after your `try/catch` scheme, a `finally` block is the way to go. Simply add one at the end of any `catch` blocks you have.

The full set, in the abstract, looks like this:

```
try {
   // risky code
}
catch (Exception ex) {
   // save data, inform the user
}
finally {
   // complete the logic
   // release allocated resources
}
```

Handling Unchecked Exceptions

So far I have carefully avoided using unchecked exceptions in my examples. It's actually quite easy to illustrate the flow of execution to a catch block with clearly bugged code, as shown in Listing 11.5.

LISTING 11.5: Catching an ArrayIndexOutOfBoundsException

```
final class CatchArraySize {
    public static void main(String args[]) {
        try {
            for (int i = 0; i < 3; i++)
                System.out.println("" + args[i]);
            }
        catch(ArrayIndexOutOfBoundsException arrx) {
            System.err.println("Array access exceeded length");
        }
    }
}
$ java CatchArraySize
Array access exceeded length
```

In one sense, the problem in the code has been solved. If the user inputs too few arguments, this program preserves its running state and informs the user. There is no data to save or an alternate path of execution to consider, but these things wouldn't be hard to support.

We haven't improved on what the JVM already does in this case, but this is a tiny piece of code. You could argue, with some force, that managing program errors this way in a very large body of code meets the basic criteria for exception handling and, in fact, allows you to customize it however you'd like.

On the other hand, catching exceptions you didn't have to throw is a hard practice to justify. It leads to more lines of code, for one. It's arguable that it improves at all on the JVM's default output. It only defers the termination of a program in a trivial way. Perhaps most important, it hides the opportunity for replacing it with better code *and* it's expensive to compute. To construct an exception object, you have to convert the stack track data to string form. The more data there is, the more expensive the object.

For this example, you have already seen a solution in the language that helps you avoid it: the enhanced for loop. By rewriting this program with it, the problem we had drops out altogether, as shown in Listing 11.6.

See Chapter 5, "Using Loops in Java Code," for a refresher on the enhanced for loop.

LISTING 11.6: Using an enhanced for loop for a variable argument count

```
final class PrintAnyArray {
    public static void main(String args[]) {
        for (String arg : args)
            System.out.println(arg);
    }
}
$ java PrintAnyArray
$ java PrintAnyArray 1 2
1
2
$ java PrintAnyArray a b r x v
a
b
r
x
v
```

Now the program reads the value of args.length itself and applies it automatically. We also could have used the args.length value as a limit in a basic for loop, which was the first approach in Java for averting an array bounds exception.

If there's something worse than handling an ArrayIndexOutOfBoundsException in a catch block, it's handling *all* unchecked exceptions using the Exception class. You'll see a lot of code that does it. I, for one, discourage the practice. The first thing catching an Exception object tells me is that the programmer has developed some lazy habits. Or what's worse, that they encountered an exception type that was strange to them, didn't track it down, and used a catch block to defer the problem.

Even if that kind of code doesn't break as I am maintaining or testing it, I'll wonder when it might break. It's a lot like having to be wary of a pit in a construction lot that has a thin plank over it. That's energy spent on my own safety I'd much rather devote to the task at hand.

You will find more than a few examples on the Internet that use runtime exceptions to inform a try/catch example. Many of them provide a disclaimer, too: Just for illustration. When does that disclaimer ever work? Don't develop this habit. Use exception handling when you can't avoid it.

Understanding Exception Types

You now have enough example code and friendly advice to feel your way through exception handling. In this part of the chapter, I explore further the difference between checked and unchecked exceptions. I'll also discuss the Error class and its descendants. Frankly, they get a bad rap, and even though you may not incorporate them into your code very often, they deserve a fair hearing.

Refer again to Figure 11.1. The Throwable class is the base of the exception system and represents the first object type the JVM knows how to throw. It is also a Serializable type, which means the JVM knows how to convert it into a byte stream.

Serializing an object is not the same as turning some aspect of it into a String value. Serializing translates a whole object into a form that retains the properties of its type. From this form, an object can be de-serialized and immediately used as an object again. When you want to share an object with another Java program or save it in its most complete object state, serializing gives you a way to do it.

However, the Serializable interface isn't a good example of Java interfaces as you've learned them. For starters, it has no methods. As source code, it looks like this:

```
package java.io;
interface Serializable { }
```

This is called a *marker interface* by some and a *tagging interface* by others. Programmers use it to indicate to the JVM which types are suitable for storing and retrieving from a persistent form. What the JVM does to serialize an object isn't a secret, but it's meant to be a hands-off operation.

You'll have no need to serialize exceptions in this chapter.

> Another interface, java.io.Externalizable, lets the programmer define how an object should be converted to a byte stream form and back.

Understanding Errors

There are two kinds of Throwable objects a program should not catch, according to the JDK documentation. Both kinds are called *unchecked exceptions*. Classes that inherit from the Error class are one kind. They represent abnormal conditions in a program that, like checked exceptions, fall outside the direct control of a program.

Unlike checked exceptions, however, unchecked exceptions are by nature difficult to manage. The problems they identify often compromise the health of the JVM itself, which may call into question the sanity of the code it is running. Thus the documentation describes Error subclasses as Throwable objects a "reasonable program" would not catch.

Here are some examples of Error subclasses:

▶ CoderMalfunctionError

▶ IOError

▶ LinkageError

▶ VirtualMachineError

A CoderMalfunctionError occurs when a subclass of either the CharsetEncoder or CharSetEncoder abstract class encounters a problem encoding or decoding a stream of bytes. The IOError encapsulates "serious" I/O errors; that's all the API documentation tells us. A LinkageError is a case in which one class has a dependency on another—for example, as a field member—but the second class has been changed and recompiled in a way that breaks the dependency.

The most descriptive of these types, from a program perspective, is a VirtualMachineError, which is a parent class to the InternalError, OutOfMemoryError, StackOverflowError, and UnknownError classes. The class names here form a descriptive picture of the problems they cover. Chances are you will rarely see these errors raised. The class documentation helps to see that such problems have nonetheless been named, categorized, and described.

Understanding Unchecked Exceptions

The other kind of unchecked exception inherits from the RuntimeException class, as shown in Figure 11.5. It can be thrown at any time, without warning, by a method or constructor. It occurs because of some disagreeable runtime event.

Many of these types, like ArrayIndexOutOfBoundsException, are conditions that arise from improper use of a language feature or operation. All arrays are subclasses of Object, for example, but their operations are built into the language. When one of those operations arrives at an insensible condition, the JVM communicates the problem by creating an exception object and sending it along.

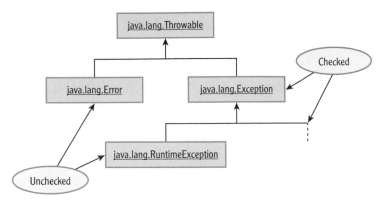

FIGURE 11.5 Checked and unchecked exceptions by class type

Up to this point, I have defined unchecked exceptions as problems you can and should correct in your code. To be honest, that's a white lie some instructors tell to motivate Java programmers. We want to make sure you focus on writing correct code before it becomes apparent that you can mask program problems with exception handling.

Some unchecked exception types, however, view JVM or system configuration as a source of invalid input. Unfortunately for beginners, these problems often appear as you're experimenting with code and seem surprising. It then takes some time to understand the problem and more time to fix it correctly.

When you've gone through that a couple of times, it's easier to understand why there are so many blocks that catch the Exception class: It covers every exception you haven't specifically called out as well as every exception you'd rather not hear about. But just because the temptation can be strong doesn't mean the practice is okay. These are still problems you should correct rather than handle silently.

Many classes fall in this category:

▶ NegativeArraySizeException

▶ IllegalArgumentException

▶ SecurityException

▶ UnsupportedOperationException

We've seen the NegativeArraySizeException class before; the JVM raises this exception any time you construct an array with a negative value. The IllegalArgumentException is the parent class to a broad category of bad arguments, including ones that have been fed to an object at the wrong time (IllegalThreadStateException). The JVM raises a NumberFormatException object when a String object that is supposed to have a numeric value can't be converted.

SecurityException objects probably inspire a great deal of try/catch work-arounds. It's not usually obvious from the error messages they generate what to do to fix them. They are thrown by the java.lang.SecurityManager class for several reasons. Most of them concern requests for resources or operations the program does not have the privileges to use or invoke. Although it's not an exam objective, you'll save time and your sanity by reviewing the SecurityManager class and learning the formats of the files it uses.

The UnsupportedOperationException class is another self-evident type with a number of subclasses. You may encounter it early (and often) when you learn to use collection classes. It so happens that some collection classes don't implement all the methods they should, according to the interfaces they have declared. Ugly as that is, it's apparently an unavoidable condition. To compensate for this, the classes will throw UnsupportedOperationException objects to alert the programmer. It's a learn-as-you-go kind of thing. On the bright side, it's yet another good reason to depend on your JDK classes only after you've verified them with testing.

This branch of classes also covers cases such as trying to write to a read-only file system or trying to invoke a GUI on a system that doesn't have a local monitor. Figure 11.6 shows this class and its direct subclasses.

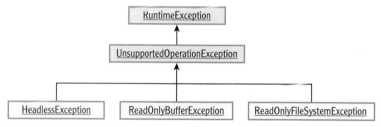

FIGURE 11.6   The UnsupportedOperationException class and its direct subclasses

These are all conditions you don't want to catch in code. It's better to let a program fail, know the system isn't configured to expectations, and fix these problems where they stand.

Understanding Checked Exceptions

The Exception class documentation defines checked exceptions as "conditions that a reasonable application might want to catch." That's not too exacting a formula. I take it to mean the distinction between checked and unchecked exceptions is, in some way, open to interpretation. I have to form my impression of the difference, more or less, by examples in the JDK core libraries.

Fortunately the practical definition is much easier to apply. As Figure 11.5 shows, checked exceptions extend the Exception class but not the RuntimeException class. And, as I said earlier, the JVM can throw an unchecked exception without warning. You the programmer, however, will not only throw and catch checked exceptions. To play the exception game properly, you'll declare them as well.

Here's the thing: Checked exceptions aren't bad. They're good. You *want* to throw them to callers. Why? Because they give you a separate way to communicate with your callers when something's wrong.

Let's take two examples, one with a constructor and one with a method. Listing 11.7 shows the familiar Customer class. In this version, its constructor accepts a String parameter. The constructor tries to match the parameter to an internal array of names. If it doesn't, the name variable retains its initial empty value.

LISTING 11.7: The Customer class with a constructor and a method

```java
final class Customer {
    // will be replaced by database access some day
    private String[] names = { "Jess", "Guy", "Samuh" };
    private String name = "";

    public Customer(String str) {
        for (String name : names)
            if (name.equals(str)) this.name = name;
    }

    public String getName() {
        return this.name;
    }

    public static void main(String args[]) {
        Customer cst = new Customer("Samuh");
        System.out.println(cst.getName());
        cst = new Customer("Lance");
        System.out.println(cst.getName());
    }
}
$ java Customer
Samuh

$
```

The program output shows the problem. The code defends against a null value for the name member. There isn't, however, such a thing as a default customer. If you start using a database later on, how can you tell the caller they've provided a name that has no match in the system?

You could *encapsulate* the constructor and use a method to return a NullCustomer subclass, like this:

```
private Customer(String name) {
    // Validation now perfomed by getCustomer()
    this.name = name;
}
public static Customer getCustomer(String str) {
    for (String name : names) {
        if (name.equals(str)) return new Customer(name);
    }
    return new NullCustomer();
}
```

This approach has an elegance I admire. Callers receive an object, as they'd expect from a constructor. The caller now has to check whether the received object is useful, but it keeps communication to one channel. That can be a good thing, especially if the idea of null objects is applied consistently.

To implement this approach, however, you have to allow inheritance. If you do, there are other obligations a caller may reasonably infer you have also observed. It's easy to remove the final keyword from the class declaration, but the practical consequences go beyond skating past the compiler.

If that prospect sounds like more work than benefit, let your constructor instead declare that it throws an exception. Create a class, such as CustomerNotFoundException. Let it extend the Exception class. Override any methods as you please, but often a good class name can cover the work you need. Then alter your constructor like this:

```
public Customer(String str) throws CustomerNotFoundException {
    for (String name : names) {
        if (name.equals(str)) this.name = name;
    }
    throw new CustomerNotFoundException();

}
```

The constructor's signature uses the keyword throws to notify callers of the CustomerNotFoundException class. The exception can then be passed to the caller wherever the throw keyword is used in the constructor body. This structure is the calling card of a checked exception. It's the same for a method:

```
public static Customer getCustomer(String str) throws
    CustomerNotFoundException {
```

◄

Chapter 9, "Inheriting Code and Data in Java," discusses the obligations you assume when allowing inheritance in a class.

```
        for (String name : names) {
            if (name.equals(str)) return new Customer(name);
        }
        throw new CustomerNotFoundException();
    }
```

A method or constructor can declare as many different exceptions as it needs to throw. Just separate the types with a comma the same way you would if you were implementing multiple interfaces.

The compiler will verify that a constructor or method throws the exception types that it declares. In these examples, the connection is obvious, but it isn't always so plain. In the next sections, you'll see how a method or constructor can also declare an exception that was thrown at it.

Calling Methods That Throw Exceptions

Certification Objective

Now you see what declared exceptions are for. They make it possible to notify callers that some responses are thrown rather than returned. The cause of those exception responses may occur within the called method, but they can also be the result of a method or constructor the called method uses to perform its own computation.

It is *assumed* that these responses result from a condition the called method can't (or shouldn't) resolve on its own. Here again is where the practice of applying exception handling well relies as much on interpretation as following set rules.

When you call a method that throws checked exceptions, you have two options. One, the calling method can handle the exception with a try/catch block. Two, you can make the calling method declare the same exception. Some people call this the *catch or declare requirement*.

Catching a Checked Exception

Early in this chapter I used the term *risky code*. I had in mind specifically methods that throw checked exceptions. The risk is clear and specific, and it's often a momentary problem. If you call a method that connects you to a remote server, any number of things can go wrong. The name you give for the server may be misspelled. Your system's connection to the Internet may go down for a minute. A network device between you and the remote system may have to reboot. The remote system itself might be down.

A good checked exception class bundles the details in a way you, the calling programmer, can easily identify. You can then decide how to manage the exception when you receive it.

The rest you have already heard: Work to save data or state, inform the user, and provide a means to keep the program running. Admittedly, these goals are easier said than done. Let's say you wanted to retry connecting to a remote server. The attempt will be futile if the server name is wrong (java.net .UnknownHostException) or the remote system stays down for a long time (java.net.ConnectException) or even something else (java.io.IOException). Listing 11.8 offers an incomplete example of this problem.

LISTING 11.8: NetProblems class with multiple possible exceptions

```
import java.net.*;
import java.io.*;

final class NetProblems {
    public static void main(String args[]) {
        Socket sock;
        try {
            sock = new Socket(args[0], 25);
        }
        catch(UnknownHostException uhx) {
            System.out.println("Bad host name: bailing out");
        }
        catch(IOException iox) {
            System.out.println("Network problem: bailing out");
        }
        System.out.println("Finished");
    }
}
$ java NetProblems
Exception in thread "main" java.lang.
ArrayIndexOutOfBoundsException: 0
        at NetProblems.main(test.java:8)
$ java NetProblems foo.bar
Bad host name: bailing out
Finished
$ java NetProblems 192.168.15.108
Finished
$ java NetProblems localhost
Finished
$ java NetProblems 192.168.15.245
Network problem: bailing out
Finished
```

You also cannot use multi-catch syntax with a parent exception and any of its subclasses.

In the NetProblems class, I try to create a Socket object by connecting with a remote system's email service. The well-known port for an email server that uses the Simple Mail Transfer Protocol (SMTP) is 25. I have implemented a catch block for each exception thrown by the Socket constructor I am using. The UnknownHostException class inherits from the IOException class, so they must appear in the order shown. I then try various command-line arguments with the class.

The program could inform the user more plainly when no argument is given. I've omitted that part for brevity. Notice when a clearly bad name is given, the code raises an UnknownHostException object. The IP addressing ending in 108 is another computer on my home network. The argument localhost is the system I ran the code on. The IP address ending in 245 does not exist. The output line Finished just shows that control transfers to the end of the try/catch block.

In each case I have only replaced the JVM's standard complaint formula with a simpler message. That's a start, albeit a shallow one. If you're going to write more resilient code, there's plenty of work ahead. The idea isn't to quit on it, however, if you're short on time. Rather, find a package that already handles this work and employ it. Just because you want resilient code doesn't mean you have to write it yourself.

Declaring a Checked Exception

Assuming it is better to pass along an exception rather than handle it, you can declare it as part of your method or constructor signature. There are some rules you have to observe because exceptions are classes, some of which are parents to others. As you've already seen, parent exceptions must be listed after child exceptions under a single try block. You also cannot use multi-catch syntax with two or more inheritance-related exceptions.

When you declare an exception received from a method or constructor you call, you can throw instead a parent exception. In the best case, this flexibility lets you capture a multitude of declared exceptions with a shorter declaration, thereby avoiding some clutter.

In the worst case, you may be tempted to declare throwing the Exception class itself. Think about this for a second. Although you can avoid throwing exceptions with a little extra work, such as making default or null versions of your return type, sometimes throwing is the right thing to do. Even so, few programmers will thank you for the extra work.

Declaring a more general exception type, however, almost always makes it less clear why you're throwing exceptions in the first place, other than to defer a legion of problems. If you think tracking a class's hierarchy back to the Object class can get tedious, wait until you have to track an exception through its method calls the same way. It's a frustrating exercise in navigation.

You cannot declare a more specific exception or break a general type down into subclasses. There's no reason to believe you should be able to, but it's a tempting thought once you've worked with exceptions for a while.

Recognizing Common Exception Types

Several exception classes come up time and again in code, either while you're learning or because the missteps they represent are pretty common. At this point, you've got the resources and the skills you need to review these classes by documentation and experiment with them.

**Certification
Objective**

Before you consider taking Oracle's OCA exam, you should also write as many of your own test cases as you can. It's a goal of the exam to ensure that you can read Java code effectively. That said, you'll never read code as carefully before you've written code that just won't compile as after. You're going to find out that, in the beginning at least, you need to learn the elements of the Java language one by one before you can build true confidence in reading large tracts of code accurately.

There isn't a place in most books of this sort to say, "Good luck to you!" So here it is: Study carefully. Don't rely completely on any one source, including this book! Write, break, and repair plenty of Java code, and you'll learn enough to move on.

I've sprinkled common exception types you should know in examples throughout the book as well as this chapter. I reprint them here for the sake of a one-stop list:

- ► ArithemticException
- ► ArrayIndexOutOfBoundsException
- ► ClassCastException
- ► IOException
- ► NullPointerException
- ► NumberFormatException
- ► SecurityException
- ► UnsupportedOperationException

THE ESSENTIALS AND BEYOND

This chapter covered the theory and application of exceptions and exception handling in Java code. Exceptions make up an entire type system, beginning with the Throwable class. Each subclass names an error and supplies information, in the form of a stack trace, about its occurrence.

There are two broad classes of exceptions: checked exceptions, which are declared, verified by the compiler, and raised by the JVM as conditions warrant; and unchecked exceptions, which specify errors in the code. Although you can use them the same way you'd use checked exceptions, declaring one is tantamount to saying there's something wrong with your code you would rather not fix. Unchecked exceptions are descendants of the Error and RuntimeException classes. All other exceptions descend from the Exception class.

Programmers who encounter exceptions have two options: handle them with a try/catch block or re-declare them in order to pass them along. It's good practice to handle exceptions whenever possible and pass them along when it doesn't make sense to handle them immediately.

ADDITIONAL EXERCISES

1. Write a CustomerNotFoundException class. Include a constructor that requires a String parameter. Override the toString() method so it will print the message. Use a main() method to test-throw the exception.

2. Write a class with a main() method that throws the Exception class. In the code body, call Thread.sleep() with some duration less than 10 seconds. Also create a Socket object that connects to foo.bar at port 80.

3. Write a Server class with a method that constructs a ServerSocket object (from the java.net package), using port 22222. Use the compiler to tell you which exception(s) you must catch for the code to compile. Add a main() method and call the method you wrote from it.

4. Add a method to the Server class from exercise 3 that declares the exception you discovered. Use port 66666 for the ServerSocket constructor. Update the main() method to call this method after the first one. Compile the code. What happens when you run it?

(Continues)

THE ESSENTIALS AND BEYOND *(Continued)*

REVIEW QUESTIONS

1. Which of the following statements is correct?

   A. You can only declare checked exceptions.

   B. You can throw `Error` subclasses.

   C. You can only handle `Exception` subclasses.

   D. You cannot extend the `Throwable` class directly.

2. Which of the following classes is a checked exception?

   A. `SecurityException`

   B. `IOError`

   C. `UnknownHostException`

   D. `IllegalArgumentException`

3. True or false: You can combine checked and unchecked exceptions in one `catch` block using multi-catch syntax.

4. Which category of `Throwable` classes is also `Serializable`?

   A. All `Exception` classes

   B. All `RuntimeException` classes

   C. All `Error` classes

   D. All of the above

5. True or false: You can throw any Java class as an exception, and you can declare any Java class as a return type.

6. When are you required to use a `finally` block?

   A. Never

   B. When the program code doesn't terminate on its own

   C. When there are two or more catch blocks

   D. Any time you use multi-catch syntax

(Continues)

THE ESSENTIALS AND BEYOND (Continued)

7. Which exception will the following code snippet throw?

    ```
    Object obj = new Integer(3);
    String str = (String)obj;
    System.out.println(str);
    ```

    A. IllegalArgumentException

    B. NumberFormatException

    C. ClassCastException

    D. UnsupportedOperationException

8. What will happen if you add the statement System.out.println(5 / 0); to a working main() method?

    A. It will not compile.

    B. It will not run.

    C. It will run and throw an IllegalArgumentException.

    D. It will run and throw an ArithmeticException.

9. Which of the following lists is a correct sequence for catching exceptions?

    A. SecurityException, IOError, Exception

    B. NumberFormatException, RuntimeException, ClassCastException

    C. IllegalArgumentException, Exception, RuntimeException

10. The UnsupportedOperationException class is used closely by which core JDK package?

    A. java.net

    B. java.io

    C. java.util

    D. java.lang

Answers to Review Questions

Chapter 1: Introducing the Basics of Java

1.   **A, D** If you missed this one, please reread the chapter!

2.   **False**

3.   **C** Object equality is a tricky concept. It will serve you well to remember that two variables *can* point to the same object in memory. They had certainly better be equal! Whether two variables, pointing to objects that have the same content, are equal is something the class programmer has to encode. Keep that information in your back pocket for now.

4.   **A** Each non-static member in an object belongs only to that object. Other objects of the same type maintain their own values.

5.   **A** A wildcard applies only to the package listed, not to nested packages. It is also not a *globbing* mechanism; it only matches class files.

6.   **A** The Java Virtual Machine adds some behind-the-scenes information. These values are called *metadata*. You don't have to worry about this aspect of a class until you're ready to look into the internals of the JVM.

7.   **B** Review the discussion on variable lifetime if this answer is not clear to you.

8.   **D** When arguments are input on the command line, they're in the control of the shell. The shell doesn't know what a `String` object is and uses unquoted or unescaped white space to separate the arguments.

9.   **True** Remember, the Java compiler will add one if the programmer does not.

10. **C** The classpath is the final link between a Java program in runtime and the shell environment of your system. The program knows where to find classes by package declaration. The system has to know where to find the packages. Between the two, the JVM is able to locate files that are Java classes and then load them into memory.

Chapter 2: Applying Data Types in Java Programming

1. **B** The JVM must create this object as instructed. Without a reference, however, you can't access it. It will be eligible for garbage collection right away.

2. **D** Immutable objects (referents) can't be modified once they are created.

3. **D** The highest bit in any integral type's range is reserved for the sign. That leaves 2^{63} possible nonnegative and negative values. We use one in the nonnegative range for zero, leaving enough for $2^{63}-1$ positive values.

4. **B** 256 is too large for a byte. Other integral types will have their bit ranges padded with zeroes.

5. **D** The initial capacity of a `StringBuilder` object is 16 plus the length of the string argument (here, 18 characters). For exams (and possibly some job interviews), you'll be expected to know by heart some technical details of well-known classes. You can't remember everything, but if we discuss a class in detail in this book, you should plan to study it thoroughly.

6. **A, D** In a `String`, the length is its capacity; only the room required by the caller is ever allocated. In a `StringBuilder`, the length value can be equal to or less than its capacity value, but never more. All empty `String`s have a length of zero.

7. **D** Java is case sensitive. Java keywords are all expressed in lowercase, but `integer` isn't one of them.

8. **D** The content of a `StringBuilder` referent is completely arbitrary: control codes, punctuation marks, white space, even nothing at all. They will all make valid objects.

9. **B** The `String` class interns a value on direct assignment for the first time only. Upon a subsequent assignment of the same literal, the reference is made to point to the already interned `String`.

10. **C** A primitive stores a copy of a literal value. An object reference stores a copy of a referent location in memory.

Chapter 3: Using Java Operators and Conditional Logic

1. **B** $2^{31} - 1$ is the maximum positive value for an int. Its bitwise complement is the maximum negative value, which is -2^{31}.

2. **D** The categories between Equality and Conditional (Bitwise and Logical) aren't listed, but the order given is still correct.

3. **A** Shifting is the other category that has compound assignment support.

4. **True** The compiler cares if a switch statement is legal. Whether it is also useful is something only the programmer can define and control.

5. **C** The parentheses change the order of evaluation but not the result. This expression evaluates to 37 before shifting, and then is right-shifted once to get 74.

6. **C** This question is tricky but instructive. The problem isn't precedence; we know the postfix operator comes first. The result of that operation, however, is a value, not a variable. The variable isn't in play anymore, so the subsequent operation becomes --2, not --x. Consequently, the compiler will tell you it expected a variable, not a value, and bail out.

7. **B** A switch test expression may evaluate to any integral type (except long), or their object-based counterparts, or a String. Boolean values are not supported.

8. **True** An enthusiastic person might contend that by modifying the source code of the Object class, you could make the correct answer False. Hypothetical dodges like that aside, the Object class by design maintains no difference between strict and effective equality. Every subclass may define effective equality as it sees fit, or not. Many classes, especially test cases like the ones we've written, have no need for it.

9. **True** The conditional operator is an expression that will return any legal type. In this case, what constitutes a legal type is defined by the variable used to accept the value.

10. **False** All if/else constructs are considered statements. The semicolon may always be replaced by code block separators, even if they contain one statement. The switch structure is also a statement, but allows only code block separators.

Chapter 4: Using Java Arrays

1. **True** Every array is a direct subclass of Object, regardless of its component type, and has access to all Object methods.

2. **C** Option B may be a crime against nature, but the compiler allows it. Option C uses the variable name as if it were a type, which is clearly illegal.

3. **True** A String object is considered equivalent to a char array that has the same content.

4. **C** Anonymous arrays aren't nameless in any respect you've learned. They aren't exceptions either. They actually restore the rules for expressions so an array can be created as part of any expression.

5. **False** There are several other validating rules that System.arraycopy() applies, including the rule that the arrays must have matching component types.

6.   **D** Capacity is a secondary property of the `ArrayList` class. The methods `ensureCapacity()` and `trimToSize()` let you modify it, but only with respect to the array it contains.

7.   **B** Lists order their components by indexing them. Duplicate values are possible because the index provides an implied key for each component.

8.   **True** An array is a direct subclass of `Object`. It does not change any `Object` behavior, including the `equals()` method, which just implements the `==` operator.

9.   **True** The documentation for `ArrayList` specifies its rules for equality, which it inherits. If two `ArrayList` objects have the same components in the same order, they are equal.

10. **C** You probably cannot answer this question correctly without writing test code for each assertion. That's what I did. This isn't really a review question, which perhaps doesn't seem fair. There is, however, a very important moral: Never assume a class is robust, that it covers edge cases and other ugliness so you don't have to. To use a Java class with complete confidence, you have to treat it skeptically. Always set out to prove with test code that it does what you think it does.

Chapter 5: Using Loops in Java Code

1.   **True** That's all it takes. An empty statement, signified by the semicolon, is sufficient under the compiler rule "It's okay if it's useless, so long as it's legal."

2.   **A, B** The legal options are infinite loops, each ghastly in its own style. Option A produces an "unreachable code" error.

3.   **D** The expression `while (false)` does not create unreachable code in a do/while loop, therefore the compiler allows it. The program will terminate shortly after it is started.

4.   **C** To better understand the answer, print out the value of `count` before and after its value changes.

5.   **C** The term *iterating* formally describes the process of traversing a Collections type but also applies to all loop constructs.

6.   **B** The for-each construction handles an array of any length the same way, including zero length.

7.   **A** The `for` statement does not open a code block, so only the `println()` method is part of that statement. The compiler complains because the `break` statement is not part of a `switch` or loop.

8.   **False** These structures help clarify the programmer's intent. There is no appreciable difference in performance.

9. **D** See the syntax presented in the text if you are unsure.

10. **False** You can define a collection object however you like. It won't work with a for-each construct, however, unless it conforms to the Collections framework defined in the `java.util` package.

Chapter 6: Encapsulating Data and Exposing Methods in Java

1. **C** The `final` keyword disallows further change to the class or member it is applied to. Subclassing is the way Java defines allowing change to a class, so a `final` class cannot be subclassed.

2. **False** The `protected` modifier adds subclasses to what would otherwise be package-private visibility.

3. **B, D** The classpath merely names directories where packages reside. A package declaration should not overlap this location but rather should detail the location of classes underneath it.

4. **False** Classes from other packages can see such a class; they just can't do anything with it.

5. **C** A final class can't be subclassed but has no effect on method behavior. Mutability isn't subject to just public methods, but to methods that change a field's value. Any method that changes the data, regardless of its name, is a mutator. Naming a method with `set` merely advertises the idea.

6. **A, B, C** Once we start using packages, we have a number of requirements to observe. You can't see a class in another package unless it is `public` and your class imports it. The environment must support the classpath at compilation time as well as runtime.

7. **False** A package is one scope. Every modifier applies equally to all classes in the same package.

8. **D** Option D, as described, leaves its implementation completely open. You can't get much more abstract than that. Option A only suggests data hiding, while option B is a bean implementation. Option C is meaningless.

9. **B** Type-safety is controlled by the compiler, not by methods. Packaging just limits the exposure of a field unless it's declared `public`. And an assignment to a field is, by definition, a mutation. What we can't do without a method is limit the range of an otherwise type-safe assignment.

10. **False** A classpath is like a path environment variable. You can supply multiple directories, which will be checked in listed order, to resolve `import` statements.

Chapter 7: Using Java Methods to Communicate

1. **B, C** The word const is reserved by the Java language and cannot be used. Identifiers can include numbers, but they can't start with a number.

2. **B, D** To overload a method, you must vary its parameter list. You can change the number, type, and/or order of the parameter list. Option B changes only the parameter name. Option D changes only the return type.

3. **C** *Chaining* isn't a compiler-sensitive activity, just a term for a technique that makes overloading a method a little easier to manage. Common sense keeps you from calling every method in a class from every other method, but it's perfectly legal.

4. **A, D** void is a return type, not a modifier; and package private is a stand-in term, not a keyword. All nonaccess modifiers are listed in Table 7.1.

5. **D** The number, type, and order of parameters all affect overloading.

6. **C** A functional method behaves like a function in that it returns a value based on (or calculated from) the parameters it receives. Option D is wrong because the definition does not restrict the type of return. Option A is wrong because the logic does not have to concern math. Option B describes an accessor method better than a functional one.

7. **A** See Table 7.2 for the descriptions. I described a procedure as a method that performs what its name suggests: no input, no returned type. A mutator uses the parameters it accepts to change a specific aspect of the object. Remember, these categories are not hard-and-fast Java rules. They are terms we're using to better define the kinds of methods we write.

8. **A, B** All parameters are passed by their value. It's just that primitive values and reference values aren't the same kind of thing.

9. **False** A static method cannot call a non-static method unless it has an instance, or object context, to use. The reverse is not true. An object of a class follows its static members in load order, so they are always available to it.

10. **False** A static method can call non-static methods, but only if it has an object reference.

Chapter 8: Using Java Constructors

1. **D** Statements A and B apply to all constructors. Statement C is true of all default constructors as well as many others.

2. **A, B, D** You can apply only access modifiers to a constructor.

3. **False** The compiler writes a default constructor in a class only if no other is present. So long as there is one constructor in the code, the default constructor is not required.

4. **B** The this keyword refers to the current object. You can use it to access members and as a parameter in a method call.

5. **False** If there is an explicit, parameterized constructor in a class, the compiler does not write in a default constructor. Therefore, the call would fail. You'd have to write in a no-arg constructor for this() to work.

6. **B** The call this() is only acceptable as the first statement in a constructor body.

7. **A** You can use the new keyword in any method or constructor. Option B is wrong: You *can't* use the this() call inside the constructor you're trying to call (try it!). Option C is also wrong: If you declare a constructor private, the compiler does not check to see if you have a static method. Without one, the class is useless, but it will compile. Option D is also wrong: If you can't see the class from outside the package, it won't matter what visibility its constructor has.

8. **True** Even though it has a specific purpose, a main() method is still a class member. It cannot access non-static members without an object reference, but it can access any constructor.

9. **B** Encapsulation describes any class element you can hide behind a method to control how it's accessed.

10. **A, C** A default-access constructor is visible to any class in its package (or file).

Chapter 9: Inheriting Code and Data in Java

1. **C, D** Option A is, of course, false; type-safety applies to all classes regardless of how you use them. Option B is false; a class can access protected members of another class if they reside in the same package. A subclass can override any non-final member from its parent or overload any method. Composed classes can be wrapped only by the containing class.

2.   **C** You can overload any method you can see. The parameter list separates one method from others that have the same name, not the same modifiers. You can reuse the name of a static method in a parent class so long as the new method is also static. You can declare a method both final and static; they are not mutually exclusive modifiers. But you can't override a method you can't see; you can only reuse the method name.

3.   **True** Try it! The final modifier doesn't do anything useful for a main() method. It also does no harm. The compiler and the JVM don't mind.

4.   **D** Options B and D are correct, but D explains why. The instanceof operator tests the type of the referent. If obj is assigned the value null, it does not refer to any type. The test in that case evaluates to false.

5.   **A** Options B, C, and D are common misunderstandings of the @Override annotation's job. The compiler normally accepts an overridden method silently. This annotation ensures that you've actually executed an override, not an overload. It also helps you distinguish between true overriding and merely reusing the name of a method in any parent class that was declared private or static.

6.   **True** A subclass constructor always invokes a super() call, whether it's implied or stated in code. If a class doesn't allow construction from a caller, it might as well be declared final. The compiler reports the problem differently but the effect is the same. There is an exception of sorts to this rule. If a class with private constructors has an *inner class*, the inner class may extend its containing class. Inner classes are a peculiar hybrid; they are part class and part class member. Since they live inside a class, they have the same visibility to that class's private constructors any member method would.

7.   **B** The super and this keywords apply to an object's context, but they are not class members. You can use them only to refer to the current object. The remaining options are therefore moot.

8.   **A or D** My technical editor is going to hate this question and call it dirty pool. He's right. Polymorphic effect, in my view, is more a product of art than craft in object-oriented programming. You probably need to pass a test on this topic, but I can't really help with an objective question. Option A is a reasonable, affirmative answer. Option D is a reasonable, dour answer. The *quality* of polymorphic effect you can achieve depends on how well you apply a common, intended meaning to the methods you override. Options B and C are out because you must have a type relationship and it does not have to be confined to a package.

9.   **C** To achieve a useful type system, you start with general behavior or attributes in your parent classes and specialize them in your child classes. Granted, proper organization can be a matter of perspective. For these types it's easy to rationalize

the `Employee` class as the most general type. A manager, director, or executive "is-a" kind of employee. Thinking the other way around requires a qualification of some sort, as in "an employee *could be* a manager, director, or executive." By the same token, you can say "a manager has one or more employees," which brings to mind composition as the best way to express that relationship in Java code.

10. **True** The `@Override` annotation makes sure the current method is an override. The `final` modifier prevents a subclass from overriding it.

It may seem odd that you can override a method but prevent subclasses from doing the same. You can in fact prevent subclasses from implementing the `toString()` and `equals()` methods you have overridden. You can apply that technique for the better or for the worse, as I see it. It's up to the programmer to apply this knowledge well. Just remember that you can make a method always visible by declaring it `public`, but you can't make it always open to overriding.

Chapter 10: Understanding Java Interfaces and Abstract Classes

1. **A** Option A is correct because an interface method cannot have default access; the compiler will make it `public` whether it is declared or not. Abstract methods can be `public` too, so that's not a difference. Any method can be overloaded, regardless of declaration.

2. **True** If you declare an interface method `protected`, the compiler will complain.

3. **B, C** To answer this question, you just need to look up the interface list for the `java.lang` package. The `Serializable` interface is listed in the `java.io` package. The `List` interface is listed in the `java.util` package.

4. **False** An interface is a type; you cannot test one as an instance of any type. However, an object made from a class that implements an interface will pass an `instanceof` test.

5. **C** Options A and B are missing a return type. Option D uses `null` as a return type, which is not a legal declaration.

6. **A, D** The `String` class is the return type and has no effect on parameter types. It is also declared `final`. An enum, while similar in some respects to an interface, cannot be implemented.

7. **False** Interface methods are always public, whether you declare the access modifier or not.

8. **D** Passing an enum element to `System.out.println()` invokes `toString()` on the element, which evaluates to the element name.

9. **True** Interface methods *are* abstract methods. It's considered bad style to include the modifier when writing an interface.

10. **A** An interface with no methods to implement is also called a marker interface. If a class implements it, it qualifies as that type. The java.io.Serializable interface is an example of a marker interface that is essential to converting objects into a stream of bytes.

Chapter 11: Throwing and Catching Exceptions in Java

1. **B** Option A is incorrect because you can declare any exception; the only standard is whether it's reasonable to do so. Option C is wrong for the same reason. Option D is wrong because the Throwable class has no particular restrictions to it. There's no need for another kind of Throwable category, but the compiler and JVM do not prohibit you from making one.

2. **C** Options A and D descend from the RuntimeException class. Option B descends from the Error class. Option C descends from the IOException class, which descends from the Exception class.

3. **True** Multi-catch syntax prohibits any two exception types that have a parent-child relationship. You could combine Error and Exception in a multi-catch clause if you wanted to. Again, the standard is what's reasonable.

4. **D** Options A, B, and C are wrong because all descendants of the Throwable class inherit the Serializable interface.

5. **False** The JVM will only throw objects that descend from the Throwable class. It does not impose any restrictions that keep you from passing them around like regular objects. It's unreasonable to use exceptions this way—but not illegal.

6. **A** You're never required to use a finally block. Its purpose is to bring control back to a common point from all possible paths of execution, including exceptions that are raised during exception handling.

7. **C** The code violation occurs in the second statement, which tries to cast the Integer object to a String object. Removing that line and replacing the argument to the println() method with the obj reference solves the problem. There are no other untoward operations in this code.

8. **D** The compiler tests the operation for a valid type, but not a valid result, so the code will still compile and run. At runtime, evaluating the parameter will precede passing it to the println() method, so an ArithmeticException object is raised. It's reasonable to infer that the result is also an illegal argument, but the order of evaluation determines which exception would occur first.

9.   **A** Option B is wrong because the `ClassCastException` class descends from the `RuntimeException` class. Option C is wrong because the `RuntimeException` class descends from the `Exception` class.

10. **C** According to the class documentation, this exception is a member of the Java Collections Framework, which resides in the `java.util` package. A class that inherits the `Collection` interface can throw this exception to show that an inherited method is not supported in that class.

OCA Certification Program

The Oracle Certified Associate, Java SE 7 Programmer certification is based on one exam (number 1Z0-803) of 90 multiple-choice questions. To pass, you need to answer at least 68 questions correctly (75). Two and a half hours are allotted to complete the exam.

The 803 exam does not include any questions that are based on recall alone. Instead, it tests your ability to interpret and analyze code and determine if it will compile, execute, and run correctly. Candidates who can read Java code accurately and are familiar with the basics of the language, as defined by the exam topics, have a strong chance of passing. Although the exam format does not allow for written code responses, the candidate who can write short Java programs has the strongest chance of passing.

Before you schedule the exam, you should feel knowledgeable in the syntax and use of common Java programming language constructs, including keywords; reserved words; operators; differences between primitive and object types; arrays and array operations; decision constructs; declaring fields and methods; defining concrete classes, abstract classes, and interfaces; and using exceptions.

This exam focuses on a few key classes in the Java core libraries, namely the `String`, `StringBuilder`, `ArrayList`, `RuntimeException`, and `Error` classes. You should expect detailed coverage of these classes. Be prepared to answer questions on any aspect of their intended use. Know their visible constructors, methods, and fields by heart.

You should also feel comfortable defining object-oriented principles such as inheritance and composition and be able to differentiate between them. Expect questions that stress techniques including declaring constructors, casting objects, overloading and overriding methods, extending classes, implementing abstract methods and interfaces, and catching and throwing exceptions. You should be able to define the principles of encapsulation and polymorphism and recognize their application in sample code.

These topic areas are all covered in this book, but the exam is not its sole focus. The topics are arranged to help the reader build skills over a course of study, whether self-directed or part of a college course, and to consider higher level goals in programming that an employable programmer is expected to understand. The book helps you to appreciate clear Java code and to apply every-day practices that help you achieve it. As you can see from Table B.1, I've mapped the exam objectives to my chapter outline with those goals in mind. Some exam elements appear outside the subcategories defined by Oracle so I could create a more natural sequence.

Certain topics that do not appear heavily weighted in the exam are given far greater weight in the book. It's my opinion that these topics cover skills that are essential for your further professional development and thus deserve strong treatment in the early stages of your practice.

Certification Objectives Map

Table B.1 provides objective mappings for the Oracle Certified Associate Java SE 7 Programmer exam. It identifies the chapter where each exam objective is covered.

TABLE B.1   OCA, Java SE7 objectives map

Objective	Chapter
Java Basics	
Define the scope of variables	1
Define the structure of a Java class	1
Create executable Java applications with a `main` method	1
Import other Java packages to make them accessible in your code	1
Working with Java Data Types	
Declare and initialize variables	2
Differentiate between object reference variables and primitive variables	2
Read or write to object fields	2

TABLE B.1 *(Continued)*

Objective	Chapter
Explain an object's lifecycle	2
Call methods on objects	7
Manipulate data using the StringBuilder class and its methods	2
Create and manipulate strings	2
Using Operators and Decision Constructs	
Use Java operators	3
Use parentheses to override operator precedence	3
Test equality between strings and other objects using == and equals ()	3
Create if and if/else constructs	3
Use a switch statement	3
Creating and Using Arrays	
Declare, instantiate, initialize and use a one-dimensional array	4
Declare, instantiate, initialize and use multi-dimensional array	4
Declare and use an ArrayList	4
Using Loop Constructs	
Create and use while loops	5
Create and use for loops including the enhanced for loop	5
Create and use do/while loops	5
Compare loop constructs	5
Use break and continue	5

(Continues)

TABLE B.1 *(Continued)*

Objective	Chapter
Working with Methods and Encapsulation	
Create methods with arguments and return values	7
Apply the `static` keyword to methods and fields	7
Create an overloaded method	7
Differentiate between default and user-defined constructors	8
Create and overload constructors	8
Apply access modifiers	6
Apply encapsulation principles to a class	6
Determine the effect upon object references and primitive values when they are passed into methods that change the values	7
Working with Inheritance	
Implement inheritance	9
Develop code that demonstrates the use of polymorphism	9
Differentiate between the type of a reference and the type of an object	9
Determine when casting is necessary	9
Use `super` and `this` to access objects and constructors	9
Use abstract classes and interfaces	10
Handling Exceptions	
Differentiate among checked exceptions, `RuntimeException` and `Error`	11
Create a `try-catch` block and determine how exceptions alter normal program flow	11
Describe what exceptions are used for in Java	11
Invoke a method that throws an exception	11
Recognize common exception classes and categories	11

INDEX

Note to the reader: Throughout this index **boldfaced** page numbers indicate primary discussions of a topic. *Italicized* page numbers indicate illustrations.